Contents

CW00546354

Chapter 1 A Death in The Family

As a young man I drifted around from one menial job to another. Like many school leavers I wasn't sure what to do with my life, until eventually I decided to act upon the only good piece of advice my father ever gave me. He'd always said how important a trade or career was in life and having seen the places my brother had visited after he'd signed up, I applied to join the Army.

After visiting the Derby careers office, I went through a process of testing and selection at Lichfield. This involved a series of interviews and a medical test, which was followed up with a physical fitness test. We had to run a mile and a half in under eleven minutes, followed by forty-five sit-ups and four heaves on a beam. I was doing the fitness test with a young man who had been on selection a few times. He was brimming with confidence and talked a good run, so I was surprised when he came last on the run, clocking up fourteen minutes in total.

I longed to travel the world and help people, spreading my young wings and venturing beyond the small town I had grown up in. I was just fifteen years old when I began my basic training program at ATR Bassing Bourne, fresh-faced and enthusiastic as I embarked upon a military career. I knew it could be a small stepping stone pushing me towards something far greater.

I didn't know it at the time but my brother, who was friends with the non-commissioned officers who were training me, had asked them to be nice to me. Obviously, this meant that, contrary to his wishes, I was occasionally treated to a beasting on the drill square, marking my first real encounter with male authority figures who would become a source of constant battle throughout the next few years. I was certainly in a male-dominated world where the men around me who were my age projected an aura of assertiveness. In retrospect it is easy to understand how this was often a front, or a compensation mechanism masking low self-esteem.

Joining the Army marked the beginning of a very long journey, and I was setting out on the winding path which would create the story of my life. In isolation, each event which was to transpire would seem relatively insignificant, but only when I would step back and view the entire picture would I truly realise how each of these events placed themselves in a larger jigsaw; each piece bringing me the clarity to write this book.

I learned a great deal from my time in the military, not least the discipline and self-drive to pursue my life passions and achieve my dreams through hard work and determination. It provided a solid foundation on which I could build my knowledge, and many of the life skills the service taught me I never truly realised at the time. Perhaps this is a reflection on the service as an environment which isn't conducive to the realisation of one's dreams and ambitions. But regardless, I'm grateful for the skills I learned, and my ability to use them to their fullest potential once I eventually left the forces.

But this point was far away, and it was during the early years of my military career when the first life-changing event emerged on the horizon, ready to challenge my perceptions and shake the foundations of my world.

Lindsay and I first met one day when I was standing at the bus station in Derby waiting to travel back to my home in Spondon. Our eyes met and we both smiled nervously at one another, as I boarded the bus and sat down, she followed, and I willed her to sit beside me with a huge smile on my face.

We began talking and I explained how I was on leave from the army. We chatted for the entire journey home and by the time we arrived it felt as if we had known one another for many years. As I'd stood up to get off the bus she asked if I'd like to meet her that evening at one of Derby's nightlife highlights at the time, the Pink Coconut, and I happily agreed. The rest of the day passed in a haze right up to the moment I was due to go out, not knowing how a single chance meeting would impact the rest of my life.

I arrived at the club later that evening with a spring in my step (and still wearing that huge smile), eager to continue our conversation. I spotted her almost immediately and we talked and danced all night. We exchanged phone numbers and before long started to date. She became my first serious girlfriend – and first love – and I cherished the way her smile beamed, lighting up any room she was in. There was a familiar air to her, and I felt as if I had known her for many lifetimes, and I thought of her with all the clichés of youthful love you can think of.

First love is a powerful phenomenon, and she ignited a feeling deep within my soul which seemed to transcend my mortal years. It was an archetypal love, and I couldn't fathom the depth and magnitude of it at such a young age. I'd never believed in the expression "love at first sight" but now I felt it for myself. It was as if I was lost in a spell of serenity and beauty, her energy drawing me towards her.

However, serving in the Royal Engineers wasn't necessarily conducive to a healthy relationship, and before long I was posted to Hamelin in Germany. The sacrifices you make when joining the army begins the moment you sign on the dotted line – once that signature is made your life is never truly yours again. There's a running joke in the military when people are asked to volunteer, to which they often respond, "I've already signed my life away!".

The challenge of making a marriage succeed during time in the military is one which everyone in the services faces, and divorce rates are higher for servicemen when compared to the general population. Marriage should be about considering your partner when making decisions, but the very nature of the armed forces is that the job comes first. Inevitably this means sacrificing holidays, risking personal injury and even having to deal with the mental scars this service can lead to.

With such a nomadic lifestyle committed to an overarching system it can be very hard to make a relationship work. The constant requirements to go on courses and away on tour means that the army ends up becoming like a mistress whom your wife has no other choice but to accept as being a part of your life.

4

Whenever I was away I would call her regularly to see how she was doing, while counting the days down to my next leave back to the United Kingdom. I'd recently passed my HGV licence and had bought a new car – a sporty Ford XR3i which surely marked me down as a boy racer of the times – and was keen to get back home to be with her.

Loading the car up with our kit, myself and three other colleagues hit the road and began the fifteen-hour trip back to the UK. Brian, a colleague who was accompanying us on the journey, insisted on playing his dance mix tapes for the full thousand miles, and the rest of us resisted the urge to grab his cheesy music tapes and throw them out of the window before we went completely insane.

We survived the travelling musical torture chamber and I arrived home and fell into Lindsay's arms, where we would hold one another longingly. The apparent purity of first love is difficult to describe – it seemed somehow totally uncomplicated, as if emboldened by the essence of youth. Looking back, this kind of purity is something I would strive for in all the romantic relationships which were to come, as the twists and turns of my love life were to unfold over the following years. This would bring with it plenty of heartache, with lessons needing learning two, sometimes three times before they would sink in. Sometimes fate has to hammer home messages before they finally reach my stubborn soul, these messages alluding to a parallel path which would come from a chance encounter.

Chance encounters seemed to play a recurring role throughout my life. Faces from the past would appear before me, their beaming smiles returning to my life. Many years later when visiting the Red Zebra bar I would go on to open, I saw Lindsay approach with a smile on her face. I'd see her again while drinking coffee many months later, and while part of me thought that these had been coincidences and nothing more, another part felt as if these moments were a way of showing me how happiness still awaited me.

Lindsay and I continued to date for a while, until eventually the pressure of being posted abroad became too much. Being just nineteen years old at the time and thinking I had been lucky enough to find the woman I could spend the rest of my life with, I toyed with the idea of leaving the army. But I was still young, and believed that it wasn't possible to meet your soul mate early in life, so I brought the relationship to an end.

The thought of a long distance relationship bore heavily on bringing about the end of my relationship with Lindsay, and when reflecting on my choice I knew that it had been the wrong decision. Being a young man this inevitably led to me going out and getting very drunk, causing a mess and being put to bed by my friend Micky. Despite the fact I was a "tough soldier" I had cried in front of him about the break up – even though I had caused it myself. I'd never cried like that before, and I would never cry this way over a break up again.

As often happens to people when their first love comes to an end, I hardened myself and built a wall so high that nobody would be able to climb it. It was a response many will be familiar with, but brings with it a huge problem: the only way to be truly loved is to love yourself first – only then will you become prepared to let people in and to love them truly in return.

I returned to the UK from Germany at great cost, both financial and emotional, to try and repair the relationship, taking a flight back to Heathrow where my brother David picked me up. Seeing Lindsay, I tried to make amends for my decision and she said she would think about it, but deep down I knew that it was over for good. So I returned to Germany feeling very sad and awaited my next leave so that I could try and win her back. But in doing so fate intervened and I bumped into Julie, a mutual friend of ours. I knew instantly that there was

something between us and recalled the time where she had shared a taxi with us shortly before. The writing had been on the wall at the time, but I hadn't been ready to read it.

But things were about to change dramatically, and while the women in my romantic life have played an important role in helping me become the person I am today, the fate of another woman closer to my heart than any other was about to intervene and reshape who I was in a way I'd never experienced before.

If you were asked to choose the one person who played the most significant role in your life, the chances are you'd name your mother.

We all love our mums and there's a very good reason why the mother figure has taken on such a significant symbolic status throughout human history, to the extent that we identify the very planet we live on as Mother Earth. Mothers provide the foundation from which we grow, their nurturing wombs and instinct for protection and care in our formative years shaping us into the people we will become.

My mother was no exception, and it was with a heavy heart that I listened to the doctor's verdict announcing that she had a shadow on her lungs. I was home on leave just prior to my wedding to Julie in the summer of 1997, the arrangements for this occasion in full flow during the two weeks I had off duty. It was the last week in July, a cold and drizzly day which seemed to pre-empt the bad news I was about to receive. The doctor explained to us the significance of the shadow on my mother's right lung – all those years of smoking finally coming home to roost in the form of malignant lung cancer.

My sisters stood outside smoking cigarettes wishing, not without a degree of pathos, that they would not face the same fate. Sometimes people are self- fulfilling prophecies creating their own future, and as the doctor delivered his diagnosis, I had a strange, inexplicable feeling that it would be terminal, and that my mother would be leaving this mortal coil soon.

Still, no amount of preparation for the worst is enough to equip a person with the emotional armour to deal with such a dreadful prognosis, and my mother's diagnosis with lung cancer was a difficult one to comprehend. I realised that it isn't just the person with the illness who goes through the stages of anger and denial – loved ones, too, share this frustration and anguish. Irrespective of my fears, the initial prognosis was promising, and the doctor reassured us that our mother stood a good chance of beating it. She'd always been a strong woman with a survival instinct, so it wasn't without good reason that my family and I were optimistic about her pulling through.

While my mother had suffered from health issues throughout her life, mostly this seemed to be an inevitable consequence of the hard life she had led. Raising eight children single-handedly would be a great task for anyone, not least when you add to this the numerous jobs, she'd worked to help provide for us all. Ironically, she had smoked to relieve the pressures of daily life, and that relief had come back to claim its toll.

It was around this time when Julie and I made preparations to return to Germany and to settle into married life together. We'd married at a wonderful ceremony at Elvaston Castle where a string quartet had played beautiful music to us in the echoing spaces of a Gothic room. My mother had been too ill to attend the ceremony and had been sadly missed during the speeches, so afterwards we'd visited her in hospital, still wearing my full number one dress uniform with Julie in her elegant wedding dress. My mother was delighted, smiling from ear to ear as her son and new spouse had stood before her proudly.

This was to be the last time I would see my mother alive.

Shortly after I set off to Germany, then on to Poland for three weeks of exercises having barely slept, fitful with excitement at the prospect of getting it over and done with so that I could be with Julie once again, while at the same time concerned for the health and well-being of my mother.

I participated in an exercise known as Ulan Eagle, a brigade level exercise which involved an amphibious squadron providing a bridging capability, while bank supports section laid track way allowing for access to the amphibious bridge or pontoon. It was a tough three-week exercise in which we were constantly on the go and had little in the way of sleep. We did five days and nights straight on the bridge sites, and by the end of the exercise I began to hallucinate due to the lack of rest.

8

This overworked schedule came down to a simple error which led the brigadier to believe that we had twenty rigs instead of the ten we actually had. When it was over some of us organised a much-needed boys' night out, complete with the luxury of real food after three weeks on rations. We ate chicken and chips with a couple of beers to wash it down; a meal fit for a king when rations have been your sole diet, and enough to leave us satisfied and in bed by 9pm, still exhausted from the exercises but with contented smiles on our faces.

When the exercises were completed, I faced a long haul back to Germany in a hired van for a brief two-day stop over at base. I then drove back to the UK to collect Julie and our belongings, before making the tiring fifteen hour drive all the way back to Germany. We finally arrived at the army base in Hamelin, famous around the world as the home of the Pied Piper, the folk legend popularised by the Brothers Grimm and the poets Goethe and Robert Browning.

I quickly readjusted to the routine of army life, the familiarity of which returned to me in no time at all, since the army is a place of repetition and regimentation which is difficult to shake. Around the world, the daily routine for the military is much the same, orders timed for each event of the day. These range from the Reveille at 6 am (even earlier if on tour) and breakfast, followed by the first parade, kit inspections and the detailing of the daily works.

It's little wonder that many soldiers become institutionalised after a few years in the service, and some don't even realise just how much their lives have become prescribed by these routines until they finally leave or are medically retired. After such intensive regimentation, readjustment to civilian life can sometimes cause major issues.

I met many career soldiers during my time in the forces. They often had families but spent their lives in the sergeant's mess. These men were devoted to the army, with no other life to speak of, and would become apprehensive when

it came to retire from the military. Many of these men had joined the army very young and spent their entire careers there, and some of them didn't seem to appreciate how

9

broad their skill set was. They'd joined the army for the adventure, but the Peter Pan inside all of us has to grow up sooner or later.

Before long I discovered that my mother's illness was far more serious than I'd previously realised, and I considered asking for compassionate leave and a posting back in the United Kingdom so that I could be closer to her. My Troop Commander at the time, however, advised against this, since I was up for a Cadre course with the prospect of a promotion to Lance Corporal. Obtaining a compassionate posting back in the United Kingdom, he said, would most likely relegate me to the bottom of the pile for selection to the cadre. I would effectively have to start again and prove myself.

He assured me the compassionate leave system was first rate, and that if anything were to happen to my mother, I would be back home and by her side by the fastest means possible. It was an assurance I was to regret taking on board, and I went against my instinct and chose to remain in Hamelin.

I had a nagging feeling inside my head that something was not right, the doctor's voice ringing in my mind, telling me that my mother was on borrowed time. I tried to rationalise against this as the feeling grew stronger, attempting to push this to the back of my mind and striving to focus on my career – the reason, after all, I'd opted to stay here in Germany in the first place.

Over a year later when I finally got onto a Cadre course, I suffered a bad back injury and would be medically removed. It took me a month to recover from this and be able to walk properly, as if fate had quite literally telling me that I

wasn't on the right path, and that I should have chosen the road of family and loved ones. It taught me never to put my job in front of my family's best interests again.

It was less than a week later when the moment I had been dreading came about – a knock came at my door and I answered it to my Troop Commander, who informed me that my family had been in contact with the military to inform them that my mother was dying. He placed an arm comfortingly around my shoulder and reassured me that I had the strength of character to see my way through this awful time. No matter how much a person prepares themselves for such news – even when they know that it is inevitable – such words will cause a chasm to open up in the pit of their stomach. The announcement filled me with a feeling of dread and sorrow.

Given that my mother's death seemed imminent, a category 1 compassionate leave was immediately granted allowing for any means necessary for me to get back to the UK. What should have been a routine journey ended up being anything but, and in hindsight entirely preventable. Had the Brigade Commander been involved I would have been permitted the use of staff cars and helicopters at their disposal.

Instead, my plans to board the next flight home were to be in vain. The Junior Officer responsible for handling my situation was inexperienced and unaware of the correct procedure – and matters were hardly improved by the fact that this took place on a Saturday, so the officer was unable to get in touch with the higher ups in Brigade. I was told that I'd have to make the journey myself by car. This was a systemic failure of the Compassionate Leave system, which was drafted precisely for moments of crisis when the army would be there to look after you. To think that just one call to the Brigadier and the outcome would have been different altogether.

Faced with a journey which would take me at least ten hours, I was hardly inspired with confidence that I would make it to my mother's side before she passed away. Expecting the quick and efficient process of being flown immediately home, only to discover that a lengthy journey now lay ahead added to my troubles considerably. Julie tried her best to lighten the mood as best she could have given the circumstances, acting silly and making jokes.

But her efforts to comfort me and distract me from what seemed inevitable were in vain. I could sense what was about to happen before it did – I was a passenger observing events passing by through a window, and Julie was an amazing companion during that time, in ways I perhaps failed to appreciate until much later.

With no alternatives to consider, Julie and I loaded up our car with essential supplies and, still in a state of shock, I gunned the engine off the base. It's strange how unsettling news can impair your better judgement: I found myself driving my new car at the recommended speed for British motorways, before I realised, I was on the Autobahn and gave myself a swift word to put my foot down and regain much needed time. I used to do this often on trips home with Julie. I'd keep the speedometer at around 80 mph until she drifted off to sleep, then put my foot down until we hit 120 mph. She would eventually wake up and chastise me for going so fast. It seemed like a suitable analogy for my life at the time; always going too fast and failing to take the time to admire the scenery.

Hungry and with a long journey ahead of us, I stopped off so that we could refresh ourselves and eat some food. It was a decision I would live to regret. I can still remember vividly the taste of the meal – steak with black peppers, which Julie joked about being peas in an effort to cheer me up. I believed her, being in a daze, and bit down unleashing a sharp taste in my mouth. It was a prophetic sensation foreshadowing what was to come.

In the 21st century it's very easy for us to take for granted the utility of modern communications – at the touch of a button we can contact anyone in the world in an instant. But back then even the most basic mobile phone wasn't something we had at our disposal, so sitting in the ferry port for what seemed like an eternity with no means of getting in touch with my loved ones back home was an agonising experience. My mind raced with the possibilities of what my mother was enduring. As much as we try not to, thoughts of the worst case scenario can often dominate our minds even as we struggle to stay positive.

The sea was choppy and wild as we crossed the Channel back to the UK, the horrendous weather delaying us even further as the blackened, portentous skies matched our miserable mood, and we drove the final stretch home in total silence.

We arrived back in Spondon – a suburb of Derby – which as a child I had often had fond memories of, despite always longing to head out and see more of the world. My seven siblings and I had been raised in a small three-bedroom house situated in a close-knit community which I would always gravitate back to, but on this occasion my return wasn't something I welcomed in the slightest.

As my mind wasn't functioning on account of the sadness and stress, I drove to my brother-in-law's house rather than heading straight to the hospital. Having last spoken to my brother-in-law I'd switched on to autopilot and gone to his home, grief clouding my thinking. It was a second costly error of judgement which I would regret. This additional diversion added another twenty precious minutes, and few decisions in my life have weighed so heavily on my mind., as I've reflected in the years since on the choices which lead us to our destinations.

I finally arrived at the hospital and was told my mother had been moved to a private side room, and it was here where her body lay as I raced towards the room. The first person I saw was my brother David, who rushed up to my side as I approached the door. I immediately knew the worst had happened and he put his arms around me, reassuring me as he told me that our mother had passed away.

She had waited up through the night to see me but by the following day her time had finally come, and she had passed away just five minutes before I had arrived. I couldn't believe it – the news itself was devastating enough, but to hear that I had been late by such a short amount of time tore me to pieces.

A crucial moment in my life was prevented by just two decisions – they were decisions which prevented me from spending time with my mother before she passed and give me the chance to say goodbye. It felt, however, as if these decisions were unavoidable, as if set in motion from the beginning. Could I have really changed what came to pass? Something told me that the outcome would always be the same, as if fixed and immutable. But the journey was a different matter, and it began to dawn on me that it is how we influence our journey which counts for the most.

13

David continued to reassure me that things would work out fine. In his eyes I had become a grown man, no longer the baby or young boy of the family, as much as the years between siblings often perpetuate that perception into adulthood. As the eldest brother he had always been very kind and gentle, and during our time growing up together he was always there if I ever needed advice.

Reflecting on our relationship as an adult, it became much clearer to me just how alike we were in many ways, and in handling our mother's illness it was apparent that his sharp sense of humour and intelligence – and the way he would be happy to help anyone – were as vibrant as they were when we were kids.

I was beside myself with an uncontrollable mixture of grief and anger. Why had I stopped for food before embarking on the ferry?
Why had I gone to my brother-in-law's house first instead of the hospital?

These were the questions any grieving person might ask, as if to understand the "what if?" that might have made things turn out for the better. Why hadn't the military arranged a flight, as I had been assured that they would as a matter of protocol? Had they followed procedure I would have had the opportunity to say goodbye. Instead, all I could do was look down on her still body as the words I wanted to say to her faded into the past.

But again, the urge to blame some external force is as strong in grief as the doubts and questions about one's own actions, and ultimately no answer would come which could bring my mother back to life. Yet these were questions which I beat myself up over for some time to come, despite their pointlessness in retrospect. When we suffer such a loss we do not think with clarity but with love.

The experience had a deadening effect on my mood, with the loss of my mother compounded by the fact that I'd been denied the opportunity to speak to her one last time and say farewell, and I fell into a daze in the long period leading up to the funeral. The chance to speak one last time had passed and I thought of this moment, replaying it over and over in my head as I wished it had turned out: arriving before the end, talking at length and seeing her gently passing over into a peaceful eternal slumber.

My family had a number of gatherings at their homes in the run up to the funeral. We arranged the ceremony together, and when I wasn't with them discussing these plans my time seemed to be spent in a dense fog, as if I were on auto pilot without any sense of orientation. Subconsciously it felt as if this would be the last time the family would be gathered together, and I knew that we would all drift apart after this.

A place in my heart had died and a part of my soul felt as if it had been removed. It would take a long time to find something that would fill that gap. Julie and my family all pulled together and provided each other with support and love, but for a time it felt as if nothing would alleviate the emptiness my mother's death had left behind.

The hole which remained in my soul for a long time was largely responsible for my inability to settle. Grief can have an awful tendency to linger, becoming an emotional burden which doesn't seem to have an expiration date, and it was only at the birth of my daughter that this chapter of my life drew to its conclusion. Like so many fathers, my daughter for me was a saviour. She became a reason to live, and a reason to hope.

Having once thought that the lessons a family teaches itself come from the parent to the child, the realisation that this is a two-way relationship which grows with the bond of love has never been clearer. Once you realise this you're never truly alone again.

One of the most difficult things I have ever had to do in my life was to carry my mother's coffin into church with my family. The death of the familial matriarch is a terrible thing for anyone to endure – as inevitable and familiar to many of us as it may be – and having been through it myself I can only have the utmost compassion for those who have experienced it for themselves.

I met with my brothers, David and Gerald, and my good friend Andrew, on the morning of the funeral, keeping ourselves in good spirits as people often do to see themselves through such a trying occasion. At the undertakers we practised carrying the coffin down the aisle, ensuring we were stepping with military precision while making light of our strange choreography, if only to counteract the sombre purpose of the day. Gallows humour set in, that necessary mechanism for survival in the armed forces, and I tried to bring a little levity to the situation and put us in a better mood. Years later David commented on my sense of humour that day, lifting our spirits and making the day easier to handle.

Andrew had become a lifelong family friend ever since he had dated my sister, Dawn. In adulthood they had a son together, and I admired Andrew for his hard- working ethos matched with a gentleness towards those in his personal life. One Christmas in 1990 he had dressed up as Santa Claus and became the life and soul of the party, lifting spirits, embodying the loving values of the holiday season and generally making everybody feel good about themselves with his cheerful disposition.

But making light of the situation was an illusory short term solution, and the true gravity of what was to come struck me: this was clearly going to be one of the hardest moments of my life. Nothing I had ever faced could ever prepare me for laying to rest the woman who had brought me into this world and made me the person I am.

Yet little did I realise the rich tapestry of life which lay ahead of me. We see moments in terms of absolutes, but in fact my mother's death was simply another staging point from which more life lessons would come – lessons which exist to prepare you for new, clear paths. At the time, the short path towards the church may have seemed like a path which brought with it an ending, but without it other avenues would never have emerged in its place.

My mother had always been a popular woman in her town. She may have been small in height, but as is often the case with diminutive people she possessed a large heart full of warmth and consideration and was known as something of a

16

pillar of the community. Still, I was taken aback by the huge crowds which had gathered for her burial, with numbers approaching four hundred in attendance,

many of whom clearly knew her well, judging by the grieving expressions on countless faces. In fact, the church was so full that people had spilled outdoors, unable to all fit inside the building. I realised how she must have helped so many people in different ways; a shining light in the community just through being her good-natured self.

As sombre an occasion as a funeral is, nothing else quite brings out the impact a person had on others during their life and I was truly heartened to see such a turn out. It seemed to me a validation of my mother's inherent goodness above and beyond my previous understanding, and I came to respect her even more than I thought was possible. A true mark of how a person has lived their life can be seen in the way they have treated those around them in life. This is reflected no more clearly than in the people who attend your funeral to celebrate the life you lived.

She had always taught me that, no matter what I did, as long as I told her the truth and explained myself with honesty, she would stand by me. She instilled a deep sense of morality and an understanding that helping others is the truest way to help yourself. She embodied the idiom that life is but a mirror, reflecting back to yourself what you put out into the universe. The most important job in life is being a parent, and my mother made me the man I am today.

Nevertheless, it was a difficult occasion to see through, and were it not for my friend Andrew I would have broken down in the church. When we placed the coffin down, he must have seen in my eyes what I was going through, and he put a hand on my shoulder and gave me a look which simultaneously dispelled some of my fears and emboldened me throughout the rest of the long and

painful day. It was a simple gesture of kindness, but it was more than enough reassurance to help me collect my composure that day. His staunch support and compassion provided me with the mental fortitude I lacked within myself, and once again I was reminded of the strength of others and the importance of the human relationships which urge us onwards through the hardest times.

Without those close to us we wouldn't be the people we are, and we should cherish them at every opportunity we get.

After the wake I arrived for the clearance of the house with all the family. I didn't realise this at the time, but this would be the last time that we would all be together.

My mother had always been the linchpin which held us all together and made the peace when arguments had arisen. We attended to the practical matters of clearing all of my mother's possessions from the house and making other arrangements. It felt strange to view someone's life through the ornaments and trinkets which lay around the house, storing memories for a later date. It was as if we were intruding on an unspoken privacy – these possessions weren't there to give you their meaning, and with the owner no longer there they become unwanted objects.

Some items carried with them a latent poignancy: there were several pieces of jewellery which sparked strong memories, including a silver pendant and the engagement ring my father had given her. There were also copious quantities of

paperwork relating to me joining the military, which brought home to me just how proud of me she was. As I eyed these documents and picked up the silver pendant it struck me that, even though I had no children at the time, I would hand this down to my future daughter for safe keeping. The engagement ring, too, would remain a part of my life, residing in its box for some time until I would resize it for my future partner, Jade.

I noted the strange occurrence of the next-door neighbour, a friendly woman called Brenda, dying within a short period of my mother from cancer, closely followed by a woman called June who lived across the road. All of these women had lived within less than a ten-metre radius of one another.

18

Was this just pure fate or was this a cancer cluster caused due to environmental issues?

The questions posed, forever to remain unanswered.

My brother later informed me of a sub-station at the rear of the house which was later removed, which may well have been the root cause of these illnesses. In statistical terminology this would be known as an aberration anomaly – a possible coincidence but an equally likely cause. Of course, this knowledge did little to alleviate the grief I felt at my mother's passing.

Upon my return to Germany I fell extremely ill and found it almost impossible to sleep, the creeping insomnia exacerbating the grief I was still feeling for the passing of my mother. She had been the centre of my life and I knew that nothing in this world would replace the void her death had left. Time may heal all wounds I thought to myself, as army life continued on around me as if shrouded in fog, but how much time would it take for me to move on?

It was a question I had no answer to.

I was put on guard duty and equipped with a loaded weapon, a decision that I couldn't help but think probably wasn't entirely appropriate for a grieving man. I raised the compassionate leave circumstances with my superiors, complaining that had they followed protocol and flown me straight home as they should have done, I would have got to see my mother before she died.

Predictably, the case was investigated in-house and promptly swept under the carpet. After filling in the claim forms for my fuel money and ferry costs I was reimbursed. But it wasn't the money that concerned me; the systemic failure which had let me down when I had needed it the most aroused feelings of bitterness and anger, compounded by the lack of sleep resulting from my grief.

I began to envisage illusory figures visiting me in the night.

Most significantly, one night my mother came and sat beside me on the bed, assuring me that she was okay and that I shouldn't be upset on account of her passing. Sitting beside me, she told me that she was happy and no longer in any pain, and that she would always be with me as long as I kept her alive in my heart and mind. I am convinced that since this moment she has guided me, warned me and protected me in times of peril.

At the time I didn't know it, but many years later I had a conversation with my mother's sister Sandra and my brother David. They too had experienced the same visitation, something which I put down to a pure coincidence far from the scientific explanation of mass hysteria, since none of us were aware of the other's encounter. It is well documented event that when someone passes over to the other side, the people left behind suffering from the trauma of this loss – and often being incapable of letting go – are often visited by the spirit of that person in the same time and place. This appears to be because our understanding of time and space is limited to this dimension, and we are bound only by our current comprehension of the laws of physics.

Shamanic healers have a principle whereupon people who pass over into the spirit world would not be communicated with for a certain period of time. This is considered a mark of respect for the spirit which has passed over; this spirit can choose to contact the living if it so wishes, and there are some people more receptive than others for experiencing this phenomenon. Like a radio transmitter tuned to the correct frequency, some pick up the signal while others don't.

I continued to spend the long two-hour stints on guard duty in a haze, my sorrow and regrets swirling uncontrollably around my head as I struggled to focus. My guard 2i/C (the second in command of the guard room, a Lance Corporal) questioned me as to why I was attending grief counselling every week and after a while my patience wore thin and I snapped, threatening him in a fit of anger. It was fortunate that he instructed me to head into the back room and calm down; I could quite easily have been charged with insubordination for such an unprofessional outburst.

During these long stretches on guard duty I was able to reflect on the events which had transpired. But this was not the kind of reflection which brought about a positive change; rather, it only served to exacerbate my mental deterioration, and eventually the counsellor and the medical officer agreed to put me on sleeping tablets and remove me from guard and onto lighter duties.

Yet the visitors at night continued, strange figures cutting through the darkness while sleep continued to elude me.

I started to think that I might be losing my mind or reliving a repressed childhood trauma. I couldn't put my finger on why I was experiencing these sleepless nights, but they were to become a common thread for me in time of high stress and duress. Sometimes these would take the form of a presence or energy flooding into the room during the night.

It wasn't the first time in my life I had had such encounters – as a fourteen-year-old my best friend's grandmother had passed over, and when staying over that night I had awoke in the middle of the night to see her face reflecting back in the mirror, smiling as if at peace. She had told me that she was happy and asked that her family didn't worry about her.

Later in life I would realise the importance of mirrors, but at the time I had simply told the family what I had seen, and it appeared to ease their grief. It is a strange sensation, one which the rational mind and cultural conditioning would have you believe was a mere dream. Some maintain the spiritual belief that mirrors allow us to see the image of the deceased. It's this superstition which used to lead people to cover up their mirrors at night in large houses. Considering this belief, I thought that it could well be possible that it is related to light waves and the frequencies which spirits in a higher dimension are vibrating at. Acting as a prism, the mirror allows a light spectrum which is otherwise unperceivable to the human eye to be seen.

There is another belief that dreams are a manifestation of the unconscious mind trying to communicate with the conscious mind. The only issue is how we choose to decipher them, with each person's dream language bringing with it its own symbology. The mind works in the symbology in order to attempt to communicate the inherent meaning of the dream. In this sense, recurring dreams can be a way for the unconscious mind to guide the dreamer towards a new path.

If you take the time to keep a dream journal of your own, you may be surprised by the profound effect it can have on your life. This method has been used effectively as a therapy tool, for instance in America for people suffering from Post-Traumatic Stress Disorder. By keeping such a record, people were able to reframe and sometimes change entirely these dreams. This in turn changes the brain's association with the trauma, allowing the person to process the emotion attached to the trauma and move on in their lives.

In hypnotherapy there is a very effective therapy called content free regression, which also allows a person to revisit a traumatic event, allowing them to process it and observe it in a different way. Years later, I would learn how to process the things which occurred in my life using very similar methods.

The dispute over my compassionate leave with my superiors was clearly a major factor contributing towards my troubled insomnia. The Japanese have a saying about the nail that sticks out being the one the hammer hits first, which is a variation on an expression perhaps more appropriate for those of us serving in the military regarding putting one's head above the parapet. Perhaps I should have heeded the advice of this idiom and remained silent, but the brisk and dismissive reaction from my superiors had angered me and I lodged a complaint over the way in which the entire matter had been dealt with.

It was a huge mistake – for my troubles I was removed from the Cadre course, the entire reason why I had not been posted back to the UK in the first place.

I learned a valuable lesson throughout this sombre and heart-rending experience that has stuck with me clearly in the years since.

No job can possibly compare to family in the scheme of life, and had I chosen to be posted back to the UK instead of pursuing the course – and my career – in Germany, I'd have had the opportunity to spend those priceless moments with my mother before she passed away. It's often said that life should be lived without regrets, but as we're all fallible human being's regrets are perhaps inevitable. The very least we can do when faced with them is to learn from them what we can and move on as human beings.

I was beginning to learn perhaps the most important lesson in life, which is to live in the moment, since ultimately this is all we truly have. But it would take more experiences before I would truly heed this lesson and learn it by heart. Failure to grasp the true meaning of something can lead to a person being stuck in a loop. Life forces them to sit the test again until they succeed. Each failure leads to a more severe lesson – a high stakes game of Karma in which the bank always wins. For me these lessons would be taught again and again, chipping away at my ego until they shattered the very fabric of the way I perceived myself.

I still miss my mother to this day, as anyone who has lost forever that warm, familiar embrace that only a mother can offer; and yet it feels as if she has always been watching over me, as if she too regretted not saying goodbye in this temporal world and part of her has remained to make sure I was okay. Her love was boundless and the four hundred people who attended her funeral served as a testament to the big-hearted, much loved woman she had been in life.

It's funny how enigmatic people are when they walk the earth, their deaths revealing to many the true extent of what their lives had meant to so many people. They help others in so many different ways, often without others even realising how much they have changed their lives. These are the world's kind souls, guiding others with their boundless capacity for love.

Perhaps this should have been more obvious to me – after all, my mother had brought up eight children whilst working two jobs to make ends meet and provide for us all. All of us in our own way have gone on to be not only successful people but, far more importantly, decent and loving human beings. For this, our mother deserves all the credit she can get. We were raised with food in our bellies and love in our hearts, and the lessons she imparted about respect, tolerance and compassion reflect that miraculous spirit inherent in the grand archetype of the Great Mother.

My father had been absent sine I was very young, and this had always bothered me as a child. But as I grew up it soon became apparent that my mother provided my siblings and I with everything that two parents could, making up

for his absence more than doubly with her love and compassion. In a way, his absence proved to be one of my best teachers, giving me the lesson that, if ever I was to be blessed with the gift of fatherhood, I should always be there for my children.

Now my mother was gone forever I felt as if I truly understood her significance in my life and the important lessons, she had taught me as a boy. She armed me with the grounding and knowledge to be the man I am today, and I never fully realised this until I became a parent myself. The gravity and responsibility of being there to guide someone, charged with taking care of their lives and upbringing, hits home on the arrival of your first born. My daughter has taught me the true magic of life, making me understand for the first time the trials and tribulations my mother had gone through.

Bringing up eight of us single-handedly was a feat worthy of a sainthood.

Recently, memories of my childhood and her part in it started to return with some clarity, as if after lying dormant for many years they realised their new- found relevance in my life. Images of the annual carnival returned to me and I could picture my mother helping out with the extravagant floats and arranging the equipment – she had a knack for talking people into helping out and pulling their weight, radiating the kind of infectious enthusiasm which brings communities together and transforms a good event into a fantastic one. Locals nicknamed her The Chief Scrounger, an affectionate moniker which captured just how good she was at pooling together resources for the good of the community.

Christmas of 1990, a time when my brother was serving in the Gulf War, also came to mind in the aftermath of my mother's death.

It was a simple affair but often it is the simplicity of an event which makes it all the more profound, in this case the preparation and cooking of a hearty Christmas dinner for twenty-five hungry mouths. My mother made such a mission appear to be totally effortless, gliding around the kitchen completely unperturbed by the vast table she was tasked with filling with good food. Reflecting on the joyful manner in which she served us this feast I couldn't help but once again praise her for the way in which she raised eight children alone; children who grew up to be successful and – more importantly – loving and considerate adults.

Her indefatigably and care at this sumptuous Christmas meal stands in my memory as a symbol of what my mother meant to myself and many others; a woman who cared, loved and nurtured all who came into her life with an attentive selflessness worthy of a saint.

It is sad to think that often it is only when we are faced with an emergency or a death in the family that we truly come to appreciate the real value of the loved ones in our lives. While often we can count on one hand the people who count the most and offer their love, support and encouragement unconditionally, we should be eternally grateful for their presence in our lives and strive above all else to reciprocate these sentiments at every available moment in our fleeting existence.

Perhaps the way family binds us together is through the memory of the time which lies behind us. The present is all that we truly have since the past is gone and the future unknown. We craft the future ourselves through our thoughts, dreams, intentions and, finally, our actions.

My mother's death brought home to me the mortality of the body, something which is simply a vessel containing the soul and allowing us to experience the material world. Through

our senses – the sights, sounds and smells, the tastes and the things we touch – the mind becomes the intellect through which the world is assimilated and interpreted.
Remembering everything that we experience is an internal modal interpretation of the world around us.

The soul or spirit can be seen as the life energy which combines every living thing together into a whole at the subatomic level, linking us all to the source of all energy. Buddhism refers to this as the three cups – mind, body and soul – all of which seek balance with each other to bring about a sense of harmony and true selfhood. Picture a Venn diagram with each circle corresponding to these three values, the central point of overlap representing balance and selfhood

The Venn diagram named after John Venn (1834-1923) used to explain a simple set of relationship theory.

Christians viewed the same principle in different metaphors, explaining it with the motif of the Father, the Son and the Holy Spirit. While the cultural iconography may differ, the message remains the same. To find our true self we must embrace introspection and allow the journey to begin from the inside in order to balance the three primary concepts of mind, body and soul. Inside, these are able to communicate with one another, quietening the chatter of the mind.

To find enlightenment one must discover their true self – the key is to find a way to where this truth lies, deep within you, waiting to be discovered.

It was a roasting hot day as I sat in the truck surrounded by traffic.

Everything had come to a complete standstill. But the atmosphere was far from static and calm, and there was no sense of frustration that the vehicles weren't moving forwards that you'd expect in gridlock.

Further up ahead I could see a commotion breaking out, as people gathered together forming into an unruly crowd.

I checked the stash of weapons and ammunition behind me in the rear of the truck and nervously appraised the situation.

The crowd were clearly agitated about something, but it was impossible to determine exactly what from the position I was at. It felt as if there were a charge of electricity firing through the air, enlivening everything it came into contact with.

Blood coursed through my veins, pumping adrenaline with increasing intensity as the crowd swelled, their anger palpable despite the hundred yards which separated them from my vehicle.

This was no ordinary crowd – this was a mob, pure and simple. And they were after blood ...

I never really appreciated just how picturesque Hamelin was until Julie's parents came to visit one Christmas.

The already rather remarkable medieval buildings took on a charming appearance once winter snows arrived, rendering the old town like an idyllic picture postcard representation of a child's imagination, while the four fortresses which surrounded the centre of the town offered something of a contrast, as if they belonged not in a fairy tale but perhaps a Gothic horror novel; imposing, mysterious yet at the same time a compelling sight. These fortresses had earned Hamelin the nickname "Gibraltar of the North", its heavy fortifications an appropriate symbol for the purpose of my stay in the area. Hamelin was a town steeped in the history of Europe, spanning from its medieval roots through to the horrors of the Second World War.

After Julie's parents had rested up following on from their journey, we headed out to the local Christmas market. It was a busy occasion, with people huddled beneath thick overcoats to keep themselves protected from the elements and the streetlights casting a golden glow over the rows of stalls. Hunger-inducing aromas spilled out as we strolled amiably from one festively decorated wooden hut to the next, the ancient Market Church, Hochzeitshaus (the Wedding House) and lovingly restored timber framed houses and Weser Renaissance buildings towering on all sides, as if acting as wind-breakers protecting us from an impending storm.

We supped on tasty mulled wine and felt its warmth reaching through the chill as we admired the impressive Christmas pyramid and the enormous advent calendar mounted on the side of the Hochzeitshaus and discussed where we should go for some much-needed dinner. Hamelin has no shortage of wonderful restaurants to choose from and we opted for Georgia's, where we tucked into a homely meal as the snow continued to fall.

Since these were the days in which I was an alpha male and ardent meat eater, naturally I tucked into a thick and juicy steak. It seemed befitting of my role in the military, and since great steaks were the speciality of Georgia's – widely regarded as the best in Hamelin – it felt like the obvious choice. I'd never have considered it at the time, but little did I know I would become a vegetarian years later.

Naturally Julie's parents commented on just what a wonderfully appealing place Hamelin was – certainly a marked contrast from the military base where I was based with the 28 Engineer Regiment – and as we worked our way through desserts I suggested we take a drive out to the surrounding countryside so they could take in the landscape in all its glory. Admittedly I wanted to see this place draped in a blanket of snow as much as they did – this was the first time I had seen this charming old German town looking quite so beautiful.

Wrapping ourselves up in our thick jumpers and overcoats, we got into the car and set off on the short drive up to Klutz, a nearby hill from which the entirety of Hamelin could be clearly seen. With such heavy snowfall in such a short space of time what should have been a short drive transformed into something of a nightmare, with the increasingly precarious conditions on the road leading me to drive with the utmost caution.

A part of me thought that it might not be worth the risk and I contemplated turning around and calling this small expedition off. But then it occurred to me that such an opportunity might not present itself again, so I pressed on through the waves of falling snow which battled with the windshield. Given that the car was still fitted with summer tyres it made for an interesting drive – at least, I thought, Julie's parents will go home happy that their holiday in Hamelin was not without a sense of adventure!

Sure enough, the slippery journey was more than worth it, and the view down on Hamelin from Klutz was as calming and pretty as we'd hoped it would be. As we stood there gazing down a serenity fell over the group, nothing but the soft winds could be heard and for the first time since my mother's death I felt at peace with myself and my life. It was the kind of happiness that settles inside you comfortably like a familiar friend resting a hand gently on your shoulder.

Little did I realise that, given what was to come, this was the calm before the storm.

Julie settled into life in Hamelin in no time at all. An outgoing and personable woman it took her no time at all to find work in the Service Sound and Vision Corporation and avoid the tedium which many partners of military servicemen often fall victim to. For a few weeks we enjoyed the process of readjustment and the routine that our new life brought with it.

Before long I was due to be posted to Macedonia, by which time Julie set off back to the United Kingdom to live with her parents while I was on my first operational tour. I was deployed with 65 Field Squadron to help establish the forward operating military base at Black Horse camp in the region, prior to North Atlantic Treaty Organization's (NATO) crossing the border into Kosovo. This was a time when the activities of the Kosovo Liberation Army (KLA) were creating increasing tensions in the region, and our base was less than five kilometres away from the border – certainly within the range of artillery fire.

We were heading out on a daily basis for reconnaissance missions to assess the surrounding areas and any potential threats to the base, at the same time as working tirelessly to establish the basic infrastructure needed for such a large-scale military operation. 65 Field Squadron was primarily an MT/HQ squadron but eight of us were attached from 23 squadron, who were artisan tradespeople for whom constructing the infrastructure was their primary task. It was hard work, to be sure, but nothing I wasn't amply prepared for thanks to the countless hours of training I had undertaken. Besides, the bracing yet refreshing Macedonian air was invigorating.

One thing that can be guaranteed about life in the army is the unfailing sense of humour which prevails amongst your fellow soldiers. This is notable when

posted away from a conflict zone but goes into overdrive once the possibility of suffering fatalities comes into play. The awareness of mortality brings with it a pervasive gallows humour, and this was exemplified by a soldier called Jason Swindlehurst whom I met at the forward base camp.

Jason was a charismatic individual who had appeared on Robert Kilroy's chat show to raise troop morale by asking for pen pals for serving troops. He had a razor-sharp sense of humour which caused much laughter on the base; he was the epitome of a role model soldier and his comrades aspired to be like him. He was much loved by everyone, and it wasn't until much later that I learned the terrible fate he had met several years later whilst serving as a private military contractor in Iraq.

In 2007, Jason had been providing security for IT consultant Peter Moore along with fellow security guards Alec MacLachlan, Alan McMenemy and Jason Cresswell. After they had picked Mr. Moore and another IT consultant, Peter Donkin, from their secure residence in Baghdad's green zone, they had set off to the Ministry of Finance armed with pistols and rifles, where the consultants were helping to establish a new IT system. They arrived at their destination without harm, but shortly afterwards between fifty and one hundred armed men dressed in police and military uniforms stormed the building and took them hostage.

It didn't matter that they were highly trained, ex-military close-protection officers – no amount of training and expertise can cope with such odds and there was nothing they could have done to prevent their kidnapping.

Peter Moore was released at a later date but Jason and his fellow contractors were not so fortunate – after being held captive for a year they were executed by the armed gang.

Moore's account upon his release was a harrowing reminder of the truly dark side of warfare, where a quick death through artillery fire or by the hands of an

unseen sniper seems like a blessing rather than an ignominious end. He told of how they were stripped to their underwear and blindfolded, subjected to mock executions and held bound in chains for days on end. He also described how the hostage would be "forced on to his knees, have a firearm pushed into the back of his head, the firearm being racked and immediately a second firearm is discharged into the room".

It was saddening indeed to hear of Jason's fate nearly a decade later, and it reminded me just how ignorant I was to the true violence of warfare up to this point in my life. Up to this point in the operational tour there was nothing to suggest that I would come into contact with such barbarism and I couldn't begin to comprehend what being in close proximity to such violence might feel like.

Fortunately, the political situation at the time was reasonably stable but not entirely without its dangers, and one of the major concerns many of us had at the time was the fact that we were currently driving around in soft top vehicles. There was a very real danger of being attacked by the KLA from above – there had been a number of incidents when military vehicles were attacked with large rocks and concrete blocks and a number of injuries had been sustained.

This wasn't the first time that a military operation had been conducted without the proper equipment and it goes without saying that each time we set out on patrol or left the base for any other reason, all eyes were looking upwards every time we passed beneath a bridge or high building. This became a particular preoccupation of my own since, despite being a qualified electrician tasked with setting up the infrastructure of the base, primarily I had been operating as a driver. While I was fortunate enough to avoid any serious incidents myself, two other servicemen were not so lucky and lost their lives after such an attack.

Every time we approached a bridge a palpable tension emerged, and we looked up checking the bridge for potential threats and watched intently for incoming concrete blocks. This created a high sense of alert at all times, sometimes distracting from the driving or mission being undertaken. We modified the soft top Land Rovers ourselves – since we were engineers it was easy to improvise a hard top, which we fitted discreetly under the soft canvas. This way, if we were unfortunate enough to be attacked at least the falling blocks and large rocks would be diverted.

But this lack of proper equipment due to the quick deployment of the operation was putting people's lives in unnecessary danger – many years later I realised that this negligence perfectly captured the futility of war. War is fundamentally driven by politicians, which in turn is controlled by money. Inevitably corners will be cut, particularly for the regular armed forces. During war and peace defence contracts can be incredibly lucrative – a modern army can be run almost like a commercial business. When the bottom line is the primary concern, it's easy to see how the soldier can become an expendable asset.

Yet on the whole the atmosphere was surprisingly absent of any real tensions and we all continued about our business in a professional manner, performing our duties to the best of our abilities.

The arrival of a steady flow of refugees would soon put our skills to the test in ways that no amount of training can prepare you for.

Once the true scale of the refugee problem became understood it was clear that I would be playing a part in building the infrastructure to house the many people who had fled their homes to escape from the conflict. I was immediately struck by the diversity of people I saw as they lined into the camp carrying whatever belongings they could in rucksacks and suitcases – war makes no distinction between age and gender, income and social status, it seemed. For every refugee who looked as if they were farmers there were others who appeared to be dressed like doctors and businessmen, all equals within the fog of war.

As I watched them arrive and saw hundreds more approaching from over the horizon I thought about how much their lives had been turned upside down and tried to imagine how I would feel if I had been forced to pack up my possessions and leave my home behind, not knowing when – or indeed if – I would return. It was a depressing sight, improved only marginally by the tenacity with which these unfortunate men, women and children marched on with a resolute determination. I wondered how far they had travelled to reach the refugee camp and what lives they had led before the war had begun. I tried to imagine how such events would shake the foundations of everyday life if it were to happen back in the United Kingdom. It was a scenario which didn't bear thinking about.

Orders came down through the chain of command that we were to begin construction of the basic amenities necessary for the well-being of the refugees – everything from latrines and water facilities through to sleeping accommodation and the effective distribution of aid was to fall under our remit. The refugees themselves also pitched in to this effort and worked as tirelessly as the soldiers to get everything up and running as quickly as possible.

Still, it was two weeks before the camps were fully constructed and running reasonably smoothly. We'd worked solidly for up to eighteen hours a day and were feeling the exhaustion. In order to limit the potentially adverse psychological impact on the refugees we were no longer dressed as soldiers but in attire more akin to a civilian humanitarian task force, and a feeling of camaraderie between the military servicemen and the displaced families began to emerge. No doubt the fact that we were no longer carrying our firearms had a great deal to do with this elevated mood, given the circumstances, and we set up makeshift football pitches on which the children could play, perhaps forgetting for a brief moment the dire circumstances they faced with their loved ones.

We were particularly enamoured with the children, who exist outside of the political ramifications of their circumstances and softened our hearts with their innocent play. We often joked with them, making glasses out of fourteen-gauge wire and generally acting like fools to make them laugh. There were two young children in particular who would follow us around, trying their best to help us out with our tasks. Despite all that had happened they were happy and oblivious to the fog of war. They have an endearing habit of seeing the good in any situation and, much like animals, possess an intuitive ability to judge a person's character.

Sky News arrived shortly after the camps construction had been completed, covering the unfolding events and the arrival of General Mike Jackson. He was a thoroughly inspiring leader with a booming voice and unshakeable presence who addressed the troops and gave us a level of motivation that made it clear to many of us how he had risen through the ranks. He was naturally charismatic and inspired the troops to do their jobs to the best of their abilities and – perhaps more significantly – that their efforts and the risks they were taking were acknowledged and appreciated by their superiors.

I later learned that back home my family had watched news reports on television, broadcast from the refugee camps, and had spotted me amongst the troops, my distinct hands giving me away. I didn't get many chances to speak to Julie and my family while on tour. We were given thirty-minute phone cards which we could use once a week. Contacting loved ones was a luxury for us all, and I looked forward to calling Julie and passing on messages to the rest of my family.

Often it was difficult to schedule time to make the call, and booking a slot still often resulted in being stood in line, queueing with everyone else waiting for the phone to be available. It brought home how a simple phone call could make the tour go quicker and easier. But it also highlighted the life you were missing back home and speaking to Julie was sometimes an emotional double-edged sword.

When the mortaring began, we were ordered to move the forward base back out of the line of fire, re-establishing it at Macedonia's airport. The alert state went up and the withdrawal began, initially moving back to a nearby underground car park for hard cover. As we retreated, I saw the Macedonian army wheeling their artillery pieces forwards. The relative safety of Pristina airport welcomed us, and we were fortunate to be safe from the reality of war.

My first operational tour was coming to an end and I had seen it through without any harrowing incidents of my own to speak of. My second tour would prove to be far more eventful and would have a profound effect on the rest of my life.

Once NATO's bombing campaign went underway, everything changed.

The bombs began to fall on Kosovo in the spring of 1999 and lasted until June.

Code named Operation Allied Force, its objective was to bring an end to the violence allegedly being perpetrated by the Slobodan Milosevic government against the people of Kosovo and force the withdrawal of all paramilitary, police and military forces from the region.

It was a controversial mission, not least on account of the fact that the campaign hadn't received the seal of approval from the United Nations, and the tactics they employed proved to be equally controversial in the eyes of many. NATO opted for an intense aerial bombing campaign rather than risk the potential loss of life of a ground invasion, and the air campaign they carried out was nothing if not large in scale.

It was during this period that we were tactically withdrawn from Black Horse camp in order to remove ourselves from the line of fire. We were relocated approximately fifty kilometres away, to a heavily defended airport equipped with Apache helicopters, tanks and surface-to-air missile batteries. Combined with multinational forces, which effectively made up a full garrison, we were probably the last place in the area anyone would target.

This didn't mean we weren't obligated to dig battle trenches on the off chance we were overrun by ground forces. The odds of this happening were incredibly slim since the garrison was in a position of great strength, but it was impossible to predict when the fog of war would come to cloud matters further so the precaution was necessary. Still, we laughed at the prospect of being overrun by the enemy, joking that thirty engineers would be enough to stop the enemy, even if the powerful, hi-tech equipment deployed at the garrison failed. It would be the modern-day version of Rourke's drift, and we impersonated Michael Caine, saying, "KLA, sir – thousands of them!"

Daily banter certainly helped to take the edge of the reality of a very real and impending threat, although more pressing on our minds was the prospect of having to sweep the concrete car park from day to day. Anyone who has served in the military will recall the dreadful feeling of the daily grind – if you're on camp and there is no pressing work then you can expect to spend much of your time picking litter and endlessly cleaning.

Here on this operation tour, rifle slung over one shoulder and brush in the other hand sweeping up a patch of concrete while the wind continually kicked up more dust, the futility of the task we were being asked to do couldn't have been more apparent. I imagined being shot or killed whilst sweeping up this car park and laughed ironically at the prospect of such an ignominious fate, hardly warranting a mention in the dispatches.

The reality of war really hit home once we were issued with our live ammunition. I'd handled and fired live rounds many times before on the range, but once we'd been given live ammo to carry at all times a different perspective on the war became clear. For the first time the conflict felt tangible and real, while the very real risk of physical harm was brought home to me even more on the next table along.

No amount of training prepares a person for those moments when they realise exactly what it was they had been training for. In a nervous rush to collect my ammunition I noticed that I'd missed two rounds and returned to the staff sergeant to collect the outstanding bullets. He questioned my error, an honest counting mistake on my part, and it was fortunate I'd noticed this. The discrepancy would have been picked up on the daily equipment checks, and had I not noticed then I could well have been facing a charge for loss of ammunition on an operational tour.

I had sixty rounds in two magazines and I seriously questioned if that would be enough in the event of a firefight. Compared to the average infantry soldier – who carried a minimum of 120 rounds, roughly equivalent to four magazines – I felt inadequately prepared for a potential deadly conflict.

Having collected the ammunition, I was then issued with my personal supply of morphine and auto injectors, to be administered in the event of an injury. If the ammunition had made me think long and hard about the prospect of shooting another man, the medical supplies brought home my own sense of mortality.

It took a mere three days for the bombs to destroy nearly all of the military targets throughout Yugoslavia, and yet despite these efforts the Yugoslav army continued to mount attacks against the KLA insurgents operating inside Kosovo.

Thus, the targets of the bombing campaign broadened to include factories, bridges, government facilities as well as additional military installations and strategy targets. Power plants, water processing plants and even media outlets were then added to the list, causing untold damage to both the country's environment as well as intensely disrupting life for the ordinary person unfortunate enough to be caught in the crossfire.

The civilian loss of life on account of this bombing might have been lower than expected for what some perceived as such a heavy-handed campaign, but the conflict was far from over.

The race to Pristina airport was the first order after the intense bombing came to an end, a mission which was already underway before I began my second tour in the region. There was a rumour going around the troops at the time, suggesting that General Mike Jackson had been ordered to take Pristina airport first and that he had responded to the General issuing the order with the line, "I don't want to be responsible for starting World War Three with the Russians!"

Immediately upon my arrival I noticed a new level of intensity in the air. The bombing campaign and push across the border had put everyone on high alert, their senses attuned to the possibility of coming under attack. The three-week period of cooling off I'd had after returning to Germany from my first tour had not been without incident, either. I'd returned to England for a party at Julie's and been inadvertently caught up in an altercation which very nearly came to blows and the experience had brought to home just how much my instincts had been honed from my first tour.

A surprise party had been arranged at my sister's house to welcome me back from Pristina. It was a much-welcomed respite from my first operational tour which I was thoroughly enjoying until a neighbour's brother had gate crashed the gathering. He was very drunk and trying his best to antagonise guests and spoil the party, and I did my best to ignore him.

But then he tried to bully my brother's friend, who wouldn't harm a fly, and it felt as if a pin had been pulled from me and I went mad. Completely out of character, I'd leapt towards him threatening to kill him, and following a brief scuffle we were separated. I wondered why I had acted in such a manner, without knowing at the time that this anger had come from a place of unresolved issues which were to come to the fore.

It was a distressing moment, not least because I had hoped to relax and try and put the imminent second tour in Kosovo out of my mind as much as possible. In a sense it was ironic that my first tour had passed without incident only to find myself squaring off against a drunken gate crasher at what was supposed to be a fun party. In a war zone you're prepared for such events and it reminded me all too clearly of mankind's propensity for violence no matter what the circumstances might be.

I'd retrained before my second tour; redeployment training which included pre deployment patrolling, radio skills and how to handle interrogation. The latter of these consisted of experienced veterans talking us through how to deal with the situation where the potential for torture arose. This taught me that if I was captured and they started to torture me I was only meant to say the big four under the rules of the Geneva Convention: name, rank, number and date of birth. Anything else I was to respond with, "I cannot answer that question, sir".

In reality, if they continued to torture me after I had given them my basic information then I was to be the grey man and simply try to survive. The iconic movie image of the tortured soldier pushing out his chest and telling the interrogator to "go to Hell" is largely a myth. For one thing, such posturing would be a pretty clear sign to the enemy that you do have information that they could extract from you via torture. Then they would really go to work on you, using any means necessary to make you talk.

The most important battle in overcoming torture, I learned from the training, was doing whatever it took to remain mentally strong under such intense duress. Easier said than done.

While I was grateful that this aspect of the training didn't feature simulated capture, detainment and torture (this level of immersive training was reserved for selection into the Special Air Services, not for regular soldiers) it brought home the realisation that the horrible fate was a very distinct possibility which no amount of psychological training could prepare you for. Again, it dawned on me that there were potentially far worse outcomes than being shot or blown up, and that the mind can be equally – if not more – fragile than the body.

If the atmosphere on the base was tenser than it had been on my first deployment when I began my second tour, it was nothing compared to the nerve-racking afternoon I was to spend while driving from the camp in Pristina to another base several miles away.

We were driving through a rural area of Kosovo, surrounded by the rough, unploughed fields which had been left untended since the conflict began, when a local man appeared on the roadside waving his arms to flag us down. Pulling over we approached the man cautiously, but soon realised that he wasn't a threat. Indeed, his concerned expression and hand gestures indicated that an unexploded piece of ordinance lay approximately one hundred yards away from the road, protruding from the ground in one of the fields.

We assessed the situation and judged that there was a danger that this could well be a minefield – meanwhile, the civilian had already casually strolled over to it and proceeded to start prodding it with his finger, as if it wasn't already clear enough where it was located. After advising him against such a foolish action and instructing him to get off the field and out of harm's way, we decided that we needed to secure a path through to the device so that it could be clearly marked for disposal.

Getting out our mine prodders – simple yet effective extended metal rods which were inserted into the ground at an angle of forty-five degrees into the ground – we slipped on our protective visors and began the laborious task of cautiously edging our way across the field to the unexploded device.

It takes a long time to cover this much ground in a safe fashion – it takes perhaps several minutes to cover only a metre, and with the device such a distance away from the side of the road we made slow progress. The relentless tension I felt for every cautious step I took forwards never once left me while I was on that field, and by the time we had reached the device and created a safe lane – marked with clear paint – we took out our Jayne's Handbook in order to identify what exactly the device was. The handbook was an incredibly useful guide to help us recognise all types of ordnance and weapons. A good Sergeant in the Engineers also had a Battle Box – a small chest which contained all military tactical aid memoires, as well as engineering pamphlets for all likely scenarios for the role.

Fortunately, on this occasion it was an expended piece of artillery and posed no threat to anyone. Had it been live then we would have been tasked with marking it off and relaying the GPS location up the chain of command so that the device could be properly destroyed.

We breathed what felt like an eternal sigh of relief once we returned to our truck, grateful that we'd made it back in one piece.

A few days later I was accompanying the Troop Commander on a short reconnaissance to an abandoned Kosovo army barracks, in order to assess what materials could be salvaged for use by the army. The lads affectionately called him Troopy T. He was a tall, lean and wiry man who looked like he could have modelled for Horse & Hound. Very funny and easy-going, unlike many higher-ranking officers, he would always listen to advice and be open to the opinions of those below his rank.

As we were sifting through the materials, we spotted a large steel radio mast which we considered ideal for reconditioning for our purposes. We began disassembling it and a man soon approached us from the distance. We assumed he was a local objecting to what he perceived as us pillaging from the abandoned base. My troop commander didn't take kindly to interference and, with a stern expression on his face began prodding him in the chest, saying with a voice of authority, "We are taking this!"

The stranger turned to my troop commander with a smile which stopped just a little short of being menacing – it was the kind of patient smile which says, "This isn't over yet – not by a long shot!" It was a smile which seemed to suggest that we might have won this conversation, but we'll be meeting again at some point in the future.

While neither of us knew this at the time, the stranger we'd encountered turned out to be a local KLA commander – the man's face later appeared on screen in an intelligence brief. When my troop commander realised this his face dropped as it dawned on him who he'd been rather unceremoniously jabbing in the chest with his finger. Needless to say, he wore his body armour religiously from that point onwards, his senses on red alert every time he left the base.

Still, he made it through the rest of the conflict without coming to any harm and returned to the United Kingdom free of any battle wounds.

The same couldn't be said for the dead horse which had lain rotting on the road leading into base camp since I had returned from leave. Its previously slumped form had been liberally spread across the ground, splayed out into a thin layer of dead meat and dried bones.

It didn't take long for everyone to find out just how the horse had ended up in such a state: the culprit, a man called Keith who was known as something of a joker, boasted loudly about his handiwork, much to the amusement of the rest of the soldiers. It was army humour at its finest, transforming death into a source of comedy. Keith even told the story of how he'd given the horse such a grisly make-over by driving over it with an industrial road roller to the brigadier who had visited Golez camp and he'd laughed obligingly too.

Everyone seemed to understand the essential function – and necessity – of a twisted sense of humour in the army. For one thing, it serves as a kind of emotional release valve when you're faced with your own mortality.

But not all death can be transformed into a source of gallows humour, and it wasn't long after Keith created his morbid work of art on the path up to camp that I found myself confronting the real horrors of war up close and personal.

I was acting as a driver for the troop sergeant on a hot afternoon and was instructed to take him from Golez to another camp on the other side of Pristina. We made the journey without incident but upon our arrival I was told that I was expected to drive back to Golez on my own. I immediately raised my objections – this was against standard operating procedures – not least on account of the fact that the back of the van which I was driving contained ten guns and stacks of ammunition which would be difficult to keep secure if something were to happen. But my objections were dismissed, and I had no choice but to make the journey back alone.

As I approached Pristina, I saw that the traffic up ahead had come to a standstill, cars and vans desperately trying to edge their way forwards amidst the deadlock which blocked the main road through the town.

Pristina bore a striking resemblance to Greece in terms of its infrastructure and architectural stylings – but now, after the intensive bombing campaign, many of the buildings were destroyed or in a state of abject disrepair. The buildings which remained standing were a mixture of materials, mostly concrete with scaffolding which had been improvised from bamboo.

43

As if to match the chaotic appearance of the town, the roads were incredibly busy, making driving feel a little like participating in Wacky Races. Driving required you to have your wits about you at all times, since observing the rules of the road seemed to be optional to most drivers. This was especially true at night, when you could be driving along one moment only to find a second later a horse and cart pulling out in front of you without any lights, forcing you to screech to a standstill or suffer a potentially fatal collision.

After spending a lot of time driving around the area to perform tasks at different locations, we'd built up a very good mental map of the city; a clear geographical understanding of the area. We knew that the city was like a warren of intertwining streets, and if you took a wrong turn you'd come up against a choke point, as if trapped in a possibly deadly maze.

For a while the atmosphere in the city and the reception we'd had from the locals had been very friendly, particularly in the early days following the overthrow of Milosevic. And yet, there was always the feeling that we were sitting on a powder keg, nervously waiting for the first spark to set it into a blaze.

It was a hot and clammy day and the atmosphere felt electrified, as if the air had been charged and primed for what was about to happen. A group of people emerged from the surrounding buildings and weaved their way through the stationary cars. They were shouting indistinctly and more people soon joined them.

I could see other cars trying to nudge forwards as if their occupants knew that something terrible was coming their way – clearly these people were angry and not knowing where this anger was being directed made me nervous as I thought again of all the weapons racked behind the driver's seat.

The crowd converged on a white car approximately thirty metres ahead of me and started pushing it back and forth, shouting with greater intensity as its occupants sat inside the rocking vehicle, frozen with fear.

The size of the mob grew even larger and suddenly two men were pulled out of the car window.

They appeared to be in their early thirties, their hands raised over their faces in a futile effort to protect themselves from the blows which began to rain down on them from all sides as the crowd's fury increased. I had no idea who they were or why they had been targeted in such a way, although we were all fully aware of the sectarian violence which had been erupting in the region.

There was nothing they could do to protect themselves from the kicks and punches which pounded them to the ground.

I wanted to do something to break up the crowd and perhaps even save their lives but knew that there was nothing I could do with so many weapons. If I left them unattended, I would be breaking protocol and running the huge risk of rifles and ammunition falling into the hands of a mob, and with no translator with me it would be impossible to reason with them anyway. There was also the very real possibility that the mob would turn their rage against myself, so it was all I could do to sit and watch the attack unfold.

It's an understatement to say that I was unnerved by the fact that the whole sections weapons and ammunition were right behind me. If things went even further south, eight rifles along with two light support weapons plus all the ammunition issued to ten men were ready for the taking. The decision to break standing orders and return alone without the sergeant weighed on my mind. I knew that there would be trouble but hadn't foreseen quite what this trouble would be. My main concern lay with my fellow soldiers on the hilltop – while I was stuck in the truck alone, they had no weapons with which to defend themselves.

Two men pushed their way through the crowd towards the victims and I saw a flashing glimmer of steel, realising with horror that they were wielding machetes.

My throat dried up and I felt beads of sweat trickling down my face as the machetes bore down on the two cowering men, cutting through their limbs and sending out huge arcs of blood.

This new level of intensity only seemed to increase the blood lust of the mob – I sat with my mouth agape as each blow cut deeper into their now immobile bodies. I saw their faces, trapped in a final anguished expression as the mob continued to tear apart their already dismembered forms.

A British Army infantry patrol arrived, pulling up behind my truck. It was followed only moments later by a contingent of Russian troops who proceeded to open fire on the crowd.

The Russians were using 7.62mm rounds which had a very distinctive sound. They also had a very distinctive effect on the human body, and my first thought was that I wasn't in an armoured vehicle. All it would take for me to make the trip to the Squadron bar in the sky, buying a round of drinks for passed over comrades, was one stray round.

My second thought was to hope that the mob didn't produce weapons which were deadlier – and with longer-range capacity – than the machetes they'd been wielding. If they did, then me and the other innocent people in the cars in the traffic jam would be caught right in the middle of the crossfire.

But then, a split second later, a calmness transcended around me, as if a guardian angel or higher power were communicating to me that it wasn't my time yet, and that I could relax. This is something that many people who have experienced traumatic situations have reported, as if all that one can do when circumstances become this fraught is to let go and accept whatever comes.

There is a belief that when you are about to die a loved one comes to collect you. The presence of this loved one allows for the transition from our humanity to our spirituality without the traumatic effects you'd expect from such a paradigm-shifting experience. As I scanned the crowds around my vehicle I realised I couldn't see anyone I knew or had known and took this as another indication that it wasn't my time, so I breathed a sigh of relief and waited for the situation to calm down and present an opportunity for me to get out of the line of fire.

The mob started to disperse and miraculously a break came in the deadlock, allowing the people who had been trapped in their cars witnessing the horrific attack to drive on. I took the opportunity to get out of this hot zone as quickly as possible, and by the time I watched the scene receding in my rear view mirror I finally was able to relax, trying not to contemplate just how badly the situation could have unfolded.

I arrived back at the Golez camp still shaken by what I had seen and told my troop Staff Sergeant of the incident. He gave me a look of concern, saying, "that sounds pretty bad," and that was the end of the conversation. The brevity of our exchange brought home to me just how commonplace the horrors of war really are when you find yourself in a conflict zone – there's little doubt in my mind that attacks as these were most likely daily occurrences, if not here in Kosovo then elsewhere around the world where conflict and war disrupts the lives of millions.

I looked at the dead horse again that evening as I gathered my thoughts about what I had witnessed, and it became clear that the only thing I could do was to put the events of the day to the back of my mind. This proved easier to accomplish than I'd expected – in fact, a little too easy – and I felt somewhat numbed to these events even within a few hours of it happening. It was as if I understood the only pragmatic thing to do would be to forget about it completely, and so my mind quickly obliged. It would be a long time before I confronted the implications of what I had seen.

I didn't realise at the time just how this would come back to haunt me later in life, and that deliberately repressing these memories was probably the worst decision I could have made. I may have survived my deployment to Kosovo physically intact but as I would discover for myself in more ways than one, some injuries aren't always visible from the outside, and often these are the wounds which take the longest to fully heal.

A quote from an anonymous author captured the essence of what I was about to experience:

A Senior NCO went by and the Soldier with PTSD called out for help.

The Senior NCO yelled at, told him to suck it up dig deep and drive on, then threw him a shovel. But the Soldier with PTSD could not suck it up and drive on, so he dug the hole deeper.

A Senior Officer went by and the Soldier with PTSD called out for help.

The Senior Officer told him to use the tools your Senior NCO has given you then threw him a bucket. But the Soldier with PTSD was using the tools his Senior NCO gave him, so he dug the hole deeper and filled the bucket.

A psychiatrist walked by. The Soldier with PTSD said, "Help! I can't get out!"

The psychiatrist gave him some drugs and said, "Take this. It will relieve the pain." The Soldier with PTSD said thanks, but when the pills ran out, he was still in the hole.

A well-known psychologist rode by and heard the Soldier with PTSD cries for help. He stopped and asked," How did you get there? Were you born there? Did your parents put you there? Tell me about yourself, it will alleviate your sense of loneliness".

So the Soldier with PTSD talked with him for an hour, then the psychologist had to leave, but he said he'd be back next week.

The Soldier with PTSD thanked him, but he was still in the hole.

A priest came by. The Soldier with PTSD called for help. The priest gave him a Bible and said, "I'll say a prayer for you".

He got down on his knees and prayed for the Soldier with PTSD, then he left.

The Soldier with PTSD was very grateful, he read the Bible, but he was still stuck in the hole.

A recovering Soldier with PTSD happened to be passing by. The Soldier with PTSD cried out, "Hey, help me. I'm stuck in this hole!"

Right away the recovering Soldier with PTSD jumped down in the hole with him. The Soldier with PTSD said, "What are you doing? Now we're both stuck here!!" But the recovering Soldier with PTSD said, "Calm down. It's okay. I've been here before. I know how to get out".

~Author Unknown

Post-traumatic stress disorder is like being lost in a strange country without a map, when suddenly a fog descends, and confusion sets in as you lose all of your bearings. All of a sudden, the person you once thought you knew completely is no longer looking back at you in the mirror. He may look the same from the outside, but the glint in the eye which once reflected back is gone, just as the spring in the step has taken flight.

As your zest for life starts to ebb away day by day, the battle to regain your former self rages on. You try to figure out how and why your life became an existence based only on survival. You look for the way back to the path you once walked with pride, but the fog which clouds your judgement is too dense.

Once you fall into this mental uncharted territory all points of navigation are lost, and you wander around dazed and confused. It's a seemingly endless cycle which leads inevitably to depression, until – if you are lucky – you find the help needed to get you back on the right path. I realised that the work needed to recover wasn't finished yet: for me, this was just the start of the path to recovery.

Chapter 3 Brain injury

Julie and I began drifting apart once I was posted to
Northern Ireland. Being a career soldier at the time I'd
always wanted to continue to serve across the water, and I
knew that a posting in Northern Ireland would be a good step
towards achieving my career goals and give me the
experience I required. I was eager to expand my experience
and qualifications as an electrician and had been
recommended for the Clerk of Work Electrical course,
something which had the potential to open up avenues well
beyond the military realm. Over a year had passed since I
had returned from Kosovo and I was eager to make
something of my life.

I'd seen a position for volunteers to be posted in Ireland and
applied immediately, thinking it was too great an opportunity
to pass up. But I never told Julie that I had volunteered. This
was a reflection on how I always seemed to put my career
before my marriage. In hindsight it was very unlikely that any
medals or army pensions would guarantee anything
approaching true happiness during my retirement, but when
we're young and career-driven it's easy to overlook the
collateral damage from our ambitions.

When I received confirmation of the posting I told Julie, and
she came with me for a period of time. We lived off the
military camp in an area which was mixed with the local
population, and for some time we were very happy. But deep
down I felt uncertain and unsettled. I didn't know why, but I
felt as if I didn't deserve to be happy yet and I ended up
pushing Julie away.

Living outside the wire in a mixed community, where political
tensions were running higher than in your average
neighbourhood, brought with it additional challenges which
stressed our relationship. One incident involved around ten

cars owned by soldiers being vandalised, their tyres slashed. In and of itself this might not have been too disturbing, but it hinted at something broader and more insidious, with the focus on soldiers' vehicles becoming a chilling reminder that potential enemies knew who we were and where we lived. It certainly did little to foster an environment conducive to a stress-free marriage.

I'd noticed this tension from the moment we moved into the married quarters. One of my boxes of belongings had split open, spilling my uniform onto the floor.

The man moving my belongings announced to the people watching, "Hey mate, your green kit is going everywhere!".

This gave me a troubling impression he had an idea who I was and I couldn't help but feel insecure.

Inevitably, Julie became too unhappy with living in Northern Ireland to stay, so we arranged for her to move back to the UK and stay with her parents. Our belongings were put into storage and she drove the car back home, but on repatriating back in the United Kingdom she almost immediately decided she wanted to come back. While it would have been possible it would also have been highly costly to pay for the move, and in my mind the fact she had left me had already damaged our relationship irreparably.

I remained, a married man essentially living the life of a single man, housed in a block with the same financial obligations and a wife many miles away. We became further estranged from one another, and I pushed her further away, as if feeling I somehow didn't deserve the relationship. It was to be a pattern which would repeat through most of my relationships, as I continued to discover myself and what I wanted when I eventually met Jade.

A friend of mine called Griff noticed what was happening and told me that I would be divorced soon if I didn't do something about it. It was the beginning of the end for us, and the beginning also for me of the sensation that I would struggle to settle for a long time. I decided that, if the dissolution of my marriage was inevitable, I would put all of my efforts into my career.

Griff was an older guy – the kind of man who fits the expression, "been there, bought the t-shirt" - and he was often frank and honest when we spoke. He told me that I was staring down the barrel of a divorce, and while I knew what was coming on one level, in reality I continued to live in ignorance and self-denial, burying my head deeper into the sand. The job – my life in the military – was the justification I turned to for this attitude, but perhaps deep down I just didn't think I was ready for or capable of being in a relationship yet.

Julie and I finally spoke openly to one another and admitted that the marriage was over, setting about putting the divorce proceedings into motion. Years later we bumped into one another while I was settling in a small village. We spoke of the past, and I could tell instantly that it was still raw for her. But the head injury I was to suffer had fragmented my memory, and aspects of this period in my life were missing. I couldn't help feel that it was unfair that she had become so burdened with the past while I'd had a clean sheet.

As our divorce proceedings started, I began to think long and hard about where to go from here with my career choices. Having had unpleasant experiences in the forces which weighed on my mind, I was starting to take thoughts of leaving the military more seriously. Regardless of the administrative debacle surrounding my mother's death, I'd been in the military for five years and had reached the point that many others arrive at.

I tried to fill the void which was expanding in my life with material possessions. I bought a convertible sports car, which was beautiful to be sure. But I had no one to take out in it, to share my enjoyment and create memories with. It marked the beginning of a pattern which was to become increasingly familiar, where I would replace relationships with materialistic objects. It saddened me deeply and I questioned why the marriage had failed. But in truth, I knew the answer long before I'd asked the question.

It was time to make a decision as to whether or not a life in the army was the right choice. Was a career wearing a uniform and taking orders really what I wanted? Or was it time to step back and return to civilian life where I would have a potentially greater say over my own destiny?

I wrestled with this dilemma for some time, but as is often the case the reality turned out somewhat differently than expected, and the moment my military career came to an end was a strange day which I could have never foreseen.

I was in Northern Ireland as part of the only engineering regiment in the theatre, providing Engineering support to the brigade. It was during the Good Friday Agreement and we had been tasked with the decommissioning of the observation towers which were located on the border. I was among the first troops to be using the roads to move the heavy equipment – since the early 1970s it had been safer to conduct movement of troops and equipment via helicopter, in order to minimise the chances of ambush.

I was starting to build up a great social life. It felt as if a taste for the finer things in life was already in my blood, while the cosmopolitan city of Belfast provided the backdrop for a thriving social scene. This was just so long as you stuck to the rules and didn't go out in large groups. I always made sure I went to the right places and in smaller groups, keeping my eyes and ears open and remaining vigilant.

I never told anyone I met what I did for a living. If anyone asked, I would allude to being there for some boring contract job – the kind of work which causes people's eyes to glaze over when you start talking about it. It was a good way of guaranteeing conversation would quickly move onto something more interesting, too. Otherwise I'd simply change the subject, and on occasion I'd go to another bar where I could avoid probing lines of questioning.

Inevitably people sometimes knew who you were, but as long as you didn't broadcast it you were safe.

One day I had an appointment at Musgrove Park hospital for a routine surgery on a varicose seal in my groin – this was hardly a major undertaking, and yet for some reason I had awoken that day with an uneasy feeling which made me inexplicably apprehensive about what was to come. I'd slept poorly the night before too, which left me feeling drained for the day and exaggerated the uneasy feeling in the pit of my stomach.

The issue for which I required the surgery was potentially causing fertility issues, having been diagnosed as infertile before. As I was becoming increasingly preoccupied with thoughts of becoming a father naturally this had concerned me a great deal, and it wasn't until years later that I discovered that the fertility test had not been processed correctly and I had been given incorrect results. It was a strange twist of fate – the pursuit of becoming a father which led me to have this operation would ultimately take me down the path towards becoming who I am now.

To this day I'm unsure where this feeling came from, but something deep in my subconscious seemed to be telling me that something bad was on the horizon. It was a strange yet somehow tangible sensation which reminded me of my mother; not a clear voice in my mind but rather a vague, distinct and familiar presence.

Shrugging the feeling aside I made my way to breakfast in the cook house, only drinking coffee on the instructions of the hospital. But the nagging feeling soon returned, and I again had an intuition that something was going to go wrong. It didn't make sense, since I was only having a local anaesthetic for a minor routine. But the feeling wouldn't go away.

I got in the car and put the roof down to welcome the morning sun. The familiar drive to Belfast felt different, but I had yet to figure out exactly what had changed and why I was feeling like this. I was young, fit and healthy with a career which was ready to take off. I led what I thought to be a very happy life.

So why was I so full of anxiety? Why did this sensation feel like an ominous premonition?

I arrived at the hospital putting this uncomfortable feeling to one side and checked in at the reception desk for my appointment. Before long a nurse came to fetch me for the operation and I was taken into surgery, where they proceeded to administer a local anaesthetic. The operation ran smoothly (notwithstanding the three female medical students watching on as the doctors applied the varicose seal – I don't consider myself a particularly bashful person but this moment was hardly the most dignified moment of my life) and for a second I thought that my previous anxiety had been unfounded. But any thoughts of relief were destroyed soon after I left the surgery.

I was being transferred back to the military side of the hospital by ambulance when the accident happened. As I lay prone on a stretcher, the medic was struggling to lift me down from the ambulance when I felt the stretcher falling away and my inert body crashing to the ground. Perhaps the medic had pressed the wrong lever or stumbled as he tried to lower me down from the ambulance – regardless of the circumstances, I hit the ground hard at a forty-five-degree angle, my skull smacking hard against the unforgiving concrete.

Immediately my world fell into pitch blackness. I couldn't move no matter how hard I tried and when I attempted to open my eyes they remained firmly shut. I panicked and tried moving again, but my entire body was refusing to cooperate with my brain. I could hear a voice calling out my name and a terrifying thought ran through my mind – this is it, I'm dying! The thought brought with it an inevitable wave of fear, taking hold of my brain with alarming intensity as once again I tried and failed to move.

But then, almost as instantly as the fear of imminent death had taken hold of my thoughts, another sudden wave overcame me, one of calm tranquillity. I don't know why this rapid change from fear to peacefulness came about any more than I can rationally explain the premonition earlier that day that something bad was going to happen, and yet this change certainly occurred, and I felt my heartbeat settling down as I realised that I was going to be alright.

Feeling my breathing becoming more calm and measured I waited patiently for my brain to reboot, then attempted to open my eyes once again. This time they opened without any objection, and as my vision came into focus the first thing I saw was the worried expression on a nurse's face, hovering over me as she gazed down at my semi-naked body lying sprawled on the cold, uncomfortable concrete.

It felt as if I must have drifted in and out of consciousness several times from this point onwards – even now my recollection comes in fits and starts, with hazy images of the inside of a moving elevator and a nondescript hospital ward full of anonymous patients, as if my brain were struggling to interpret reality.

A doctor soon came to check up on my condition, but as I tried to speak the words came out slurred and the doctor mistook this for the after effects of a general anaesthetic which hadn't yet worn off. I attempted to correct him but again my voice was incoherent. I tried to figure out what time it was but I had slipped in and out of consciousness so much I'd become completely disorientated. I was phasing in and out of reality, the sequence of events playing out like fragments of memories.

The sound of the medic's voice – the one who had caused me to fall, whether through carelessness or because of a genuine mistake – could be heard alongside the doctor. He was laughing about the accident and joking to the other hospital staff, saying how it was my fault that he'd dropped me. He tried to claim that I was too heavy, which instantly struck me as an absurd justification for his own actions – actions which were to change my life forever.

Despite my muddled head these words infuriated me and if I'd had the energy to move, I'd have been more than tempted to get up and throttle him for his crude attempt to absolve himself of any blame for my injury. But it was hard enough for me to simply remain conscious, and I lay there helpless as the medic walked away from my bed, his casual laughter disappearing down the hospital corridors. I often wondered over the years if he ever realised just how much his simple error was to change my life forever. Part of me thought that he might realise and feel guilty one day, but really I knew that this incident would never enter his thoughts again.

The doctor examined me – a superficial series of tests conducted in what felt like a perfunctory manner which would reveal very little about the severity of my injury – and I slipped back into unconsciousness once again, too tired now to think about anything.

I roused once again later that day at around 7 o'clock in the evening feeling incredibly sick and nauseous. My vision was blurred, and while initially I put this down to being unconscious for such a length of time, as the minutes passed and images failed to gain any clarity my understandable concern for my eyesight began to grow. The hospital kept me in overnight for further observation, but by the next morning they decided to discharge me and, with what felt like the worst hangover I had ever experienced – not to mention the feeling that my dignity had been taken apart and ripped into tatters – I climbed uneasily into my car and began the journey back to camp.

For much of the following week it felt as if I were in a vague dream.
I remained in Ireland working on the preparation for clearance from the regiment for my course, sleeping frequently and tired when I was awake, dismissing this lethargy as a consequence of the bang on my head. As hard as I tried, I found it almost impossible to concentrate. In addition to the persistent blurred vision I was also getting frequent headaches which pounded the inside of my skull. At first I thought that this must be a normal reaction to my fall and hoped that it would pass in time, but as the days went by and there was no sign that these symptoms would alleviate I started to become increasingly concerned that something more serious was amiss.

Still, I resolved to do my best to get on with my life until something could be done about it – I was in the midst of making preparations for leaving Ireland after six years stationed there and tried to focus on my upcoming plans following the end of my tour of duty. I was due to continue with my Clerk of Works (COW) Electrical qualifications – something I'd been working towards taking on for the previous eight years – and this highly specialised role required a great deal of dedication simply to get onto the course. I hoped to continue on from this qualification to pursue a degree in electrical engineering. Progression through the ranks could mean an exciting career leading up to retirement at the rank of Major, and I had mapped out the next 25 years of my military service doing a job which I thoroughly loved.

At any one time there are around sixty COW (E) in the Royal Engineers, which gives a good impression of just how highly specialised this job really is. With a career path leading up to the rank of Major I was understandably keen to deliver my all and prove myself capable of handling the work, and this resolve gave me the encouragement I needed to try and put aside the after effects of being knocked unconscious.

I had started working towards the course as a Lance Corporal, but even during the four years prior to that as a Sapper I had consistently applied myself and earned promotion at every available opportunity. I'd been excelling at my work during this time and had been getting some exceptional confidential reports tracking and assessing my performance, so it was not without good reason that I was confident in my ability to rise to the occasion.

Recalling the time, I went on the Senior Non-Commissioned Officer Education Command Leadership Management course when I was a Lance Corporal was amusing, if only in that ironic way that becomes clear later in life, since when I walked into the classroom some of the other people on the course told me I was in the wrong room. It seemed to point towards my head injury ahead of the curve, as if foreshadowing the neurological problems which were to come.

The incident reminded me how often people judged the knowledge I held within me based upon simple categorisations such as my appearance and status in life. It's a shorthand many of us use to assess the people we meet, and it can affect how we view ourselves as well. But this was something which would change dramatically after the accident, when I would eventually put all the pieces together and uncover the real me. As I experienced more and grew

59

as an individual, years later and after studying many subjects I realised how my intellectual capacity and my depth of knowledge had deepened.

On my first look at promotion I had been promoted to the rank of Corporal, a promotion attributed to the excellent performance I put in during the annual section completions. Out of thirty sections I had left over men from the regiment with no training and won third place, despite the fact that I was a Lance Corporal while the other sections were being led by experienced Corporals.

We were just three points off winning, and I found out later from a friend who was on the directing staff that I had at one point been storming ahead with winning the completion. This, combined with the highly technical trade task I was in charge of, earned me a personal letter of recommendation when I submitted my application to the board for selection. I even saw an email saying it was the best application they had seen in four years.

I had a week's leave prior to starting the COW (E) course and seemed to sleep far more than I would usually. The problems with my vision and excruciating headaches continued, and as much as I tried to focus beyond the pain, I was unable to focus on reading and revision. Just as the blurred vision made the words on the page indiscernible, so too did the throbbing pain in my head make it almost impossible to hold onto a train of thought. I spent most of this week on leave preparing for the course with daily mathematics and other academic work, but as I tried to focus, I found that this was incredibly difficult, and I became easily distracted and tired. The week flew by, and the next thing I knew I was reporting for duty.

I reported to Chatham 1 Royal School of Military Engineering to begin the course in earnest, but already within the first week of attending the classes I noticed that things were wrong, and my condition was deteriorating. We were introduced to the civilian instructors and our fellow classmates, and during the first three weeks of mathematics classes I began to daydream, my attention drifting away as the teacher delivered his instructions. It felt as if I were losing control of my mind, my thoughts no longer under my own

60

volition. These ailments became infused in my daily experience and I would find myself easily distracted, often breaking away from someone during mid-sentence. I frequently arrived late at the classroom and missed out on crucial information required for the course.

It is to be expected when an experienced soldier is undertaking a critical career- changing course and his frequently late for the lessons, alarm bells begin to ring within the system. One of the first assumptions is that the person is experiencing personal problems: the stress of the course may be taking its toll, or personal relationships have become strained. But for me this was clearly not the case. While the erratic vision and headaches were causing some frustration

this hadn't led to stress, and my relationship with my former girlfriend Emma was a happy and compassionate one which gave me strength and encouragement.

I'd first met Emma when I was back in England on leave, finalising the divorce proceedings with Julie. We met when I was on a night out with friends – I was standing at the bar and she'd walked past and pinched my bum and continued on with a cheeky smile on her face. A few moments later she approached me again, and I caught her attention and said, "If you're going to do that again, you'd better do it properly!"

She laughed and I introduced myself, and a relationship which held me strong and steadfast began with an evening of non-stop conversation which seemed to cover every topic under the sun. She became a wonderful companion and helped me overcome numerous obstacles. We'd separated amicably prior to the beginning of my course but had remained good friends, and I often rang her for advice.

It was Emma who considered that me failing the maths test suggested something was amiss, and that this was not like me at all. We began spending more time together when I was on sick leave and during this time I began to long for someone close to support me; a confidante and lover to be there during the darkness which was to come.

When I'd told my family about the head injury they had seemed distant and unconcerned – since we'd drifted apart following on from the death of my mother a closeness had been lost. My brothers and sisters even laughed and joked about it, and while later I understood that this was simply a coping mechanism on their part for processing the news, at the time their apparent lack of consideration left me feeling hurt.

After this failure just three weeks into the course, it hit me hard just how negatively the brain injury was affecting my life. My blurred vision and foggy thinking were seriously putting my future in jeopardy. Emma thought that something must be glaringly wrong, but I thought that perhaps simply wearing glasses might be the answer to the problem with my eyes, so I informed the Army about my condition and they referred me to an optician.

The examination led me to wearing glasses, but even with them on I found that my vision would still shift out of focus making it difficult to read. Strange optical phenomenon started to occur – sometimes the text before me would shift around the page, with letters and numbers reversing as I tried to take them in. It would be some time from now before I would discover that this is a symptom of acquired dyslexia.

Understandably, the combination of reading difficulties and the pain from the regular headaches meant that before long I fell behind on what was already a high uptake course – the strict interview process was designed to be so rigorous in order to ensure that all the candidates possessed the necessary high attention rate, and my neurological condition was completely hindering me in this respect. To get on the course a selection process had been put in place.

The year before I had been for the interview but had failed as I had just received my divorce from Julie. Obviously, I had not been in the correct frame of mind and should have deferred this for a year. It was recommended to me that I didn't apply again, words which rang loudly in my head. Yet being very determined I decided to focus on any shortcomings and eventually reapplied, this time with a personal recommendation from the Office Commanding the Special Team of Royal Engineers.

The second set of interviews saw me in a completely different mind-set. The interview consisted of a panel of specialists: A Lieutenant Colonel, a Warrant Officer and Captain of the Wing. The interview lasted over half an hour and ranged from questions about military capabilities to more specific technical understandings. I was asked about the special Live Line Tapping I had done in Northern Ireland and gave textbook answers.

The Lieutenant Colonel said to me, "it hasn't changed that much since I wrote the manual on it" and I knew at that point that I was going to get on the course this time.

I explained why I had changed so much since my previous application: "The divorce had taken the wind out of my sails," I said. "But now I am more focused than ever".

Despite all of this hard work to get on the course, my neurological condition now worked against me. It seemed as if there was nothing I could do about it, and as much as I fought to stay positive about my situation once again anxiety began to creep in.

It was as if I felt the uncertainty of what was going to transpire. I felt lost and without a compass. I'd focused primarily on my career in the military for years – often at the expense of my personal relationships – and given everything I had to get on this course. Now, in the cold, hard light of day, fate had intervened and changed my path forever. I questioned this endlessly at the time and cursed the reasons why, only to look back now and see that it was all meant to be.

After speaking to my superiors I was referred to an ophthalmologist (not the kind of word you want in your vocabulary, no matter how much you might admire the beauty of language) at Maidstone hospital where they carried out further tests on my vision. They discovered that when they shone a bright light directly into my eyes it triggered an intense headache, and further tests from the consultant revealed a shadow in my left eye. To say that this was a distressing thing to hear would be a huge understatement, and when he sent me home with instructions to return the next day for additional tests, it was all I could do to

remain as calm as possible and avoid contemplating what the worst-case scenario might be.

I spent the first night after the prognosis lying wide awake in bed, as all the worst-case scenarios ran wildly through my mind. My worst fears had been set free and cutting through the paranoia was a certainty that it was serious. I didn't realise yet the full extent of the matter and how serious it truly was. I had terrible notions that the shadow in my eye could have been a tumour, or something else equally dreadful and potentially fatal.

Like many people in times of personal crisis, my mind ran with these thoughts. In such moments, our fears throw a party and go to town pondering the worst-case scenarios. The thought of losing my vision – closing the window to the world around me – also raced through my mind, and only the presence of a contrasting calm voice telling me not to worry about things I didn't yet know managed to ease the sense of dread.

The following day's tests baffled the consultant – after examining my eyes once again he turned to me and informed me that the shadow had now completely vanished and that he was at a loss as to what the root cause of my problems were. I was sent on sick leave until my next consultation with Dr. Patrick Trend, an incredible doctor specialising in neurology with a frank yet pleasant demeanour which put me at ease the moment I met him. Thanks to his stylish suits – which looked as if they had been cut by the finest tailors of Savile Row and his debonair manner – he quickly earned the nickname "Doctor Trendy". After conducting a variety of tests, including an MRI scan, Dr. Trend referred me to a psychiatrist for psychometric testing, and by now the seemingly endless round of referrals and tedious stretches of waiting for results was beginning to take an emotional toll.

By this point I had been on sick leave for too long and was rather unceremoniously removed from the course, my personal belongings being taken and put into the QM storage. Until I received a clear diagnosis on my condition I was to remain on sick leave, and I was posted to the Y list reserved for soldiers on long term sickness. My only options from this point on were to either recover my health soon and return to active duty or receive a medical discharge.

Which one of these it was to be there was simply no way of predicting.

After convalescing at home for some time, Dr. Trend eventually referred me to Headley Court Defence Medical Rehabilitation Centre. It was here that I had the great fortune to meet Kit Malia and Ann Brannigan, two experts in brain injury and rehabilitation who were to contribute immensely to my road to recovery, and I am forever indebted to them for their care and professionalism. Kit was the only Certificated Cognitive Rehabilitation Therapist in the United Kingdom – having spent several years working with people with learning difficulties, he then spent an additional two decades at Headly Court working as a cognitive rehabilitation therapist with adults who have acquired neurological injuries.

As Project Officer for the mild Traumatic Brain Injury Program it's fair to say that he was the best suited individual to assess my condition. Ann, too, had an impressive background in her field: also specialising in the cognitive and executive sequel of acquired brain injury, she has lectured around the world and sits on the board of a number of key organisations which study brain injury rehabilitation. Indeed, her efforts were notable enough for her to receive an Order of the British Empire (OBE) in 2010 for her services provided to rehabilitation. It is fair to say that I was without a doubt in good hands.

Kit was the first person to inform me that my condition could be permanent and that matters were unlikely to improve, and this news was devastating to hear – to think that my mind and brain would never be the same again was a realisation that I wouldn't wish upon a single soul. At the same time, it was his kind demeanour and gentle personality – not to mention his intellect and calm wit – which helped me to take this news on board with enough strength to see through the darkness towards a potentially bright future.

Most importantly of all, Kit was the first person to be honest with me, telling me exactly how it was with no evasions or beating about the bush. The news changed my world, although in reality this had all changed the second my skull cracked on the concrete in Ireland. But Kit's words brought it all home in full; it was as if I was receiving a telegram to inform me of the gravity of the situation.

It dawned on me with finality that my military career was over and all that remained was for me to try and pick up the pieces of my shattered life and move forwards as best I could. Looking back over my military career I couldn't help but find it ironic that, after serving in Kosovo and Northern Ireland, it would be something like careless negligence which would end my time in the armed forces.

I felt somewhat ashamed when I thought of my fellow soldiers who had been shot or blown up in the line of duty – to be dropped off a stretcher in what should have been a safe environment and landing on one's head seemed an indignity compared to the sacrifices others had made, proving that you can never second guess what fate has in store for you.

After these assessments I was given a date to be admitted to a head injury ward; a controlled environment in which I was to be under constant supervision where everything I said would be logged by the staff. When I finally arrived there I couldn't help but note that the place had the feel of a prison, both in terms of the walls which surrounded the complex and the treatment I was soon to experience. In some ways the ward was conducive to recovery, and yet I felt that the constant observation and recording of everything I said ended up becoming very intrusive. I understood the rationale behind it, but being fiercely independent and then having to have a nurse accompany me every time I left the ward was a crushing reminder of how far I had really fallen.

I often thought of the film One Flew Over the Cuckoo's Nest starring Jack Nicholson. The film takes place inside a psychiatric ward, and it bore a strong resemblance to the constant monitoring required for people recovering from a head injury. To a private and independent person like me, this constant observation soon becomes very suffocating.

The highlight of my week came when I was allowed to go into town at the weekend, escaping the confines of the ward walls and the aura of illness which pervaded the air. Outside I felt liberated, accompanied by two nurses who came along for my safety, dressed in civilian clothes (had they been in uniform there's no doubt I'd have got a few strange looks, although my blue tinted glasses did create a few curious expressions anyway).

The manner in which the head consultant dealt with my condition almost led me to lose my mind completely. The trauma in the back of my head where I had sustained the injury had damaged the occipital lobe – the part of the brain which deals with visual processing – which accounted for the strange visual spasms I had been experiencing. The consultant, however, seemed to be unaware of the extent of the damage I'd experienced in this region and instead put my condition down to a psychological complex, repeatedly making this suggestion and brushing off the possibility of a neurological root cause.

On one occasion he arrived at my bed along with a junior doctor and together they repeatedly pushed upon me the idea that the cause was psychological – their manner was by turns aggressive and consoling and I couldn't help thinking they were putting me through the good cop, bad cop routine. They seemed intent on making me feel like a criminal who was deliberately deceiving them about my condition.

Coming after the reassuring professionalism displayed by Kit and Ann, this turn of events was thoroughly depressing, leaving me shattered and in tears. After all that I'd been through up to this point I'd never have expected the system to react with such unwarranted suspicion, and as I lay sobbing on my bed I felt utterly inconsolable. A kind nurse tried to lift my spirits and offer me comfort but my thoughts were whirring around my head, trying to figure out what I'd done to deserve such treatment. Soon, I sank towards my lowest ebb; frustrated, tired and exasperated at my situation.

The following morning, after yet another fitful and sleepless night, I filled my day sack with the heaviest items I could find and headed down to the nearby deep pond, sitting at the water's edge and considering ending it all. I'd never been suicidal before, but the thought of just walking into the water and letting everything go seemed incredibly appealing – death, I thought, would solve everything, the cold water's embrace offering a resolution to my situation that nothing else could match. During these dark times until this point the thought of committing suicide had never occurred to me. But then something seemed to resonate deep inside me, triggered by the awful experience of the junior doctor that day. It seemed completely unfair to me that, during this time of vulnerability, I didn't have the razor sharp brain that would have rebuffed such issues the doctor raised with a sharp rhetorical comment. But in that moment I had lacked the faculty to respond as I otherwise normally would, and this had left me feeling disempowered and depressed, as if a voice in my head were declaring "it's sink or swim time".

As I looked at my reflection in the still waters a familiar voice sounded inside my head urging me to strengthen my resolve and face up to these issues. I'd heard this voice before in my darkest hours, echoing from my subconscious instructing me to fight through this and not take the coward's way out. The voice counselled that I had done nothing wrong and that the state of my life at this point was through no fault of my own.

Was this the presence I had heard the day of the accident that reminded me of my mother? Or was it something else – something beyond the temporal realm? Some higher power, perhaps?

Whatever the source of these messages (whether it was the deep realms of the subconscious or something utterly outside of myself, although I'd never considered myself religious in the dogmatic sense) the impression it left was profound, ultimately sending me on the path to question my very existence.

I needed to get back on my feet and fight the system that was supposed to be there to help and protect me but had utterly failed me, so with a new sense of conviction and purpose I stood tall and left the edge of the pond behind, determined to avoid hitting such a low point ever again.

Kit had previously spoken to me about a barrister by the name of Allison Eddy QC who was a senior partner at Irwin Mitchell, and I took it under advisement to pursue a claim for clinical negligence. Engaging Allison's services, I began to fight back, my remaining time at Headly Court becoming a game of patience as I sat through ward round after ward round in which my disbelief at the attitude of the consultant was matched only by my sheer dismay and loss of respect for the military. It seemed crystal clear to me now that the institution had an unpleasant side the public remains in the dark about, and that once a serviceman is not operational or politically expedient, the army is quite happy to cut them loose without a second thought for past services rendered.

There were many heroes convalescing at Headly Court who had suffered permanent injuries in the course of serving Queen and Country, and while their treatment in the facility was largely commendable, the truth of the matter is that the real battle for many veterans begins once they've been discharged, where a return to civilian life brings with it a series of challenges they have to contend with without the appropriate support networks.

My six months stay at Headly Court passed excruciatingly slowly – I had a myriad of endless tests and assessments to face as well as a strategy of medication and counselling allowing me to come to terms with the new me. It is sometimes said that after a head injury like mine it takes up to seven years to adjust to the changes you experience, and the thought of such a long, drawn out process of change and adaptation was a traumatic realisation to come to terms with. Sometimes I hoped that a new diagnosis would bring with it a miracle cure and I would be able to return to my former life, but such a dream never manifested itself in my reality, and the truth of the matter is my condition was outside the realms of the neurological understanding of the time.

Indeed, the methods to diagnose the extent of my brain injury were perhaps twenty years away from the current medical abilities, made up as it was of a group of symptoms clustered together to form a new, as yet unnamed, condition unfamiliar to science. Hearing that the source of my trauma was something unknown only made my emotional state worsen, as I questioned the very essence of my own mind. With the persistent questioning from the consultant continuing to insinuate that the root cause might be psychological, I became deeply introspective. Were these symptoms real? Or were they products of my imagination? Lost in this unknown wilderness I started questioning my own sanity.

My saviour and guide through these uncertain and troubling times was without a doubt Kit. As well as being the first person to offer me a truly honest prognosis, he seemed to understand from the beginning that I was being

completely honest about my problems and that I was in desperate need of his professional help. There was no doubt a degree of professional curiosity underlying his commitment to my case, with the cluster of strange symptoms which characterised my brain injury pointing away from the frontal lobe – where most brain injuries tend to manifest themselves –to the rear of the head, transpiring from the rare downward-tilted motion as my head was driven into the concrete from the angle of the stretcher. This may well have compressed the top of my spine into the Chalria 1 malformation affecting the larger brain stem.

Without this malformation most people would simply experience minor concussion. In my case, since this area of the brain includes the occipital lobe which deals with vision, along with the parietal occipital temporal lobe which deals with immersing sound and vision in the brain, my post-trauma symptoms conformed to expectations for such an injury.

While very little is known about these areas of the brain and consequently injuries sustained to this area are difficult to diagnose, Kit seemed to understand the implications and put the pieces together very quickly, emailing his findings to a colleague in America who was considered a leading voice in this field. While their prognosis was speculative it reassured me that, contrary to the insistence of the consultants at

Headly Court, this was indeed a neurological rather than psychological condition. While this may have done nothing to counteract the debilitating effects I continued to experience, it at least took away the doubts I'd been feeling about my sanity.

Still, with more questions than answers remaining and a military career in tatters, my mood remained erratic and prone to dips into despair, accentuated by the frequent headaches and problems with my vision. The medication which had been my crutch with which to deal with my symptoms inevitably transformed into something of a curse as my addiction to the drugs began to increase, and before long it began to feel as if I were little more than a zombie wasting my life away. Indeed, without the much-needed support I got from friends, family and professionals I fear that I may not have recovered at all.

I contacted Kit during the process of writing this book, to see if he remembered my case and to explain what I was planning with this project. I was very surprised to hear that the approach he used with me, including blue sunglasses which reduced the amount of light going into the eyes (and would become a trademark feature for me during my period of recovery), had been adopted for seven other patients of his. Such a low number is a clear indication of just how rare this condition was. At the same time, I felt a sense of pride that my injury and Kit's research had led to others being helped with this treatment path. I gladly offered Kit my help if he required anyone to talk through with his patients the effects of such a head injury.

One person for whom I shall be eternally grateful for their friendship and compassion was a veteran called Karl Hinnet. At first glance you'd be forgiven for thinking he was a rather quiet and unassuming fellow; a softly spoken man from Birmingham, in truth Karl was a real hero who had been through far more than most could ever imagine. When serving in Iraq he had been in a tank trying to rescue SAS soldiers from an operation when his vehicle was struck with petrol bombs, dousing him in flames and severely burning his flesh.

The horrific imagery of this attack made it onto the news, imprinted in the minds of millions of people as they watched the conflict unfold. When we first met at Headly Court he was undergoing massive reconstructive surgery, and we stuck up a rapport which soon developed into a close friendship. I didn't know it at the time, but Karl would end up playing a significant role in my future.

My time at Headly Court was finally coming to an end.

After the fateful ward round which had reduced me to tears, I had decided to keep my head down and see my time through. After all the tests I had been through and the constant battle with the hierarchy of the system it was finally time for me to be discharged. I'd gone from being a completely independent person to living in a residential ward, and for much of the time if I wanted to leave the ward I had to be accompanied by a nurse.

But now it was time to reintegrate with the real world. I left the ward at Headly Court a quiet and humbled man, entirely different from when I'd first arrived there. My time there had taken a severe toll on my well-being and highlighted to me a number of issues I didn't realise I was facing.

As I packed up my belongings ready to go home and be with Emma I couldn't help feeling that my independence was gone. Transitioning from the military to civilian life can be hard, but with all the added stresses surrounding my injury and the way I had been dealt with I felt detached.

Emma and I found a suitable house and moved in together, but at the time all I could focus on was what I couldn't do, not what I was capable of achieving. The road to recovery was about to begin in earnest.

Chapter 4 Recovery

After being discharged from Headley Court and medically
retired at the grand old age of 30, a period of trauma
recovery began. I felt as if I had been cast on the scrap heap
of life by the military, and with a once-promising career in the
military now over I was living in the shadow of my former life.
Even my driving license had been taken away from me by
the DVLA.

Fortunately, I had Emma by my side. She was a caring and
stoic nurse to me, helping me through the darkest of these
times at Headley Court, a place which had compounded my
symptoms rather than give me any hope. With a long drawn
out legal case for suing the military impending, my stress
levels were high.

It was a long and protracted case, during which time in the
course of gathering evidence I had to travel extensively. I
visited a range of specialists dealing with different fields of
expertise. I also had to see specialists who had been signed
up to represent the other side of the case. In all, the opinions
of ten different specialists were drawn upon when assessing
my case.

Eventually this became a blur of consultancies and
meetings, often concluding with uncertainty as to what was
actually causing the symptoms. One conclusion was that it
was entirely psychosomatic. The suggestion that I had
woken up one morning and decided to throw away my
military career on a whim was completely preposterous. It
did nothing to lower my stress levels and I was put on
medication to stop me from becoming depressed. I'd thought

to myself ironically, what on earth could I possibly be depressed about? To help with my

visual symptoms I had been left with a pair of dark blue sunglasses, but initially all these seemed to do was put up another barrier between myself and the real world. I was left with medication to help with sleep and avoiding depression, small comfort considering the fact that the entirety of my world had changed into something very limiting.

It was a time when stress and nightmares returned with a vengeance, something which I would later learn correlates directly to experiences of trauma. You can try your hardest to stack life traumas in boxes hidden deep in the recesses of the mind, but when stress occurs it has a habit of knocking all the lids off in one fell swoop!

As part of my hypnotherapy training many years later we covered the subject of content regression, and at this point I was finally able to return and empty some of these boxes. In doing so, I unlocked the realisation that all of my life traumas had been leading up to the point of this training. It was the trauma itself which equipped me to become a clinical hypnotherapist; the perfect training for understanding and dealing with the darker recesses of the mind and the boxes which lay within. My trauma unveiled itself as not a curse, but a blessing.

As I opened these boxes during the training the pieces began falling steadily into place, allowing me to formulate the ideas which are expressed in this book. When Chris, a colleague of mine, regressed me to the point in which my issues were clearly focused, there was an immediate seismic shift. I could feel the issues rising up inside me and screaming – it was as if they wanted nothing less than to tear me apart. My body began to shake and the more I fought against it the harder it seemed to fight back.

But then there was a voice – the familiar voice I'd heard before when contemplating suicide – of a woman telling me to simply relax and go with it. Heeding the advice, I let this strange, cathartic shift take place, and a wave of tranquillity washed over me, taking away with its tide the issues I had

74

carried for years. They dissolved away in a moment, losing their grip on me.

Our minds love to dwell on drama, but when you move your attention it quickly loses interest in the issue which had caused so much suffering. I came out of the trance and told Chris of the changes which had transpired, feeling like a physically different person. Looking back on my recovery from the head injury through the lens granted me by this session has enabled me to see the effects of trauma – and the process of overcoming it – with far more clarity.

One thing which is apparent now is how the treatment had the capacity to harm as well as heal. The medication I was taking for the stress seemed to bring with it recollections of the events of that day in Kosovo, searing them on my mind and somehow morphing as the chemicals from the medication interacted in my brain.

It reminded me of the anti-malaria drug Larium I had taken in South Africa, now well known for the long term effects – and the lucid nightmares – people had experienced while taking it.

I saw myself in the crowd as machetes raised up into the air around me, glinting in the hot sun.

I saw them swinging down towards me, tearing into my body and cutting away huge chunks of flesh.

I would wake up screaming, drenched in a thick coat of sweat from head to toe and terrified of falling asleep again. The fear became so profound that for some time I would sleep with a light on in an attempt to ease the anxiety.

These recurring nightmares were commonplace during the legal case – variations on a dark theme, sometimes with my flesh burning through to the bone, pain searing through my body until I awoke. I realise now how these nightmares managed to persist for so long: having failed to process the emotion which connected to the original sensitising event – the moment I had been trapped in the traffic jam as bloodthirsty carnage ensued – those emotions lay dormant, hiding under the carpet and waiting to reach out and grab us when we reach our lowest ebb.

The emotional problems I experienced during this legal case were compounded by an issue which came from serving for five years across the water in Northern Ireland. This was known as Northern Ireland Syndrome, which relates to a feeling where you feel as if you are being constantly followed. The syndrome derives from the high periods of alertness felt when patrolling a province in civilian clothing whilst carrying a pistol. As you become aware of your surroundings and your senses become heightened, you find yourself constantly thinking of potential ambush points and potential imminent attacks.

After leaving a theatre of operations, when experiencing times of stress, the sensation that you are being constantly followed comes back with a vengeance. Any person you pass on the street is suddenly seen as a potential threat, and the sound of a car backfiring can cause you to reach for a pistol which isn't there. In one sense this is another variation on Post Traumatic Stress Disorder – a variant specific to a particular theatre of operations.

Since being medically retired I had shaken off this sensation many times, but then one day I decided to leave the house for a tai chi session and again the feeling of being followed returned as I walked to the bus stop. I shrugged the sensation off as best I could as I got on the bus and proceeded to town, but when I got off at the destination the feeling returned.

Thinking now that maybe someone was really following me, I decided to merge with a crowd of pedestrians, taking a different route than usual to tai chi. I thought I was being completely paranoid, but nevertheless this incident caused me to stay in the house even more than I had been. I began to check the cars in the street and monitored people outside walking near the house.

While it might have appeared as if I had been going crazy, things took a very different turn once the other side of the legal case I was involved in disclosed their evidence to try and disprove my symptoms. It turned out that they had hired a private detective to put surveillance on me for three weeks, proving that far from being paranoid I was fully justified in my suspicions.

Prior to going to court they were obliged to disclose their evidence, tactically releasing a DVD showing the surveillance to my solicitor who then gave me a copy. It felt like a warning, as if they understood that I would watch this and know that they were watching me. The videos showed me leaving the house, and the revelation of this information made a bad situation far worse.

At the same time, I was full of anger towards the military for the way they had treated me. Having given years of loyal service to the Forces – and lost friends and suffered personally – I was being repaid as if I were a criminal. Fortunately for me Karma was on my side – the three-week long surveillance only recorded me leaving the house a couple of times, adding weight to the foundation of my case and confirming what I had been telling them all along. But the psychological damage had already been done, and it felt as if they were softening up the enemy before a battle, engaging in a psychological war of attrition.

The inner journey changes once everything you knew becomes torn apart.

When the model of your world is ripped at the seams, your hopes, dreams and ambitions are destroyed along with it. You are left with the ashes of your life, sifting through them for new meaning in a haze of fog. Not knowing how to rebuild and recover – or even if you can – you end up sinking into the depths of despair, trying to realise the truth which lies within.

But then you rise like the phoenix from the ashes, a rebirth forged in the first of adversity and tempered by torment. You become stronger, more grounded and resilient as a person. I started rebuilding my life minute by minute, hour by hour, my energy slowly renewing from one day to the next. I began to grasp at what I thought my dreams were and what I had wanted, and a new perspective emerged where I understood that if you want something the real point is the journey towards the achievement of that goal. Reflecting on my military career it dawned on me that sometimes when you achieve your goals you might not want the finished outcome. But regardless, invaluable lessons can be learned along the way.

My thoughts, my self-belief and my creative flair and inspiration allowed me to come to this conclusion. To heal oneself one must first learn to give oneself over to the servitude of others, since only when you heal others do you truly begin to heal yourself. This understanding has struck me several times during my life.

When I took part in my training to become a Clinical Hypnotherapist, many of the practices we covered helped me to deal with these issues which I'd previously swept under the carpet. It was also apparent when conducting my training to become a Reiki master, where we were taught that if you heal others you become a channel for universal energy, or chi. As this energy flows through you to the recipient its healing properties work on yourself as well, proving to be more beneficial than other hands-on healing which can deplete your own energy. With Reiki this energy is universal and flows through all life, including your own.

Other people can often teach you more than you realise – it is a constant exchange of energy and wisdom. Each time you communicate with someone, the more you can understand their words, the more you will notice messages of guidance. I am grateful to have had many conversations with people from all walks of life; a diverse mix of people who have fortunately gravitated towards me, confided their secrets and opened their hearts.

It isn't until now, ten years later, that I realised on reflection that it was only when I removed my ego from the conversation that I really started to listen to what people were really trying to say to me. The next time you have a conversation yourself, pause to leave a gap for the thoughts to manifest, and then you will be able to process the real conversation.

I learned the importance of dialogue and healthy debate during my hypnotherapy training with Chris, who helped me in many ways as I embarked on course. His background lay in commercial banking as a director at a large company, but years of living and working in the corporate world had left him yearning for more. Our mutual warped sense of humour led to a good friendship, and he was happy to share his knowledge with me, which extended to a high level of skill in neuro-linguistic programming, or NLP. An exceptionally well-read man, he'd come on the course to consolidate his knowledge, having studied psychology – and especially hypnosis – for many years. His encyclopaedic memory led to some very interesting debates and questions in class; a testament to the importance of the inquisitive and critical mind.

As part of the training we were also able to go through many modalities, as well as practice some of the techniques on one another. I was able to deal with issues I had ignored for a long time, finally letting go of a lot of baggage. Chris and I often joked that I was like King's Cross left luggage department, but the hypnotherapy was making quick work of removing whatever luggage remained to be collected.

During the time of my recovery it felt as if I were stranded in an endless darkness looking for the light switch to illuminate the way out, but that there was no light or peace on the horizon. It was a difficult time, but in hindsight I can see that this period of my life was also a period of reframing my perspective with more life knowledge. Such a long period of convalescence taught me to closely observe people and their interactions, and I realised that such interactions often resembled a choreographed dance. It was often mesmerising watching human interaction forming intricate patterns

After the final discharge from Headley Court I spent many months in a cyclical pattern of medicated sleep, intermittently watching television, only half paying attention to the images on the screen. This period provided me with the requisite time to heal and contemplate the stark transition from an independent career soldier – in charge of some complex engineering projects – to being confined in a house like a shadow of my former self. At times I felt like a medicated zombie, barely existing.

Yet during these times, which I often considered to be my darkest hours, I learned more about myself and my inner strength than I realised. These months were invaluable to the person I became, my perception incrementally but definitively shifting from the negative to the positive.

I had been living on the same street in the same house for two years, something which was new to me, given that I had become accustomed to living out of bags while in the military. This newly settled life became essential to the stages of recovery I was going through, although initially I hardly went outdoors, preferring to keep myself to myself. I thought that my neighbours must view me as something of a ghost, and people seemed to walk past me without seeing me.

Perhaps my posture and mannerisms at the time had caused this; physical manifestations of the mental processes evolving in my mind. When soldiers leave the military, we often think civilians are a strange breed of people, but in reality, the real issue is to shake off our conditioning in order to fit in with civilisation again. The things we have seen often stay with and haunt us in times of trauma. But though we carry these demons with us – and sometimes these demons win battles inside us – ultimately, they never really define who we are. They only have the power to affect our lives if we allow them to.

My demons stayed hidden and haunted me for some time, taunting me at my lowest ebb. It was only with the fortune of training to be a clinical hypnotherapist that I finally put these demons to rest.

Once a very confident man who walked, talked and looked people in the eye, I had become pale and slumped over, gazing at my feet as I walked down the street. Much later I would learn how much physiology was the key to interaction, and when I understood this I saw that during this time of recovery I simply wasn't ready to engage with the world around me. Solitude and rest were what I needed to heal, and this was largely what I indulged in.

The introduction of Dylan to my life triggered the beginning of real change. Dylan was a Welsh terrier Emma had bought be for my birthday, named after the appropriately Welsh poet and author Dylan Thomas. I admired Thomas greatly for his work and his own life struggles with alcoholism and his intense creativity in the face of adversity. I felt a deep sense of compassion for his problems with alcohol.

As any ex-military person will tell you, alcohol can easily become a crutch to help you through dark times. But inevitably this crutch eventually breaks, and while you believe this is helping at the time it merely masks the underlying cause. Ultimately it acts as it always does as a depressant, lowering the person's mood and causing them to spiral down further into despair. Initially it numbs the pain and stops the nightmares, but in the end alcohol itself becomes the problem.

I was fortunate in this regard and never took to drinking to alleviate my problems – the medication I had been given for the injury had made me highly sensitive to alcohol, so at most I would only drink the occasional glass of wine with a meal. If I drank any more it would only ramp up the zombie effects of the drugs the following day, driving me deeper into the thick fog I'd been trying to find my way out of for so long.

Dylan the dog was equally full of life and vivacity as his namesake, as well as being as strong-willed as terriers are noted for being (as any terrier owner will attest to). His vitality reminded me of how I had been before the accident, and I thought to myself, "Is this a sign that I can be that way again?"

The underlying idea behind getting a dog had been to get me out of the house, since up to this point it was possible for me to go for weeks without leaving the house while Emma was at work. She also thought that exercise would do me a lot of good, changing my daily patterns for the better.

In the end Dylan's presence in my life contributed so much more than simply an excuse to go for a walk.

Since he was such a boisterous and friendly dog I found that strangers started interacting with me, chipping away at the mind-set I had created from my reclusive behaviour, causing it to dwindle day by day. I grasped just how much I had allowed to isolate myself, and Dylan gave me the courage to re-engage with humanity. Dylan's warm, affectionate company and the love he exuded to these strangers changed my outlook entirely, giving me the opportunity to see the spiralling patterns I had allowed myself to fall into and slowly energise me.

I began to look forward to my daily walk with Dylan in a way which I hadn't looked forward to anything for some time. He provided the spark I'd needed to passionately fight to regain my life as it had once been, as if his wagging tail finally wafted away the mist which had surrounded me. We'd take to the nearby woods, the fresh air invigorating me and slowly blowing the fog from my mind. The world breathed new life into me for the first time since the injury.

With my health improving considerably from these walks I decided to stop taking the medication which had been turning me into a zombie. Emma expressed her concerns and I was clearly going against the advice of the doctor who had prescribed them, but I felt it was time to step out from the chemically induced haze which had surrounded me. I'd been taking them at 8pm and not waking up until mid-afternoon the following day. The dazed feeling from the drugs would lift for perhaps a few hours before it was time for more medication, plunging me back into the haze.

While it's undeniable that the medication helped me to sleep and possibly avoid depression in the early days following the head injury, now I had to concede that they muddled my thoughts and stripped me of any passion for life. There was no way I was going to spend the rest of my life functioning at such a low level.

The craziest thing about my situation was that the doctor had me taking Amitriptyline in order to help prevent depression and help me with sleeping. Amitriptyline can be an effective drug for these conditions, but on the flipside, it is known to bring with it some potentially serious and counterproductive side effects. One such side effect is increased blurred vision, and the drug was exacerbating the issues I'd been experiencing since the head injury. My changes in mood –

82

and the overall effects on my state of consciousness – were also attributable to the side effects of the drug.

After any type of head injury, a person is known to become highly sensitive to medication, and this was certainly the case for me – in addition to the mood adjustments and blurred vision I started to suffer from tinnitus, a constant ringing in my ears proving to be incredibly unsettling. To this day I suffer from this condition, although I have since come to learn that tinnitus is believed by some spiritual teachings to be a consequence of going through a period of spiritual transformation.

This belief is intrinsically linked to the way in which undergoing a period of spiritual enhancement factors shifts your vibrational frequency, and it is these vibrational changes which can bring about tinnitus. It is as if you are hearing the frequencies between the dimensions – at first, it seems like meaningless noise or static, but if you quieten the mind with meditation this noise starts to take on new meanings, and you begin to hear the guides which are there to show you the correct path in life. The more you take on board this guidance, the more congruent events – or signposts – move you along the spiritual path.

The side effects of the Amitriptyline reached their peak when I suffered from debilitating bouts of vomiting combined with violent spells of dizziness and loss of balance, very close to the symptoms of Meniere's disease. These attacks came on suddenly and could last for up to three hours, with episodes of vertigo adding to the sense of disorientation.

I decided it was time to reclaim my old brain and the creative thought patterns I used to have. I would do whatever it took to get any of it back. At the time I didn't expect to be able to turn time back to my pre-accident cognitive functioning, little did I know what was about to happen to my brain and thought process.

Over time my head cleared itself of the fog which the chemicals had brought with them, and I started to notice that things were different. At first it felt to me as if I had had a software update. And yet, the hardware still had to figure out how exactly it should operate the newly installed system.

Finally, my brain synapses started firing again.

After six long years the fire which sat deep in my soul was finally glowing.

Emma and I were married at the Priest House Hotel, a beautiful old stone building nestled in the Derbyshire countryside, which bloomed with colourful vegetation trailing down to the banks of the river Trent. It was an amazing day featuring classic cars complimenting the gorgeous setting and – most importantly of all – beautiful people there to help us celebrate the special occasion. I felt so proud as I listened to the after-dinner speeches, glowing with happiness for a special day and thinking that finally I had found the love I'd been searching for.

We followed this with a dream honeymoon to South Africa, taking in a penguin beach, safari and the luxury suite at the Mauritius. I'd wanted to visit South Africa ever since I was a young boy. The thought of going on a safari – and the thrill of seeing such majestic and exotic creatures in their natural habitat – is one which no doubt appeals to the adventurous side of every child.

There is something raw and primal about the continent of Africa which speaks to our ancestral past; it is a land where nature seems to overwhelm everything with its incredible beauty.

Early one morning while on a daily safari drive, Emma and I were fortunate enough to see a pride of lions taking down a zebra. Having been briefed by our guide not to make any noise or sudden movements, our vehicle pulled to a halt around ten metres away from the action.

The pride of lions was eating away at the carcass, surgically stripping it of its meat with a tenacious eagerness.

Suddenly, an Italian tourist who was sat in the seat in front of me stood up abruptly, ignorant of the dangers of making such a quick movement. He seemed to be oblivious to the fact that the vehicle we were in was open, too, and that if the lions had noticed him and perceived him as a threat, they would have been on him – and most likely the rest of us – in a split second.

I grabbed his shoulders and firmly but politely pushed him back into his seat. He turned around giving me a funny look, but a quick stern nod in the direction of the pride set him straight as to the nature of my intentions and a different look fell over his face showing that he registered the gravity of the situation. When you're literally metres away from being devoured by hungry predators, the fragility of life and gratitude for living is not a hard thing to find.

As the sun bore down on Emma and I something still felt out of place. I was still awaiting the outcome of the legal case and moments of stress came throughout this process. How many more medical experts would I have to see before the case would be settled? How long until I could truly move on with my life? I was in the midst of a legal battle with the Ministry of Defence for my injuries and had no idea how it would end.

I brushed these thoughts aside – for the moment I was in paradise and I was happy. It is easy to miss the true purpose of being in the moment without worry or concern of what might be in an uncertain world. To create the future you desire, only focusing on the new while letting go of the old will achieve the desired ends. The past can exist as an anchor which stops us from sailing forwards, and only when the chain is detached are we able to move onwards.

I felt deeply for Emma at the time and understood how the odds were, in a sense at least, stacked against us. The man she had fallen in love with hadn't truly existed since the head injury, and during my time of recovery – complete with all the stress of the legal case in the aftermath – we often simply existed, without truly living.

During my recovery I had started tai chi, which introduced me to a new way of understanding the concept of energy. I had an amazing teacher called Elly who taught me about Ki, or qigong, the life energy which flows within each and every one of us. It was a concept which was to help me heal far more quickly, both physically and emotionally.

I discovered tai chi by chance, since Elly had also taught me in the photography classes I'd been going to. At the start of the photography course I'd discussed some of my other problems with her and she'd suggested tai chi as a solution. Like tai chi itself, sometimes life seems to flow naturally from one event to the next.

The tai chi that I studied was based on the methods used by Dr. Paul Lam. Lam had been a family doctor working in Australia who had taken up tai chi to control his arthritis, having been told in his early twenties that he would be crippled and wheelchair bound. Refusing to accept this diagnosis and feeling that the mind could be used to strengthen the body, he developed a specific system of tai chi to tackle his arthritis. His story is another example of how personal adversity can lead to important lessons which can help others.

Lam went on to lead an active and healthy life, even going on to win the gold medal at the 1993 World Wushu Championships for his interpretation of Yang Tai Chi. This story reaffirmed my long-held opinion that if you believe you can recover then you will, and that the state of mind is critical to the process.

I also started getting involved in photography during this period, another method to break my patterns and routines. Before long it had entirely reframed the way, I saw the world, allowing me to integrate with it once again and shifting my focus from the negativity of the past to a bright and positive future.

For the first time I truly saw the beauty and details, like a child in a wonderful new world. I even went so far as to invest in studio equipment, helping out when my niece was born by taking some family portraits for them. We used this equipment later for Allison's birthday, taking family photos of the event. A talented photographer friend of mine helped out with these sessions, expanding further my knowledge of this new and invigorating activity.

Picture your life as a photograph you are about to take, with the viewfinder representing the present moment. As you look through the viewfinder the camera lens will show you everything there is in the field of view at that particular point in time.

But then, as you twist the rings on the lens to adjust the focus, objects in front of you become either sharper or out of focus. Exactly the same principle applies to the eye in the mind – our focus and intent will shift towards what we are currently observing in the present moment, but this can be tainted by emotional filters from the past, clouding this perspective rather than enhancing.

Once we understand how we can control and change these filters to a positive experience, the current image itself will become bright and positive. Continuing the photography analogy, we can also adjust our focus and perspective by moving our feet, allowing us to move further away, closer to or around the

subject. As we do this, our perspective and understanding of the situation begins to change dramatically, on the one hand allowing for additional clarity, but also putting things out of focus. It is only through seeing life through these varying perspectives that we can choose to focus on the truly important things in life.

Photography had changed the way in which I saw and understood the world and my relationship with it – in allowing me to see the finer details it had built up a much bigger picture, and in some ways it was a precursor to my later Neuro Linguistic Programming training. Looking back, these experiences themselves formed a smaller part of the bigger picture of my life; a piece of a jigsaw slotting smoothly into place, bringing the whole picture into focus for the first time.

The protracted legal case combined with the recovery and my reaction to the medication increasingly took its toll on my relationship with Emma, and the love which had once been there between us started to fade away. Once the legal case was finally settled out of court and we were financially secure, the damage had already been done, and we had gone from being close lovers to strangers who hardly recognised one another.

After ten years of moving around, dragging the legal paperwork with me wherever I went, it was finally over. I decided to burn it all and let it go for good. I watched as the attachment I had to the papers – and the implicit troubles they signalled – drift into the air above the flames. It was almost like a confirmation from the universe it was time to let go and move forward.

An even more profound discovery in the box than any legal paperwork could hope to be was a stuffed toy of the Bagpuss cat, famous from children's television when I was a child. I'd seen clearing out this legal paperwork as an exercise in realising the past and letting it go but hadn't expected to find an object so intrinsically linked to something so personal.

I picked up the toy and turned it over to read the attached label. It read: "A little friend to keep you company. Love Em X". Bagpuss had been my favourite show as a boy, and something which Emma had sometimes called me during my recovery on account of me exhibiting the same characteristics of sleepiness.

Bagpuss has been there as one of the few constants in my life for the best part of a decade, always watching over me as if I had been on a wild adventure. Emma might not have known it but the words she had inscribed on the label were literal. Was this a coincidence, or was it another example of the synchronicities which life seems to exhibit?

But now things had changed. Everything I thought I had wanted in life became meaningless, and as the distance between Emma and I continued to expand and my recovery came to its end, I realised that I wanted more from life. The road to recovery was at an end and feeling as if I'd been released from a long prison sentence, it became clear to me that I wanted to experience life in ways I'd never considered before.

The settlement from the legal case brought with it a resolution to a problem I had faced for a long time, but in its place a new set of problems arose. The settlement acknowledged that I had been right to take the issue to the courts and vindicated me for my decision to do so, but now I had the money I realised that it wasn't enough to bring me happiness. Having sufficient money to survive and pursue other goals may well relieve the everyday financial stresses many people go through, but being able to do whatever you want when you're not at all sure what it is you want to do proves that having money can be something of a double edged sword.

Sensibly prioritising our needs, the first thing I did was pay off the mortgage on the house and set about making plans for renovation, as if I knew that up until now the place had never truly felt like a home. I took to this task with a hands-on approach, emptying the garden, putting in drainage by hand, building a decking area and transforming it into a show garden.

It was hard graft – not something I've ever been afraid of – and the physical toil did wonders for my self-esteem. This raw physical exercise of lifting and carrying tons of soil reconnected me with my body, which had been wasting away under the duress of my recovery. From one day to the next I found myself capable of more and more.

Despite our relationship taking a downward turn, Emma and I were certainly in a better position than most, and I decided to invest in an old Volkswagen camper van from Jersey. It was to be a restoration project which would teach me new skills and, more importantly, keep me occupied.

I bought a new car for Emma too, noticing that she appeared to be more excited by the free pen which came with it. At the time I had thought this strange, but now I realise that her reaction made an important point about the small details

in life mattering the most, not the grand gestures. Nevertheless, I'd been able to pay for a brand-new black Mercedes SLK convertible with cash. I never thought I'd be in a position to splash out cash on a luxury car before and the feeling was strange.

I was eager to move to a new house and work on developing another property, but Emma was happy where we were. I was increasingly feeling like I now had a second chance at life, along with the funds necessary to transform my dreams and ambitions into reality. My sense of independence was growing, and I wanted to see more of the world, and the pressure this had on our relationship finally built up to a climax.

When I finally ended the relationship, it felt as if I was ready to explode and I had to leave, and while I was not proud of what I did at the time I knew that it was essential for my journey towards a full recovery. I took my camera bag and moved out and checked into a nearby hotel, beginning a pattern I would repeat over the next few years where hotel rooms became an all too familiar sight. Part of me felt as if I didn't deserve a home of my own, and I adopted a life almost like a nomadic traveller of indeterminate origin.

The journey of recovery would not have been possible without the help I had from Emma over the years, and without the down time and alternative therapy I sincerely doubt that I would have recovered at all. And yet there was a heavy price for this, and the damage to our relationship was irreversible, leading inevitably to divorce. Life moves in mysterious ways, and I owe a huge debt of gratitude to Emma for everything she did for me, nursing me through the

hardest time of my life. I never made it clear enough just how much she had done, something which I deeply regretted.

Sometimes we are merely passengers in the lives of those around us and must part when the journey reaches a crossroads. But the help I received will never be forgotten.

It is said that it can take as long as seven years to become the person you're going to be following a head injury. I had gone through ten long years in which so much had happened, and it is only when I stopped and paused to quiet my mind that the pieces start falling into place. I seemed to be learning new skills faster than ever before, my passion for knowledge driving me onto new fascinating subjects.

I realised I hadn't been able to recognise and appreciate what I had when I had it, only glimpsing it in the reflections of the past. I'd failed to take the time to truly be in the moment and smell the flowers – I'd been given the option to do anything and initially chose materialism. But then something inside me had changed, and I took my destiny in my own hands for the first time in my life.

After the separation from Emma I ended up renting a small one-bedroom apartment, wondering how I was going to repair the mess that my life had seemed to become. Focusing on my health I started to get fit again, building on the work I had done through renovating the house and garden by taking up rock climbing. Even though I was new to climbing and learning the techniques I found that a daily climb further helped to reduce the stress. It provided a natural release of endorphins and would often leave me feeling happy for the rest of the day.

The local climbing centre I went to was based inside an old church, and as such the curved walls and ceilings provided a perfect challenge for novice and expert climbers alike. As I improved over time, I'd head out to the Peak District with my friend John. He was nearly sixty-five years old but climbed better than Spider-Man.

We did a few thirty metre ascents, which felt much more exhilarating than those inside the confines of the church, before abseiling back down to the ground with no safety ropes. The expression of getting our lives back in our hands never felt truer, both literally, as I slid through the air kicking away from the rocks, and metaphorically. Grappling with nature and pushing my body to such limits was a liberating experience.

One of the wonderful things about the chemicals released from exercising is that they don't have any side effects, something which I immediately noticed. Much like climbing itself, I learned to focus on the next move ahead. Often I would come up with my best ideas and clearest thoughts during or shortly after a climb, as if the exertion had put me into a meditative state, allowing clarity of mind.

One day I bumped into Allison, a strikingly attractive woman with blonde hair who lived in the same building as myself, and after a handful of encounters filled with small talk, we soon hit it off. We started dating, going out for meals and drinks in Derby, and on one of these evenings out fate seemed to intervene again.

We walked into a bar called Red Zebra and sat at the bar to order a drink. The owner was having a conversation with someone else about his desire to sell the business, and immediately cogs started to whirl in my mind. Although I had never run a business before I asked him about the bar and he provided some more details, and even though I knew very little about wine my instincts told me to go for it and that things would work out fine.

It was later, once my business venture with Red Zebra was well underway, that I saw Emma briefly one more time. She had come to the bar on a date, moving forwards with her life, and saw me behind the bar. As soon as our eyes met she turned around and left, and I felt as if I'd had a glimpse of the past. There were clearly unresolved issues between us about the manner in which our relationship had ended, and I wish we had been able to remain friends.

I wish we'd had a chance to sit down together and discuss what had happened to me over my period of recovery. I wanted to tell her how my behaviour at the time wasn't representative of the real me.

I'd have welcomed her and her date if I'd had the chance and offered them a meal on the house, a small gesture towards clearing the air. But it wasn't to be, and I am forever in gratitude to Emma for all the love and support she had shown me at a very difficult time in my life. Without Emma my story would have turned out very differently indeed. Contemplating these difficult times I regret, as we often do with the benefit of hindsight, not telling her just how much her compassion and support meant to me.

On reflection I feel truly sorry for not reciprocating and giving back as much care and support as I had received. Such is the nature of the intertwining paths we traverse in life, often blindly and without a guiding map. It is only when we look back that we can see the obstacles we overcame and the significant people who lifted us up in the face of adversity, helping us to continue on our journey through life. I also realised that my recovery led me on a path to this point in my life for a reason. While Emma and I may have drifted apart, by the same token these events led me to becoming stronger.

My recovery had improved considerably once I'd stopped taking the medication, with the process of detoxification triggering a change which was to have a profound effect on my future. As I noticed my brain began to fire up again I felt my confidence begin to return. It came back slowly at first but soon surpassed my pre-injury capacity. I felt enlivened, excited by what was happening after three long and arduous years as my brain finally got the reboot it had been crying out for.

My creative urges quickly came back to the fore and I started to take my photography more seriously. Eager to learn the craft as quickly as possible, I signed up for a course in landscape photography run by a talented photographer called Simon Wilkinson. He suggested that we go on a trip to Nepal – somewhere I had long hoped to visit – where we could trek and take photographs of the stunning scenery. Taking a leap of faith, I booked the flight and a short while later the two of us landed in Kathmandu.

I felt a strong resonance with Nepal on this trip, something which stirred deep within my soul. An ardent meat lover before this visit, I returned a vegetarian and continued this diet for another nine months. At first it seemed to suit my body and I initially felt wonderful, losing approximately two stone in weight and feeling completely energised. The return flight from Nepal brought with it a severe chest infection on my right lung which made organising the business venture at Red Zebra and finding tradesmen to commit to the bar refurbishment very difficult, since I was barely able to stand up.

It was the hectic pace of the business – and the constant late nights striving to build up the company – which eventually led me to eating meat again. Returning home one evening I had felt incredibly weak and then fainted. Fear of the symptoms of my head injury re-emerging appeared like a spectre in my mind. While several tests including a CT scan reassured me that everything was fine, I realised that the stress of overworking wasn't good for me and was leaving me feeling debilitated.

Fainting was clearly my body's way of telling me to slow down and look after myself, and it certainly got my attention. My vegetarian diet had brought with it a deficiency in B12 and protein, so I made the decision to revert back to eating meat simply out of necessity. I needed a physical boost and sure enough once I started eating meat again my energy returned swiftly.

The real change which came about from this trip, however, couldn't be seen on the surface and yet had a far more significant impact than changes in my diet. It was a sense of peace and tranquillity I had never experienced before, shaking the foundations of my belief system and making me aware of the bigger possibility of modality, more complex than I had thought possible. I had been a

Christian during my time in the military (few people faced with the possibility of a violent death will truly contemplate the absence of God), but since then I had re-evaluated my position and considered myself broadly atheist.

With my visit to Nepal behind me, a world of spiritual and metaphysical possibilities opened up. At the same time a new life as an entrepreneur lay ahead of me, bringing with it a range of new opportunities and possibilities of its own.

It was time to make my mark on the business world.

<u>Chapter 5 - Materialism (Self-Belief)</u>

Allison and I began dating and at the same time I started to go through a period of change characterised by a much-needed improvement in my appearance. Gone were the casual jeans and t-shirts and the general lack of care about my presentation. Instead I began wearing business suits while growing my hair out in long curls. Allison had reminded me of the old adage which says that if you look the part, you feel the part and then you are the part. In business the first thing people notice is your appearance, and in the business world the only credible look is the smart suit.

When Allison and I went to the country for a hotel break we made sure that we dressed the part. On one occasion we booked a penthouse suite in a hotel in Birmingham for the weekend, my friend Carl joining us. I booked a luxury room for Carl as well, thinking how such opulence is surely a sign you've hit the big time. But I would also come to learn some valuable lessons about my identity and how happiness and materialistic objects and the lifestyle that goes with success aren't necessarily compatible ideals.

In traditional Japanese theatre there is the idea that people all wear different masks depending on their social situation, and by the same token we often transform our identities through the clothes we wear and the way we present ourselves to the people we meet. I was beginning to formulate a new mask of my own, one which signified a new era in my life.

A similar principle to the one found many decades ago in Japanese Noh theatre exists in modern psychology. The Johari window technique consists of four

areas – much like windowpanes – which represent aspects of our psychological make-up. These aspects range from what is known to others and what is unknown by ourselves. Extending the Japanese metaphor to the Johari window and it can be said that we wear four masks – only when we accept ourselves and remove these does our true self become apparent.

I was becoming more comfortable in my skin and Allison and I would joke to one another about our stylistic choices when we went out to restaurants, calling ourselves the "Posh and Becks" of Derby whenever we hit the town. In our own way we became known around town for our old-fashioned approach to dressing up for a date. Allison always looked elegant and refined, her style and classiness often turning heads when we walked into a room, with me complimenting her with well-tailored suits and a sharp tie. We emitted happiness, as if affording me a glimpse of what could lie ahead and what joys the future might hold, and often strangers would address Allison as my wife.

The ironic thing was that I knew that Allison would never marry me since she knew that my heart lay in becoming a father. It was a sign of her selflessness – she seemed to know long before I did where my true destiny lay. We often had long conversations about children, and I'm certain that she could see the passion and longing in my eyes. I knew that my role was to be a father – it was something I had increasingly started to feel deep in my soul, allowing me to become the best I could be.

My own father had taught me the best lesson ever simply by not being there. His absence cut to the core, and I vowed that, if ever I was blessed with children of my own, I would never be like that.

I bumped into my father during the period when Allison and I were setting up Red Zebra. I was checking out a motorbike in a shop window when I saw a familiar figure on the other side. I decided to go and speak to him, and even though I hadn't seen him for many years I knew instantly that it was him. I looked like a spitting image of him when he was my age.

"What are you looking at?" he said in a gruff and aggressive tone of voice. "Don't you recognise me?" I replied, watching as a flicker of recognition lit up in his eyes.

But instead of acknowledging me, my father said, "No, I've got no idea who you are. I've got a bad memory".

I could have told him who I was there and then, but instead I smiled at him and said, "When you work it out, find me".

I walked away dazed by the encounter, as if in a state of shock. His indifference and evasiveness were difficult to take on board in that moment, but it soon strengthened my resolution to become a father myself and avoid the pitfalls he'd slipped into.

I saw my father again after my cousin informed me about the passing of my uncle. I hadn't been in touch for a while and had a sense that I should contact her. It was the day before the funeral, and I met up with many members of the Harris side of the family.

My father's identical twin was there and spoke to me. He was a calmer and more settled version of my father, very different in temperament despite looking just like him. After the solemn funeral came to a close, we went outside into the bracing air. My aunt – who by strange coincidence also had a twin sibling – tried to encourage my father to show some warmth.

"Aren't you going to say hello to your son?" she said.

But my father seemed to be intractable. He simply shook my hand and muttered, "Hello" as if I were a complete stranger.

The sad truth of that moment was that my father essentially was a stranger to me, and I to him. He might have given me life, but the buck stopped there. He would never know his granddaughter or be a part of her life. A tragic reality, but often it is through tragedy that goodness is able to blossom.

Allison and I closed the Red Zebra bar for thirty days and got to work on refurbishing downstairs and the cellar first, as I started working on a concept of a westernised Moroccan theme. While my engineering background was ideal for the project management side of things, I came into my element when switching to the creative side of my brain. I'd always wanted to travel to Marrakesh and thought a Moroccan theme would work perfectly in the bar.

I'd long wished to make Marrakesh the subject of a photography expedition, visiting the markets and observing the culture. It is a place full of vibrant colours and lifestyles which would make for some stunning photographs, and when it came to thinking up a theme for the bar the Moroccan concept stood out by a mile. Immediately I knew it would be a success.

As I began building an image of the finished bar in my mind, I started to procure piece by piece the things I'd need from eBay. I had beautiful furniture, elegant rugs and Moroccan-style tables and lamps arriving from all over the country. I didn't know this at the time, but I was to influence the bar culture in Derby, my ideas being taken on by other people in the business. They say that

imitation is the sincerest form of flattery, but if you can't come up with new ideas as well you run the risk of ending up a pale imitation.

When we purchased Red Zebra, it was originally a wine shop owned by a man called David, who had had a wonderful relationship with his father. He'd travelled to vineyards throughout Europe when David was young, planting the seeds for his life-long passion for wine and also building the foundations for his incredible knowledge. I saw the future of the business from the outset: a bespoke bar where people could come for a civilised drink. I also envisaged setting up an online wine merchant once the brand had grown – a new source of revenue to sustain the business.

As the Red Zebra project gathered pace, I continued to absorb knowledge of fine wines in an effort to constantly improve the venue. I attended wine courses and had numerous consultations with different wine merchants to ensure that the wine list was unique. Every detail had to be perfect, and I believe that if you're going to succeed in business it's important to do what you know well and to the very best of your abilities. Through understanding the core of your business and sticking to these principles it is possible to constantly review and improve, keeping a keen eye on new creative ways to move the business forward.

As well as studying wine extensively and establishing the theme for the bar, I also paid attention to the finer details such as designing the menus. I considered it all an organic process of learning. Creating something from scratch teaches you all manner of new skills, and I was able to apply my recent foray into the world of photography too, using my photographs for the website and marketing material. It was a very creative period in my life aided immensely by the challenge of constructing a clear vision for the business.

I worked so hard in the first year trying to establish the business and build it up. Originally, we opened Red Zebra for six days a week for very long hours, but soon realised that in order to make it exclusive we'd have to limit the market. I achieved this by building a solid customer base then reducing the hours. It may have run contrary to most business models – and some people certainly thought I was mad – but I had a vision and was sticking to it.

I can still recall the long evenings shortly after we'd opened when no customers would come in, but I utilised the time and designed the rest of the bar, constructing the business in my head and bringing it into reality stage by stage.

So, we adjusted the business model and opened for just twenty-two hours per week on Thursday, Friday and Saturday, catering towards a more specialised clientele to avoid watering down the market while making the venue feel more unique and special. Desiring a more niche customer base meant that it took more time to establish the business, but before long word of mouth generated a buzz which led to footballers and managers coming in for drinks from Derby and beyond.

One of the most satisfying aspects of the work was to see people coming in straight from work and watching the stress of the day disappear within the first drink. It was in moments such as these, seeing people truly relaxing after a hard day, which made me realise that Allison and I had created something special. We were proud that all the hard work getting the venue ready had finally paid off.

It really struck home just how successful the business had become when we won the Food & Drink Awards for Derby, beating a company which had won for the previous four years straight. They had invested considerable sums into new designs and extensive refurbishments, while I had revamped Red Zebra using my creative side. I felt like I had pulled all the elements together and created a very special place, and the award validated all the efforts which had been made.

Often people assumed that it was Allison who had come up with the designs and crafted the ambience of the bar. While she had helped out with some of the design elements, for the most part it had been the inspiration I had felt for Morocco which had made it all happen.

After collecting the award, we asked our staff where they wanted to go for a meal and took them all to Pizza Express. As we sat down to eat I felt on top of the world, but in truth it was largely driven by ego and fed with a diet of materialistic objects. I was to find this out much later, when I realised that a far more magical moment in life is doing something simple with my daughter.

But during this period, I became increasingly materialistic, desiring nothing but the best clothes, watches and cars which I felt lined up with my new image and lifestyle choices. I had a lovely Mercedes SLK convertible which I paid for in cash and a stunning Omega Olympic special edition watch. And yet, despite owning these luxury items I was still missing something inside. I realised I was trying to buy my own happiness, and that while material possessions can give you the illusion of contentment – and a fleeting feeling of happiness – it remains brief and intangible. Materialistic satisfaction never lasts and you always end up desiring new trinkets once you get bored of the last ones. Like any addiction it doesn't take long until you need another fix to stay on a level.

In reality, it is working towards your next goal in life which makes you happy, and while at the time it felt as if I had the

Midas touch and these brief distractions made me happy, deep down I knew I was searching for something deeper and more meaningful.

There is a story about a man who thought he knew exactly what he wanted, so set about to obtain his dreams. In the process he ended up losing the most important thing of all.

As he pursued his dream it became his only focus and he would obsess over it to the point where it would consume his every waking moment.
Along the way he lost his way, his single-minded pursuit of his dream leading him to miss all of the beautiful details which presented themselves to him. He failed to realise that sometimes it's the chasing of the dream which counts the most, not the dream itself.

The journey is the true experience – the destination is an illusion or mirage, forever on the horizon. If you don't look out of the window during the ride, before you know it you will arrive at your destination wondering where the time has gone. These moments cannot be retrieved; once traversed, the journey cannot be re-trodden.

Before the business became all-consuming Allison and I decided that we'd take a break and booked a ten-day holiday in the Maldives. After a long flight we landed on a beautiful island, settling into the hotel and relaxing by the pool. The holiday was hampered slightly by Allison's injured knee brought about by an old back injury, but with such beautiful weather to enjoy and plenty of wine it certainly didn't spoil our enjoyment of the occasion.

One day by the pool I caught a glimpse of someone I thought I knew. I looked again but she was gone – was it the sun blinding my vision, or something else, gently prodding me towards the path I should be on?
It had seemed to me that a friend I had known for years had been stood next to the pool before mysteriously disappearing. I don't know why but it felt as if this had been a glimpse of my future, in some way indicating a path I should take. Like the junction on a road, if you take one path it may end up being a diversion which keeps bringing you back to the same crossroads. I don't know why but the vision of this

friend by the pool seemed to point to a future in which Allison and I parted ways. Maybe the way we continue to return to these same junctions is simply a matter of divine timing, and that the path to true happiness and love – coming from a position where one first loves oneself – will be worth the wait. Still, I put the vision to the back of my mind and continued to make the most of the holiday.

Our palates had become incredibly refined as a consequence of Red Zebra and Allison and I had become wine snobs, so the house wine available from the all-inclusive package we were on wasn't up to our new standards. We ended up drinking imported Chablis Premiere Cru which cost a small fortune for a bottle, and I realised that once you get a taste for the finer things in life it's very hard to go back.

Before Red Zebra I thought that the average supermarket wine tasted pleasant enough, but with more knowledge and understanding I realised that fine wine was an altogether different experience. A great wine is rather like theatre in the glass: it creates an environment of its own – a sensorial familiarity linked to a specific moment as if taking you back through time.

Naturally, once you've experienced the taste of such wines it's very hard to go back to an inferior product. This became particularly difficult after my wine consultant had kindly arranged for a tasting for my birthday, providing ten world class wines with a trade price that would make most people cringe and hide their wallets. As a business inducer it was totally free, but I knew that I'd reached the pinnacle now, and afterwards I only drank wine again on very special occasions.

With my newfound taste for the finer things in life we thought about upgrading our accommodation to a water villa. The decision was made for us later that day when a German couple staying in the hotel room adjacent to ours got into a prolonged and heated argument. I could tell that the husband was very drunk as he screamed at her, and I had to stop myself from interjecting as I knew there were children involved. Still, I left our room to check, just as she was leaving the room and heading towards the reception. I asked

102

her if she was okay in my broken German and the situation seemed to have been defused, but the incident was enough for Allison and I to prepare to move to another accommodation.

The next day we moved to the water villa, an amazing, opulent place which sat in dream-like suspension over the water on stilts. Allison's knee continued playing up so we even had our own butler and chauffeur who would collect us and drive us around the island. The villa was plush, with an open deck with a Jacuzzi, and steps which led down into the crystal-clear water so we could go swimming directly from our room.

The food at the restaurant was on par with a high-end eating establishment and the wine list was superb. As we sat down for meals with Allison in her elegant evening gowns and myself in my new suits, I felt that I was finally living the dream. For the first time in my life I felt I had everything I thought I had ever wanted.

This decadence didn't leave me any time soon. Later while I was with Jade we went to World Service and I ate the best meal of my life. Dining in such opulent surroundings is an intoxicating experience and the 1976 Chateau Margaux was the best wine I had ever tasted. I'd never expected wine to be able to reach such heights, but it seemed to create a sense of soaking in its bouquet for a lifetime. Luckily, they only had one bottle of Margaux in the wine cellar – it had cost more than my first car.

The memories, however, remain priceless.

Yet during all this time living the high life a constant nagging voice remained which triggered a latent unease. I could not settle and simply be in the moment despite being in such a paradise, as if I knew what lay on the horizon. I was trying to look towards the future but instead dragged my past along with me: as a consequence, I never really lived in the present.

When Allison and I had first met the age difference between us hadn't been a problem. On our first date I'd had a vision which I'd tried to shake off, dismissing it as a dream. I'd looked at her face and saw her go from beautiful to ageing in an instant, and when I looked away and glanced back, she'd returned to normal. I tried to think nothing of it at the time, but a voice rang out in my head which pointed to this image as a premonition of what would eventually end the relationship. I chose to ignore the writing on the wall, but the problem with creating a mirage is that it takes a great deal of energy to maintain, ultimately becoming unsustainable.

Had this premonition been an echo of a potential future, the point at which was predetermined with just the time remaining to be set? Are our lives little more than a series of random events which we try desperately to add our own meaning to, if only to justify our own existence? Like a dot to dot picture, it's only once these are joined up that the picture is finally revealed.

Looking back at the time Allison and I spent together, once again I saw how I was never truly appreciative of the moments we'd shared. I seemed to be incapable of being in the moment, truly seeing what I had and understanding that this is the true path to happiness. All the fun times and enjoyment we had lie in the memories of our minds, and when we look back they surface in ways they hadn't manifested before. Our memories are never fixed, and each time we interact with it the memory changes. This depends on our current model of the world. Life experiences change the person we are and the beliefs we have, forever altering the perspective we view our memories.

During this period in my life in which my creativity began to flourish, my family thought I was insane. They often made remarks to the effect that I'd never run a bar or a business before and didn't know anything about it, and yet I had a deep and burning sense of passion about where I was going in life. Even before the bar was opened, I could envision myself standing on a stage, accepting an award for Derby's finest wine bar.

The first customers we had might have agreed with my family – they too thought I was crazy, and that a high-end wine bar would never work in Derby. And yet, like most entrepreneurs, I had a clear vision and knew where I could take the bar. Feeling energetic and recharged following my trip to Nepal – as well as being deeply in love with Allison – I knew that anything really was possible.

I'd arrived at a point where the highly creative state of mind I was in meant that ideas and projects were flowing fast. It was one of the most prolific periods in my life. Speak to any creative person – whether it's a painter, sculptor, artist or musician – and they'll tell you how these creative phases can often transform into something vibrant and magical. You can literally achieve anything artistic which you set your mind to.

It was one of the first customers, a gentleman named Boz, who first said to me, "I'll give you six months until you're bankrupt". He always wore a smart three- piece suit and an eccentric hat and he was sometimes perceived by others who didn't know him well to be a loud and occasionally obnoxious character. But he was really the epitome of the adage "never judge a book by its cover"; beneath the loud exterior he was charming, intellectual and worldly.

We became friends and I explained to him how the pursuit of a dream isn't the same as the pursuit of money. No amount of financial remuneration can compare to the feeling of satisfaction from doing something well and with passion, while also enjoying every moment of it.

I admired his frankness even if I disagreed with his assessment, especially when we passed the six-month mark and the bar continued to thrive. Not only was the business proving to be a success, we were starting to get more high-profile clientele coming through the doors, including top paid footballers and their wives.

Since I was heavily involved on a day to day basis in the nightlife of the city I started to become known to more and more people. Thanks to the success I was beginning to enjoy the high life - driving expensive cars and frequently eating out at the best restaurants on offer. I continued to buy designer clothes and booked luxury holidays and yet, throughout it all, the more I thought about my success, the more I suspected that it was leading me away from my true being.

Providing a great service for wine enthusiasts felt like helping people in the wrong kind of way and I began to spend many hours in Red Zebra closely observing social interactions between people and engaging them in conversation. People would come to the bar and tell me all sorts of things that most wouldn't ordinarily speak about with a relative stranger – and probably wouldn't even tell their priest, if they had one.

Slowly but surely, I started to realise that I had an innate ability to listen to people and understand their concerns and problems. Perhaps it was easier to really get to the heart of the matter. After all, alcohol combined with the relaxed atmosphere of the venue lubricated conversation in most circumstances. Even so, for me it became a learning ground for what was to come later in life.

Since the bar was located next to Derby Cathedral it had a good energy about it, as if possessed with a cleansing agent which drew people towards it like a magnet. The good vibes seemed to amplify my ability to talk to people and try to help. At the time I was thirsty for more and neglecting my grasp on the here and now – I was too busy constantly speeding to the next goal in life, always looking forward and failing to take the time to look out of the window and think, "Wow! I am so blessed!" As having a child reveals to many people, time is a precious commodity which you can't get back, and whether or not we have used it effectively is reflected in the quality of our memories.

I continued returning to writing this book during this period, but it felt as if I were being stopped by some unseen force as only half the story was there. I needed to wait for the right timing to proceed, as well as the clarity to formulate the book into its current guise. People would sometimes joke about the fact that I was still working on a book which had its genesis five years ago – but any writer will tell you that a creative process requires focus and contemplation. With the solid foundations I had worked on establishing, the clarity of my writing would transform into a totally different style.

Besides, I had other projects I was eager to complete.

I pushed myself close to the limit during the first six months of working on Red Zebra. But whenever I had some time, I kept myself busy working on assembling my camper van which I'd invested in while I was with Emma.

During my recovery I'd spend hours at a time ordering broken things from eBay – an assortment of cameras, Apple Mac laptops and other gadgets which men seem to love tinkering with – and working on repairing them. I even contemplated becoming a certified Apple technician and repair them for a living, but it was really only a passing interest to keep my mind occupied during the recovery.

I learned a great deal about the inner workings of technology, but perhaps I was really just living out a metaphor, externalising the feeling that something in my life was broken by focusing my attention on unwanted damaged goods. I expect Emma must have been surprised to see the contents of the attic when we'd cleared it out, with all the unfinished projects I'd toyed with over the last few months out of sight and gathering dust. To me they were symbolic of the brain injury and my post-traumatic stress, emblems of the anxieties I had repressed in the attic of my mind.

But the camper van was an altogether different project, for which I felt a genuine passion. It was a Volkswagen 21 window 1967 Samba in red oxide primer and the moment I saw it I knew it was the one for me. It was located in Jersey, so I arranged for the shipping and the import tax to be paid, as well as a storage unit where it could reside until I was ready to get started on the project in earnest. The original owner, Henk, was an engineer who sadly had recently had a debilitating stroke, forcing him to sell it. I assured him and his wife Catherine that it was now in good hands and promised to myself to restore it to the best of my abilities.

It arrived along with an array of new parts which had cost almost as much as the van itself, including a brand-new engine resting on a pallet, built and ready to go. Once Red Zebra was underway, I threw myself into the restoration, eager to get it back on the road so Allison and I could go on a few adventures. I was initially obsessed with the project despite my commitments to the bar and would spend many hours learning everything I could about restoring classic vehicles and the inner workings of the camper van, trying to be as well-versed in the subject as I possibly could. After a while of this intensive research I became something of an expert.

During the research phase of the project I read every single book, article and blog I could find on the subject. I also soaked in every photograph of the 21 window Samba line as well as purchasing the technical manual and reading it from cover to cover. From there I'd set about breaking down every system into its constituent parts, allowing me to form an inventory. This allowed me to organise all the parts into the relevant system and label up boxes. From here I was able to tally up any missing parts and place orders for them.

Then it was time to look for the best people to do the work, based on various recommendations as well as reviews of their work. Once these craftsmen were found I wrote a detailed scheme of the works, planning each phase and making the necessary bookings. After all of this organisation had been done it was a case of managing the project efficiently and continually checking the quality of the work.

As I continued to work on the bus, I sent progress shots of the build to Henk and Catherine, hoping they would lift Henk's mood while he recovered from the stroke. I knew it was his beloved project and wanted to reassure him that it was being looked after and restored correctly.

This included getting a bespoke oak interior constructed for the van, which was sent to Vaughn, an award-winning trimmer well known on the Volkswagen scene who had a lengthy waiting list. I was determined to make sure everything was done correctly, and on the day, Vaughn finished the work Allison and I drove up in my black Mercedes to collect the van. It looked amazing – far more impressive than I'd hoped for – and we stopped to refuel on the way home. As Allison filled up the Mercedes while I attended to the camper van, a man looked at Allison then at me and the VW. Realising Allison and I were together, he gave me a knowing look as if to acknowledge how lucky I was.

As much as I was loving working on the Volkswagen project and wanted to see it through to completion, lying on the concrete floor underneath the van and working on the reassembly started to take its toll, especially after a long day

working on the Red Zebra refurbish. If I carried on at the rate, I was going I'd either kill myself or make myself seriously ill, so I sent the camper to a Volkswagen specialist who could finish the remaining rebuilding work. Rather than risk my health, I visited them weekly to keep an eye on the progress and settle the bill for that week's work.

When I handed it over to the new restoration team they were hugely impressed with the condition of the van when I delivered it to them. All the parts were neatly arranged in boxes and correctly labelled and the sub system was all ready to be reassembled.

They remarked how they had never seen anyone so organised when rebuilding one of these Volkswagen campers and I was proud this comment reflected my ability to organise and add structure where none existed. This ability was one of the main reasons why Red Zebra ended up performing so well, despite the expectations of some.

Work on the bar was so consuming that sometimes I'd completely lose track of time. One morning, for instance, I arrived early and parked and didn't return to the car until twelve hours later, only to find that my two-hour parking had long since expired and a ticket welcomed me, stuck to my window screen. The time dilation I'd felt before had returned and that day had passed in a blur, reminding me just how all observed time is relative to our actions. The dizziness and head injury symptoms were starting to return, and I realised that I was pushing myself too hard.

I learned the importance of tempering my creative side with the impatient side of me which always wanted things to happen at the speed of light. If only they could happen at the speed of light, harnessing the energy attached to it. That would be a different matter.

The ideas for many of my projects started in this way: a simple thought permeating the consciousness, energised into growth by the internal world before finally becoming a reality. During this time, I was certainly at my most prolific, as if my energy vibration was functioning at a higher resonance due to the love and happiness I was feeling.

There's an expression which says that "love can give you wings", and in my case it literally felt as if this was the case, as everything I put my mind to came into being in a very short space of time. Looking back, I realise that this period of my life was a time when I had everything I'd been searching for. Yet it still felt as if there was something missing; something deep inside lying dormant and waiting to stir into life.

Again, the voice I'd heard before returned. Again it told me that not only was there more to learn, but that there was more to come. As much as I thought I had everything I wanted, the truth is that I was still not happy with myself.

It was going to take more life lessons before I would obtain that elusive inner peace.

Once the camper van was complete it soon gathered a lot of attention. Every time I took it out people would wave and smile, sometimes taking photographs. I even had a photo shoot lined up with VW Camper and Bus Magazine at Kedleston Hall. I'd contacted them initially, sending them a set of photographs for their consideration, unaware that ironically it would be the appearance in this magazine that would catch the eye of James Dyson, someone whom I had admired a great deal for some time.

The photographer met us at Kedleston Hall, and we managed to block the main drive. We'd parked the camper van in the centre of the driveway, framing the shot with the large stately home in the background since the photographer thought this would make for a great cover shot.

It wasn't long before the lord of the manor sent his gamekeeper across to move us on, and I apologised for the trouble caused, giving him a bottle of wine as a small token of my appreciation for being allowed access to such a great location.

The camper van – surrounded as it was by some impressive studio lighting equipment and a professional photographer – certainly drew a lot of attention from the other visitors to the Hall, some of whom clearly thought it was a celebrity photo shoot of some kind. While I was no celebrity myself, it was hugely rewarding to see the VW getting so much attention (the real star of the day, after all), and that I was receiving some recognition for the hard work and research I'd put into making the van one of the best in the country.

After the photo shoot the magazine writers contacted Allison while I had been away at Everest. For some strange reason they wanted her to comment on the project, and despite the fact that by this point we had separated they put her down as my partner in life, even including quotes from her in the magazine piece. Either it was a mix up on their part or she was trying to share credit for my work.

It was a vibrant and eventful time in my life. Yet despite all of these seemingly miraculous events taking place I was still incapable of truly living in the moment and appreciating what I had, searching for the next project to throw myself into. It would be some time until I'd finally find the key to unlock the real happiness, I'd been seeking for so long. Of course, each and every one of us carries the keys and knowledge leading to our own happiness – we just have to believe that we deserve happiness and set ourselves free.

Love of one's self was the key which allowed me to unlock my potential and discover the creative mind to build the wine bar. It felt as if this creative energy allowed me to sculpt the world around me and model my thoughts, transforming them into action. The more positive the thoughts – and the more powerful the self-belief – the quicker these ideas would manifest into the reality of my world.

I use this tactic on a daily basis now with all the projects I engage in, always making sure I organise and research thoroughly before committing to anything physically. I believe that the key to any success or achievement in life is to have clear, logical steps and a plan to achieve those steps. Even if others tell you that something is impossible, self-belief and determination to achieve your goals will overcome any doubts and bring it into reality.

Anything is possible, and if you haven't achieved it yet it is often only because you haven't yet thought of the right solution. I have been fortunate enough when project managing to be able to envision the final outcome from the very beginning. The moment I laid eyes on the camper van I could see the project finished down to the very last detail. Likewise, with Red Zebra, the picture in my mind's eye allowed it to come to fruition and turn out the way it did.

I also realised that I was often doing other projects which seemed to be for the benefit of others, as if until now I thought I didn't deserve what I had created. But this wasn't true – I now understand that I created these things in order to help me realise my true potential and unlock previously concealed gifts.

Having completed the camper van, I ended up putting it up for sale on eBay. In a bizarre twist of fate, the son of one of my all-time heroes ended up buying it. He sent an email telling me he would be happy to pay the full asking price, having only just seen it in the magazine article the previous day.

I noticed the name on the email and immediately thought to myself, "Is that really who I think it is?" but I didn't want to make any assumptions.

He asked if I knew if there was an airport close by to the heated storage where the camper was being housed and I thought to myself that he must be arriving by helicopter before driving to the location. I arrived at the storage facility early to admire the camper van one last time before parting with it, and despite the fact that everyone else thought it looked perfect, I could still see all the little flaws which remained.

As I would later learn, nothing is ever perfect, and while you continue to chase perfection you end up missing the moment. Sometimes the imperfections are what makes something more unique.

The customer arrived and sure enough I'd been right about who it was. His name was Sam Dyson, son of the entrepreneur and businessman Sir James Dyson, world famous for his revolutionary vacuum cleaners. I showed him the camper van and he was very impressed with the work. As he looked it over he said two things which really stood out to me, firstly, he told me how his children would grow up and have childhood memories in something I had created myself, and then said he couldn't wait to show off the level of engineering and attention to detail to his father, who is undoubtedly one of the most famous inventors and engineers alive today.

I'd always wanted to meet James Dyson and here I stood chatting with his son about a project which for me had been a labour of love. As the saying goes, "be careful what you wish for!" but in this instance I can safely say it is a memory I hold truly dear. This, despite the fact that the banker's draft Sam handed me was from the same bank the Queen uses! I had to laugh when I handed it in to the bank when they said I would have to wait five days for it to clear, just in case it bounced. I said to the bank teller, "If it bounces from a billionaire then that will be funny!"

I thought I had everything I wanted and yet the drive to become a father was leaving a feeling of emptiness inside me which wouldn't go away. It was as if my sole purpose was to be a father, and until I achieved that nothing would satisfy this deeply felt longing. Here I was, a thirty-five-year-old successful man with a beautiful partner and a business which was thriving. I was living the high life, yet deep down I knew that this success only brought happiness on the surface, changing my surroundings but inevitably leaving what lies within untouched and unchanged.

Materialistic objects bring with them a finite degree of happiness, as sure to fade as the items themselves. The pursuit of material goods can easily become something of an addiction, the ever-accumulating pile of clothes and gadgets never enough to satiate these desires.

But when you reach a place in life where you can have whatever you want, soon the addiction begins to wane, as you realise that it is often the idea of the possessions which counts for more than the possessions themselves. The items become illusions – while you appear to be focusing on them, in reality you're moving towards a grander goal or dream.

Allison's birthday was approaching fast.

She'd never had a surprise party before, so I set about organising one for her, paying attention to every little detail to make it as close to perfection as I could. Firstly, I took her to Emily Bridgens and bought her a gorgeous dress, then told her we'd be heading out for a meal to Darleys, our favourite restaurant with a number of prestigious awards, which overlooked the river Derwent.

I also organised a private function that evening at Red Zebra, booking a five- piece swing band to provide the music and arranging for all of her friends to be there. Our catering firm made up some exquisite French food and I had a cake sculpture made in the shape of an angel, using a photograph of Allison to ensure a perfect likeness. My dear friend Simon set up an impromptu studio to photograph all the guests on their arrival, where they were each met with a glass of champagne.

The only thing I was struggling to arrange was the transport to the venue from our house. I really wanted to hire a classic car – preferably an E-type Jaguar – but couldn't find anywhere who could help. In the end I rang for a taxi and a green Jaguar estate turned up and I laughed thinking how I'd almost got that part right as well – albeit completely by congruent.

The night passed quickly, since we all had a great deal of fun, and the guests were impressed with the level of attention to detail I'd brought to the celebrations. I realised how much I loved organising for other people and could seem to perform minor miracles when others were involved in the outcome. But I never seemed to do this for myself and part of me ached for someone to know me well enough to be able to arrange a similar party for me. I'd hoped that my fortieth would turn out as special as Allison's fiftieth.

It appeared at this time my ability to manifest my dreams down to such accurate details came about because of love; my vibrational frequency was emitting out into the universe, amplified by my love for Allison. As a result, these manifestations were simultaneously magnified and sped up, as I lived my own dreams and made them a daily reality.

Allison had two adult daughters when I met her named Claudia and Maddy, whom I treated as my own, and tried to build bridges with them whenever I could. I bought Claudia her first car when she passed her driving test and in the two years, we'd known one another it was the first time she'd kissed and hugged me. Maddy was about to begin her university degree, but clearing had messed up her accommodation, so I made several phone calls and spoke to the right people to make sure she had the accommodation she desired. I even funded her until her grant came through, helping to invest in a bright future.

Seeing how these simple gestures of support made them so happy gave me a glimpse of what it might be like being a father to my own children, and I felt a pride of my own, as if becoming a father by proxy. I started to think about the possibility of Allison and I having a child, despite the fact that when we had first met I was of course aware of the age difference. But her genetics beguiled her age, and she knew deep down that my longing for fatherhood would ultimately lead to the end of our relationship.

When we found out that we couldn't have children together it broke my heart, changing something inside me permanently. There was always the possibility of adoption, but Allison had already had children and seen them through to adulthood and understandably did not want to go through the rigors of parenting once again. Her children had grown up and left the nest and it was time for her to enjoy her life.

The news devastated me, and I knew that this was the end of things for Allison and I; by some cruel twist of fate I'd found someone I thought I could spend the rest of my life with, but it wasn't to be.

In retrospect I can see the reasons for the inevitability of our breakup, but at the time the blow felt severe and left me feeling sad and empty. We separated and I moved to the mill – unbeknown to me a new pattern had begun; a new safety net which I would cling to in times of crisis.

When Jade walked into the bar it almost seemed as if one door was closing while another was about to open. It would be another door I walked through which would change my life, altering the fundamental bedrock of the person I was. Without this catalyst I wouldn't be the person I am today – we either stand still in life, or we choose to make a change and move forwards.

Jade came into my life while I was building the Red Zebra business. She'd come in to apply for a job we'd advertised in the window, and the moment she'd entered I'd known that something was going to happen between us. Even though at the time I was perfectly happy with Allison, I'd just found out that we couldn't have children together, and it was a blow which had devastated me. I thought I'd found someone who was complex and spiritual and who understood me better than anyone else, only to discover it wasn't to be.

Jade walked in wearing her Audrey Hepburn glasses framing her big blue eyes above her winning smile. When I looked at her it felt as if I'd glimpsed the future, and I knew our paths were about to intertwine.

Had she been sent to help me move on from Allison and help mend my broken heart? Only time would tell. After interviewing her I knew she was perfect for the job and she told me that her mother had seen the sign and suggest she apply. I didn't realise this at the time, but the relevance of this would become apparent later.

Whilst living with Jade I became increasingly isolated from the business I had built, going from being hands-on on a daily basis to something of a silent partner. I took nothing out of the business, only becoming re-engaged with it once the business awards for best bar came up on the horizon. I reviewed the business and made some financial improvements to make sure it was in good stead. Allison had lost heart when I'd left to live with Jade, and the old adage "never mix business with pleasure" rang in my ears.

That year I arrived at the Food & Drink Awards and watched as all my staff stood with Allison, as people congratulated them on being a finalist. I'd said to Allison in the taxi on the way there that we'd already won, confident that Red Zebra continued to be a cut above the competition, but Allison and the staff had laughed. Yet I knew that this was going to happen, the outcome presented to me in another premonition.

During the event I stood there as the press photographer prepared to take a picture of the business I had built. I was standing in the shadows like a stranger, so I walked over and suggested that I was also in the photograph. The photographer wanted to take a picture with just the ladies in the shot, but I retorted that since it was my business it seemed only fair that I was included as well.

He laughed as if I was joking, but soon realised that I was very serious. I'd dedicated so much time working to get the business off the ground and turn it into a success story, yet now it felt as if others were willing to take the credit for my work.

We sat there waiting for the winner of best bar to be announced, then the host called out, "and the winner is Red Zebra Wine Bar!"
The staff gave me a bemused look and I smiled back. We walked up to the stage passing the photographer and I said to him, "I told you it was my business!"

I'd got the recognition I thought I'd always wanted for a second time, but it felt like a hollow victory and doubts were raging in my mind. I saw for the first time all these people from the business community and the respect I'd wanted for so long. But in reality, it was only how I saw myself and how I felt about my achievements that truly mattered.

I understood that another cycle in my life was coming to a close and it was time to take on board what I had learned from these lessons and move forward in order to continue to evolve. Soon after we'd received this award Allison and I decided to put the business up for sale and go our separate ways. I'd built a very successful business and pushed it to winning awards, but everyone seemed to assume that Allison had been the driving force behind the success.

When we finally sold the bar, I threw a party as a final goodbye to the business. I invited around twenty people to the bar for the night, putting on a spread of food and sitting back as I watched them enjoy the evening. But I knew that I had changed. The approval of others – and the satisfaction I'd felt from the materialistic items I'd been able to buy – was becoming a thing of the past for me. For real change to happen you have to realise the old patterns you have engaged in and by saying goodbye to the old part of my life I had to make way for a new beginning.

I had learned a great deal about business from building and running Red Zebra, but in doing so I also learned a lot more about the real me. I wanted to become that person, not just an image presented for the sake of other people. I needed to discover my authentic self, beyond the trappings of success and materialism.

When evaluating this period in my life I was struck by the parable of an imprisoned man, stuck in his cell with no door barring his way to freedom. When asked why he didn't just walk out of the door, he said, "I'm still trying to work out how I got in here."
We are all guilty of this to one degree or another. We become so involved in the details of our life situations we're unable to take a step back from it. But in doing this we get to see the bigger picture, allowing us to get a clearer perspective on what is actually important.

I always believed that Jade came into the bar not only for a job but in many ways for me to be in a position to help her. But now I see the true aspect of what would transpire, and that it was I who was helped by Jade. She inadvertently taught me about a greater – and truer – meaning to life, which transcended the things which had preoccupied me at the time.

It wasn't materialism, or power, or wealth which counted the most.

It was love. Love of oneself. Love of others.
This is what truly leads to a higher perspective, gifting the thought process with a new openness and allowing it to fully develop.

I'd often seen myself as helping others at the exclusion of myself, but in reality it was a two-way exchange, and I too was learning some valuable lessons which would shape the way I saw the world.

It's only now, having finally put my ego aside, that I was able to allow that love and wisdom to permeate throughout my being. As I started to realise the superficiality of the trappings of wealth and materialism, I became a much deeper and more content soul, prepared to embrace humanity with a deeper respect and understanding.

After our first meeting at Headly Court, Karl and I had kept in touch with one another and remained friends long after we'd been discharged from the medical facility. He'd sometimes visit me in Derby, and it was on one such visit when he told me of his involvement with the Walking Wounded charity. He had recently been selected to climb Everest and my immediate thought was what a perfect candidate he was.

Karl was one of the few people in the military I stayed in contact with. It wasn't until nearly ten years had passed since my head injury that I finally felt as if I could reintegrate with my old military friends. I was invited to another former colleague Matthew's wedding, where due to my long hair no one would have guessed I was ex-military. I also eventually hooked up with my old friend Danny at the twenty-four-year dining out in the Warrant Officers' and Sergeants' Mess. Danny and I had served together in Northern Ireland and our meeting brought back strong memories of a life I'd long since left behind.

Walking Wounded had been set up to support military veterans with physical, mental or social injuries to help them gain the necessary skills, support and qualifications to develop new careers outside of the armed forces and reintegrate into civilian life while providing long-term support for themselves and their families. It was started by three patients at Headley Court, initially with the sole aim of raising £10,000 for a swimming pool to be used by recovering veterans. Due to the fact that there were no charities out there performing the same services, it quickly went commercial and became an overnight success.

This was clearly a charity close to my heart, not least on account of my close friendship with Karl, for whom such a charity had been life changing. Their name was not without a degree of irony. In military parlance, the walking wounded are considered low priority on the battlefield; they are the soldiers who are conscious and breathing and whose injuries might be relatively minor at the time, they are therefore often the last to receive medical attention. On the battlefield such neglect is perhaps understandable – back in civilian life it is inexcusable.

I decided I would do anything I could to support him in his venture and prepared to take on the walk to Base Camp along with the rest of the Walking Wounded team. I realised from the beginning that this was going to be something of a challenge. Prior to the trek many people told me how gruelling such a walk would be and that most people go through at least six months of training before even attempting such a challenge.

Unfortunately, my commitments to work – not to mention my personal life – meant that I had very little spare time in which to prepare myself, so it was not without a degree of trepidation that I set off to tackle the world's highest mountain.

Many people would have ended up cancelling such a trek under these conditions, but I thought this made the prospect more interesting – and certainly more of a challenge. It was also a chance to prove myself to myself, tackling something I'd never thought I would until now.

Unfit, overweight and still suffering from the effects of the brain injury, it was perhaps unsurprising that I was concerned not only about my ability to physically accomplish the walk but also whether I'd even be able to handle the atmospheric conditions experienced at such high altitudes. I was about to embark on perhaps the most challenging endeavour of my entire life.

Despite the complete lack of training I knew that my old military ethos would keep me in good stead.

I was also confident that I would get fitter as I went along. So, I booked the trip online, making all the arrangements necessary via email, then packed up all my belongings and checked my flight details.

All that remained now was to fly halfway across the world and meet up with the rest of the group in Kathmandu.

I met the Walking Wounded team in the Hyatt Regency hotel in Kathmandu. As would be expected from a Hyatt hotel this was a plush, five-star hotel lavishly laid out in the traditional Newari style of Nepalese architecture featuring striking brickwork and a unique wood carving of a kind I had never seen before. The tiered structures which made up the bulk of the hotel resembled the rising levels of the surrounding monasteries, adapted for the purposes of hospitality rather than spiritual introspection.

It was positioned in an ideal location for tourists: on one side the view from the hotel overlooked the lush gardens, neat lawns and expansive swimming pools and the mountain ranges which spilled out along the horizon. Just a short distance away lay the UNESCO World Heritage site of the Kathmandu Valley, home of the Boudhanath Stupa, the near-mythical mound-like dome with mounted spire and gigantic mandala which drew in the large populations of refugees from Tibet over the decades. It was a strange yet, at the same time, enthralling and impressive sight and truly brought home to me just how unique and distinct this culture was compared to the one I was familiar with back home.

The juxtaposition between the sacred Boudhanath and the hotel couldn't have been more striking, bringing to my attention the gulf between the Eastern philosophies indigenous to the region and the materialism of the Western world. Given that the Hyatt Regency was a five-star hotel there was an abundance of wealth and opulence on display, with sports cars and expensive watches a characteristic of many of the hotel's guests.

The hotel even sported its own helipad, which seemed to me about as clear an indication as you could possibly get that money was no object for some of the more esteemed guests. Yet this overt display of wealth sat uncomfortably with me, particularly in the context of my visit to this part of the world and the cause for which I was hoping to raise money. It seemed to me that the materialism so highly valued by people in the modern world – myself included, for much of my life – sat in direct conflict with the purpose of the Walking Wounded charity trek, and while I wasn't so naïve as to be unaware of the negative impact of inequality in the world, seeing such opulence first hand is always a stark and inescapable reminder of the gap between the haves and the have-nots.

I realised that my own desire for material possessions and financial gain was mere window dressing for the theatre that was my life up until now and that any deeper meaning or sense of satisfaction with the decisions I made would come not from the accumulation of physical things, but through a deeper understanding of humanity and a commitment to improving the lives of others through selfless acts.

Chris was the first person I met, a thick-set and muscular man in his early twenties; a former soldier who had been medically retired from the military after being blown up in Iraq. The explosion had deafened him in his left ear, and he wore a hearing aid on account of this. His experiences certainly hadn't dulled his sense of humour – Chris possessed a razor-sharp wit of the kind often seen in those who have experienced such traumatic events and lived to tell the tale.

Another veteran with considerably more noticeable wounds was Andy, a still serving Colour Sergeant who had been badly burned when the Land Rover he'd been in was hit by an Improvised Explosive Device on tour. The severe scars down the side of his body led to more than a few stares as we reclined by the hotel swimming pool; strangers looking on and no doubt wondering what had happened, not knowing that he'd earned them in the line of duty.

The third person I met was a quiet and unassuming man by the name of Simon, who we'd later discover was a currently serving member of the special forces. This certainly went some way to explaining his almost superhuman level of fitness to the level you only usually see in Hollywood movies. His large beard was more than familiar to me from my time in the army – I'd seen similar looking men whilst serving abroad and they're against regulation facial hair was known to everyone as an indication that they were in special forces. It was the same look worn by the highly paid mercenaries who worked for the private sector, pooled from the cream of military training circles. Dave, an ex-military man in his mid-50s with razor sharp eyes and striking grey hair, also came from a military background.

As our trek progressed it became clear from several things, he talked about that Dave was possibly former SAS. This was never spoken of directly – former assumed SAS members are reticent to discuss their past in detail, not least because talk of past missions is prohibited – but some of his remarks could only have eluded to his prior service. The first hint came when we were discussing the military and Dave described the intelligence corps "green slime" - in the trade, this comment alone was something of a giveaway.

Like most assumed former SAS, Dave gave nothing specific away and never spoke in detail of any operations he might have been on. All we had were brief insights lacking in detail, descriptions and names, and we counted ourselves as privileged to hear what we did. Even these minor titbits of information were incredibly illuminating; a slight peek into a clandestine world which exists far beyond even the outskirts of normal society. These small insights perhaps gave me more satisfaction than the rest of the group – as a young boy I'd spent many hours engrossed in Andy McNab's books about his time in the SAS.

The first woman we were introduced to became affectionately known to the rest of the team as "Princess"; a slight, attractive woman who came from a very wealthy background of Russian nobility noted for their business acumen.

Princess had been sent travelling by her parents so that she might find a husband. As quaint and slightly antiquated as that might sound to the modern reader, the root of it apparently lay in how her own parents had met – they too had met during travels of their own and thought that their daughter might follow in their footsteps, if not literally then at least metaphorically.

The final member of the team, Sally, was a veterinarian who had health issues and had opted to come along on the Everest trek for similar reasons to my own – she was up for a real challenge which might lead to a refreshing perspective and a new direction in life. I was to accompany Sally for almost the entire walk, staying at the back of the group encouraging her to keep up the pace for the first four days. This unofficial role I had chosen to take on was not without its advantages for myself – indeed, in finding the energy and willpower to urge Sally onwards I found the drive to keep myself moving forwards, too. But this was yet to come – in the meantime we had some time to kill before setting out on our trek, so we decided to soak up the atmosphere of the local markets.

One of the most notable aspects of visiting parts of the world so utterly different from what you're familiar with is the way in which your senses feel as if they've become heightened, and the markets of Kathmandu opened up the palette of sights, sounds and smells to their full capacity. A wild array of intricately crafted, colourful trinkets lay sprawling across a sea of stalls; brightly patterned bangles and bracelets presented alongside handmade shawls, scarves and headdresses which seemed designed to appeal to the scattered groups of tourists as much as the locals who mingled amongst them.

Eccentric-looking handicrafts were also there in abundance – red, yellow and

golden carved elephant masks hanging next to Buddhist effigies and unusual marionette dolls dressed in wonderfully patterned clothing – all of which piled up in haphazard fashion, enticing the souvenir hunters with their arresting traditional designs.

While many of these stalls seemed as eager to lure in travellers and tourists, the range of the food and spices on display seemed to point to the diversity of cultures in Kathmandu, a place where both the mixture of ethnic groups of the geographical variety of the region have created a wide-ranging cuisine. Nepalese ingredients and dishes sit comfortably alongside Tibetan and Indian culinary creations, and the effect of this in the marketplace was a heady concoction of aromas which offered a stark contrast to the meat and vegetables I was used to back home.

I couldn't help but notice how much tourism played a role in the dishes available, as if the presence of foreigners had only encouraged restaurateurs to be even more creative with their menus and offer strange hybrid dishes which fused ingredients and cooking methods from around the world. If the markets of Kathmandu perhaps didn't represent a truly cultural melting pot with regards to the trinkets and handicrafts on display, their food was certainly much closer in spirit.

In spite of the diverse range of food available to us, we all sat down to a continental breakfast with full English as our preferred choice. It felt like a strange dichotomy to be in such a different culture, but in light of the physical exertion which lay ahead a high calorie meal seemed to be the only logical choice, so we tucked into the food to store as much energy as possible. As I

glanced around the table I wondered what the deeper reasons for everyone being here might be, and what demons they had come to exorcise.

After we'd eaten, Sally, Princess and I visited Swayambhunath Stupa, its golden spire illuminated in the glowing afternoon sun. A significant Buddhist pilgrimage destination since the fifth century, this was a truly revered, spiritual site where a miraculous lotus is said to have been planted many centuries ago by a past Buddha. While the light which was alleged to have radiated from this lotus may have dimmed and the saints, sages and spiritual men have largely been replaced by tourists, the aura of the place itself retained an undeniably calming and introspective allure.

Sally, Princess and I digested our dinner we gazed up admiringly at the Swayambhunath Stupa, still radiating the same golden aura I'd see when visiting with Simon. This time it felt more serene and peaceful. Of course, this being affectionately known as Monkey Temple there were plenty of our primate friends scurrying around the walls and alcoves, swinging from the gently swaying trees which offered some respite from the sun. Some would approach us closer, eyeing us up for potential treats and gauging our friendliness. They were admirable creatures and it wasn't difficult to see in their actions the hints of evolution that link humanity to our deeper ancestral roots.

As I sat admiring the elegant temple buildings and intricate designs which adorned the walls, I couldn't help but think that I had perhaps been a monk myself, in some long since forgotten past life many years before. A wave of peace washed over me and for the first time since I was a child I felt as if I were truly at home.

Before heading back to the Hyatt we decided to take one final detour away from the bustling throngs of Kathmandu's busy centre, exploring the hidden garden which lay within the city boundaries. Called the Garden of Dreams, this was a spot of beauty and tranquillity just a short walk from the hectic marketplace, where the still waters of ancient ponds reflected the clear skies overhead.

Famous as the garden of Six Seasons – which had been created by Field Marshal Kaiser Sumsher Rana – it struck me as an exceptionally peaceful spot, especially considering it was a stone's throw from the bustling city. It was beautifully designed in the Edwardian style and featured pavilions, fountains and ornately decorated garden furniture surrounded by lush flowering plants which clung to the verandas.

We rested some more and soaked up the ambience, watching the breeze drifting gently through the leaves of the palm trees swaying above. It dawned on us that this would be the last true moment of relaxation before we kitted up and set out on the long trek up the side of the world's most impressive mountain.

Soon we would be leaving behind all of this – the ancient structures and spiritual sanctuaries; the gleaming sports cars and immaculately tailored clothing of the Hyatt's guests; the lush greens and brightly coloured flowers of Kathmandu's fauna and flora – and trading it in for endless white vistas stretching as far as the eye can see.

But before we could get to the trek, we still had one last challenge to face up to that would test even the most hardened adventurer.

The dangerous flight into Lukla was the next mission on our agenda.

When I'd heard claims that the flight from Kathmandu to Lukla was said to be the most dangerous flight in the world I'd dismissed them as little more than fear mongering. After all, it's not uncommon for people to blow their own experiences out of all proportion in order to enhance the effect of the storytelling, so I'd thought little of it as I'd boarded the small plane which was to take us away from the capital. I'd flown thousands of miles in my life up to this point and had experienced countless episodes of turbulence so was unperturbed by the prospect of a bumpy flight and settled into my seat feeling both comfortable and confident.

Half an hour later and my confidence had been completely stripped away by the constant jolts, twists and tumbles the small plane had been thrown into by the raging winds which surrounded us. Pale and sickly, the passengers on board all seemed to be going through the same experience as myself – that is, all except for a young American boy who sat smiling throughout the entire journey, even occasionally laughing as the plane dipped several meters in a split second

We landed safely – and more than a little shaken up – in Lukla airport and disembarked to gather our belongings and met our guide, Knarly. Knarly was a lovable Kiwi man who was something of an expert climber and skier, having travelled the globe and tackled some of the most challenging peaks possible. He was thin and wiry with short curly hair and a daredevil look in his eyes. Unassuming to look at, but in my experience the most capable people of all don't put on airs to convince others of their true worth. Knarly had broken his back climbing in the past but this hadn't deterred him in the slightest – after recovering he'd gone straight back to climbing.

His experience and knowledge were second to none and he was close friends with some of the most renowned climbers in the world. He led our team with a mixture of dedication and professionalism, not to mention a killer sense of humour and a sharp wit which you could see from just looking in his eyes. The way in which he spoke alluded to his own pain and it was clear that he too was in the process of overcoming obstacles and challenges in his life.

We were all on this trek for different reasons, but a common underlying current clearly bound us all together. Faced with immense trauma we had chosen not to bow down to it, but to fight. On a subconscious level all of us recognised this in one another, and we respected each of us all the more because of it.

As we walked up to the nearby lodge to have lunch, the effects of altitude began to make themselves known. Knarly, Andy and I suddenly burst into uncontrollable fits of laughter, giggling like children for no real reason as we tried to acclimatise to the changes in altitude. Princess misinterpreted our outburst and thought we had been drinking alcohol – one of the cardinal sins of trekking at high altitude – and lectured us sternly for our perceived transgression. We maintained our innocence, but it seemed clear that she didn't believe us one bit, and her outburst of morality made us laugh even harder.

After lunch we set off on the first leg of our trek.

Full of energy and eager to prove to myself that I could get through the first day comfortably, I pushed myself as hard as I could and walked most of the day alone, reflecting on an unusual day and the multitude of emotions which had swirled through my mind. I'd left home to seek solace and find some answers to the problems in my life, having been morally judged by a relative stranger based on her own subjective perceptions of the world.

Now I was standing close to the top of the world. It's hard to think of another place more suitable for reflecting and putting things into context, and I spent much of the day away from the group processing these events.

As I trekked towards the dome of the sky above me, I bumped into the boy who had found the turbulent flight earlier so entertaining walking with his father. As often happens the conversation soon turned to discussing our professions, a trait which demonstrates how often people make judgements on one another based on what they do, as if this signifies who they really are. He seemed to be in competition with me, a touch of bravado to his talks of his business ventures. I remember thinking to myself, in reality we're only in competition with ourselves. Once you understand that, there is no competition.

Nevertheless, the close relationship between this father and son brought home to me once again the fact that Allison and I would not be able to have children of our own. If we look hard enough, we can see reflections of our own troubles and anxieties wherever we choose, and the young boy was a reminder of my longing to be a father

On the first evening I also felt the truly unpleasant effects of altitude for the first time.

It felt as if I was underwater or trapped inside a goldfish bowl struggling to breathe, so before I went to bed that evening, I made sure I drank plenty of water and tried to get an early night. Having failed to take the Diamox which was recommended to us I had a fitful and restless night's sleep in which my companion Knarly suffered himself from one of the unfortunate side-effects – he was forced to listen to my incessant snoring throughout the night.

For my part I experienced incredibly vivid lucid dreams which made me question my own existence – the kind of dreams which sear themselves in your brain upon awaking, then slide into the unconscious in a brief instant, leaving behind a fading message. I sensed the importance of these messages and tried to retain them. It felt as if the high altitude exacerbated the luridness of these dreams – I can imagine hallucinogenic drugs created a similar effect of clarity and disorientation fighting for domination over each other.

I felt completely fatigued the following morning, so I decided to make sure I took the Diamox the next evening, as we ate breakfast and readied ourselves to continue onwards.

130

The ascent up the mountain was slow going and we plodded along with determination until we reached the lunch stop. Sally was starting to show signs that she was suffering on the trek, so I walked with her to make sure she was okay, motivating and encouraging her to help keep her moving. We were at the rear of the group now, with only Knarly behind us, there to ensure our safety and to keep us on the right track. It was a surprisingly hot and humid day, and I concentrated on taking care of Sally to make sure she made it to the next stop without incident.

We stopped for lunch and were taken to a large two storey building and guided upstairs to a dining area. I removed my day sack and advised Sally to take in fluids slowly and try to eat something for lunch, but she said she wasn't hungry. I became increasingly concerned for her health, as she appeared to be going into a daze, unresponsive when spoken to. This is something I had seen before in the military with soldiers who were about to faint, but as I was about to continue helping her, I suddenly felt light-headed myself and the room began to spin.

I had been so concerned with monitoring Sally's progress that I had committed a cardinal sin of mountaineering and failed to keep to my own fluid intake regime. Quickly swallowing some refreshing water, I ate to lift up my energy levels. Sally sat there in something of a trance, completely silent for the duration of our dinner.

We finished our food and filled our water bottles ready for the next leg of the trek. I stayed with Sally all afternoon as we continued up the mountain, the intensified heat of the sun – which glared brightly on the white snow – draining our energy and making each step feel like a mammoth task. I questioned whether I'd be able to make it to the camp that day, but eventually Sally, myself and the other members of the expedition arrived at our tents and collapsed with exhaustion.

I immediately expressed my concerns about Sally's condition to Knarly. By now she was looking completely drained of energy as she sat on the ground supping at her water bottle in an attempt to slowly bring up her fluid levels, resolving to take Diamox that evening in order to help her acclimatise to the altitude.

She was discovering the hard way how failure to acclimatise, combined with the lack of good sleep, can severely impact the body's ability to perform. This combination of altitude and sleep deprivation can be a very dangerous thing and as I settled down in my tent that evening, I hoped that a good night's rest would lift Sally's spirits and give her the energy she needed to complete the trek.

The following day we set off on the next leg of the trek, moving up the mountain from Khumjung to Phortse. I faced a short but very hard climb of around 200 metres and was beginning to regret bringing along my camera equipment, particularly since I had decided to see how far I could push myself on this day to see how my body would react to the challenge. Taking my 20-kilo camera bag and all its accessories was clearly an unwise move – before long I was puffing and wheezing like an asthmatic. I noticed that the guides and safety team had stopped a short way ahead of me for a water break, so I struggled over to them for a chat and an excuse to try and regain my breath.

"What weight is it you're carrying there?" I asked one of the guides, trying to sound calm and collected but still gasping for air.

"I don't know, maybe forty kilograms?" he replied, lifting it up and down as if to weight it like a pair of scales. "Your pack a little heavy today, Mr. Harris?" he asked, looking at my backpack.

I slung it off my shoulder and he took it, feeling the weight of it for himself. After this brief assessment he passed it back, giving me a look as if to say that I was crazy for carrying such a load on such a difficult stretch before smiling with sympathy. With my breathing almost back to normal I too returned my backpack to my shoulders and continued onwards, hunched over with the increasingly heavy weight on my back yet pressing forwards with a determination to make it to the next checkpoint.

Pressing on in this stooped fashion might have made the load a little more bearable to carry, but this soon changed when I saw a beautiful blonde woman coming towards me, working her way back down the mountainside. I immediately straightened my back and tried to look far more fit and healthy than I actually was, casually saying "Morning! Lovely walk isn't it?" as if I were out on a gentle stroll in the park on a Sunday afternoon.

She smiled back and continued onwards, and I waited until she had gone out of view before resuming my stooped posture. I laughed lightly to myself at this unexpected moment of unguarded ego, before hunching down and pressing on up the steep slopes. Things might have been getting tougher for me, but for another member of our team the climb was bringing with it far greater problems.

As we moved further up the mountainside, Sally's condition began to deteriorate as altitude sickness started to take its effect. I stuck close by her side and told her to follow my footsteps so she could get into a rhythm and help her to focus. She would later tell me how she had taken a photograph of my feet as a reminder of what had inspired her to continue onwards.

Again, the atmosphere on the walk was oppressively humid, which slowed our progress and didn't do anything to improve Sally's condition. At one point she saw a helicopter and remarked wryly, "I'm going to be in one of those soon".

It was an accurate prediction of what was to come.

Fortunately for Sally there was a medical station nearby: she started to cough up blood just a short distance from this station and it became clear that the altitude sickness from which she was suffering was severe. She was admitted to the centre immediately and monitored overnight, while me and the rest of the expedition tried to keep her spirits up as we hoped for the best outcome. Having been rehydrated via IV fluid and given oxygen, the doctors then diagnosed her with pulmonary edema; her heart unable to pump effectively leading to a build-up of fluid due to the high altitude. As if to add insult to injury to the pulmonary edema she was charged $650 by the medical staff for their services (it goes without saying that venturing on such an expedition is not permitted without each member having full medical insurance).

After spending the night in the medical station, Knarly and I carried her with her oxygen bottle to the helicopter. By this point Sally was barely conscious, with Knarly and I standing either side acting as a human crutch, we guided her towards the waiting helicopter and assisted her into her seat. Part of me questioned whether I should get in the helicopter myself and call it a day, but I had to prove I could finish the trek.

So Knarly and I stood back as the helicopter lifted up off the ground, and Sally was evacuated off the hill.

Knarly was invaluable not only throughout the situation with Sally's altitude sickness but for the entire trip. While we all carried our own rudimentary first aid kits and monitored our health, Knarly was a trained medic and brought with him expertise we all lacked along with more advanced trauma equipment and, if required, morphine. He constantly looked over the group, travelling at the rear to ensure no one fell behind. In the military this is known as tail end Charlie; the rear guard of the patrol.

His presence ensured Sally's safety as the altitude sickness worsened. She was sent to the local hospital in Nepal where she was kept for five days – the payment for her medical treatment no doubt sounded like small change to Sally once she faced the $10,000 bill for the helicopter ride, and her long stay in the hospital had very little to do with her condition and everything to do with resolving the issue of payment with her insurance company.

After we'd left Sally, as she flew away in the helicopter, the thought struck me for the first time that I might well die out here. I'd been aware of the potentially deadly effects of such high altitudes before I'd left the UK, but seeing Sally coughing up blood made me think again about my brain condition and the very likely possibility of suffering a similar – or even worse – fate.

I'd had the basic medical check out – along with the required jabs – before I'd set out to Nepal, but since I'd been before this was little more than a formality. That said, if I'd brought up the issue of my traumatic brain injury – and how this might be affected by the high altitudes – I'm sure the doctor would have advised me not to go.

At the same time, I couldn't help but worry about my insurance coverage, which looking back seems like a sad reflection of the importance of money in today's culture, where even our own health and very life plays second fiddle to financial concerns. This false concern (I knew full well I had the correct insurance) seems in hindsight a moment of madness, where my own mortality inexplicably became less relevant than something as ultimately irrelevant as an insurance policy.

With Sally gone the expedition seemed to reach something of a low point, each of its members locked in their own thoughts. We were all concerned for Sally's health and hoped that the return to a lower altitude would alleviate her symptoms as quickly as possible. It was a moment for introspection and in a sense facing up to our own personal demons. A sombre mood permeated the air as the realities of the harshness of our environment came close to home.

Still, we pressed onwards and shortly after 2pm we arrived at Lobuche, snow- capped mountains surrounding the bright yellow tents which stood out in stark contrast to the landscape. We were shown to our tents and reunited with the bags which the porters had taken up the mountain ahead of us, and I slumped into an exhausted heap, eager to rest my weary legs.

How the porters could manage such a climb with so much baggage was to me something approaching a miraculous feat. I wasn't surprised by the fact that they were all used to the high altitudes as they were Nepalese it was only natural, they were accustomed to the environment. But their hard-working nature and endurance was something else, effortlessly arranging for the movement of our large bags and other supplies up the mountain; always ready when we arrived at the next stop. Despite their bright blue jackets, they still somehow blended into the background, and they would wake up long before we did to help prepare for the next leg.

135

I admired the resourcefulness of the porters and thought that a lot could be learned from them. For my part, I was just grateful to have made it to camp in one piece.

For obvious reasons, most evenings in the camp were spent relaxing. We often played cards and chatted with one another about the highlights of our day. But mostly it would be a time for reflection. Each of us had our own reasons for being there and we would contemplate this as we took stock of everything and wound down for a good night's sleep. We all had our demons to confront or problems to overcome and the trek was something of a cathartic exercise; a means of exorcising the demons from within. We needed the mental space and time to mull these issues over and the vast physical expanses of Everest were the perfect climate for such reflections.

We'd also tuck into a well-deserved evening meal as we talked about more pragmatic things such as the plan for the day ahead. The routines we established became a way in which we also learned and adjusted to each other's idiosyncrasies. Each day had become a new challenge – often in more ways than we had expected – so there was always plenty to discuss. Beyond that, I would quietly observe the group, my fascination for the intricacies of human interaction growing.

I awoke the next morning with frost inside my tent and sleeping bag but otherwise feeling refreshed and invigorated. I was ready and enthusiastic to make the final leg up to base camp.

A porter soon came to the tent with a warm towel and the traditional morning nectar of sweet tea, the taste of which shook the last vestiges of tiredness as I climbed out of the warm cocoon of the sleeping bag. This task would have been so much more arduous were it not for this enlivening beverage, which took the chill out of the atmosphere and made the transition from tent to open air much easier.

It reminded me of being on military exercises and being awoken early at dawn for my turn on stage duty. Speak to anyone either serving in the military or ex- military about being woken up early for guard duty on an exercise and it's all but guaranteed they will shudder at the thought. One moment you're fast asleep in a nice, warm sleeping bag, then suddenly you hear the thudding footsteps followed by the fatal instructions. A voice announces you're on guard duty or stag next, and you draw upon all your willpower to drag yourself out of the warm cocoon you've created for yourself into the cold, dark night. It takes all the effort you can muster to try and stay warm and alert throughout your shift.

These were memories I had long since thought were buried in the sealed boxes in the attic of my mind – memories labelled "do not open" – returned to me: the horrors of war and the violence I had witnessed in Kosovo; the brutality of mankind and the remnants of post-traumatic stress disorder. It's strange how our senses can trigger memories we thought we had long forgotten – a simple drink, tasted in the crisp morning air, weaving back through time to form a most unexpected and unpleasant association.

Dismissing these thoughts as best I could I climbed out of my tent and headed to the cook tent. I ate a hearty breakfast to prepare myself for the final push up to base camp, meeting up with the team before setting out for the day.

We'd all taken a blow to our morale on account of Sally being evacuated off the mountain a few days before, but we were still confident that we'd make it to the end, even if some of us were perhaps in quiet contemplation about our abilities. Sally had apparently improved considerably once the helicopter had lowered altitude.

It wasn't until much later, while discussing with various people the prospect of writing this book, that I spoke to Sally again. I was asking her about recounting these events in case she had any objections to appearing in the book herself. For some time after being flown off the mountain, she said, she'd had a continuous headache and had been sent for a CAT scan. This had led to complications, resulting in reduced vision in her left eye. It made me think how easily potentially severe long-term effects our actions can lead to. I felt lucky to have avoided such adverse effects myself.

Shortly after breakfast we packed up our belongings and set out from Lobuche with Simon and the other more experienced climbers taking up the lead. Once again, the scale and beauty of the scenery struck me to the core of my being, and I felt full of energy and focus on achieving my goal.

It might be somewhat clichéd to say but few words can truly describe what it is like to stand and witness this raw and primal part of our planet. At times the landscape would resemble the barren rocks of an alien world, but then the vast mountains themselves loomed above like the teeth of the world, illuminated by a perfect sky free of all pollution. It was a photographer's dream too, but even then, no lens has been invented which can capture the scale and magnitude and the affect this has on you.

Just as this view was stunning to look at, there was also an undeniable feeling of underlying hostility, and again I thought about the Sherpas who so effortlessly guided us. Without these indefatigable men and their seemingly instinctive grasp of this harsh landscape our journey wouldn't be possible. Sherpas had made Everest their home countless generations ago and the awe and reverence they feel for the landscape is deep and committed. To them, Everest is known as Chomolungma and is respected as the "Mother of the World" - a place of protected deities for whom ritual ceremonies are dutifully carried out.

We witnessed some of these rituals one day when the Sherpas blessed our equipment at Base Camp.

It was called the Puja ceremony and was used to bless the expedition. The ceremony was officiated by a Lama with two monks in attendance and took place in front of an altar built of stone. The Lama performing the Puja asked the gods for good fortune for the Sherpas and the others on the trek.

Then, they approached the altar with their offerings: a selection of food including fried dough, fruit and chocolate, along with drinks which included yak's milk. It was a very respectful blessing and a traditional event in which the Lama would also bless anything you asked him to. It was a tradition which went back many years, asking the mountain

138

deity for good luck and weather while climbing. In essence, it was paying respect to the mountain itself.

Many climbers had their ice axes and other climbing equipment blessed by the Lama, since these items were the ones which would come into direct contact with the mountain itself. As a sign of respect and energy exchange, a donation was given by each of us to the holy man for his service.

My time in the military had certainly served me well on this expedition, giving me both the physical resolve and mental fortitude to press onwards and see it through. We stopped for lunch at a pleasingly quaint trail side cafe and I reflected once again on the matters of my life over a warm bowl of soup.

As the broth heated my insides it dawned on me in an instant how insignificant all the stresses of my life had been up to this point. It was only my perception of events that allowed them to become problems and the trivial reality of them was brought home to me in this moment. I had embarked on this trek to see if I could push myself physically, but the real epiphany had been something far deeper, illuminating a sense of purpose in my life and the very essence of who it was I really wanted to become as a human being.

I had been trying to help others as best as I could in my personal life for a long time, but now there was a feeling that there was so much more I could do. The only thing that was stopping me was myself.

I thought of all the people in my life and how I had done my best to help them. But then it dawned on me.

What could I do for other people – those in need I hadn't even met?

How could I change myself to find the strength to help others to the best of my ability?

I remembered when I used to question if I was good enough to do this, allowing the shadow of self-doubt cast over me by the head injury to impose limitations. Now, for the first time since the injury, those doubts had melted away and I felt myself reconnecting with my inner strength.

Beneath the layers of ego and self-doubt, of questions and negativity, stood the real me. For the first time in my life I truly understood that anything is possible.

I snapped out of this moment of introspection just as a familiar face shrouded in long hair appeared on the brow of a peak.

"Hello there, James!" an even more familiar voice called out and I grinned when I realised that it was Karl, casually strolling in my direction as he returned my smile.

"Karl!" I exclaimed, extending my hand to greet him. "It's so good to see you!"

"Enjoying the walk, I see?"

I laughed. "A little out of breath perhaps," I said, "but worth it for the view, that's for sure!"

"It doesn't get much better than this," Karl replied, gesturing to the endless mountains which surrounded us on every side. We embraced and continued the walk to Base Camp, catching up on the multitude of events we'd experienced in life since we'd last met.

As we got closer to Base Camp the effects of the altitude were becoming almost overbearing and it took all my effort just to put these feelings to the back of my mind. When I finally reached our final destination, I was overcome with a wave of relief and excitement – it felt as if I exhaled for an eternity, every fibre of my being relaxing to an extent I had never felt before in my life.

One of the more experienced trekkers came over to me with a guide and the two of them complimented me on my strength. Having had virtually no training and starting from a position of ill health, I'd had no idea whether or not I'd be standing where I was, so to have finally hit Base Camp gave me a deep feeling of pride and satisfaction.

Unfortunately, the final leg added another casualty to our team in addition to Sally.

The last leg from Lobuche up to Base Camp was meant to be a four to five-hour trek. Simon, on account of his background, made the climb in less than four hours, although this speedy time was to be to his detriment later on. With high altitude climbs slower is always better, allowing the climber's body to adjust more gradually as the air becomes thinner. As Simon had gone up so quickly it became clear over the next couple of days that he had followed in Sally's footsteps and was also suffering from mild altitude sickness, which soon worsened at an alarming rate.

On the second day at Base Camp we decided that I would take Simon back down to Lobuche where he could recover more quickly. While it took Simon three hours and forty-five minutes to make the ascent, the return trip took the two of us eight and a half hours. Obviously the descent should usually be much quicker than the climb, but Simon's condition was so bad that we had to stop at the cafe at the half way point, where I helped him into his sleeping bag for an hour so that he could get warm, rest up and rehydrate.

Once he was rested up, I took his backpack and we completed the journey to Lobuche. Once there, he ate another hearty meal and got plenty of rest in a warm bed.

The next morning, he was like a new person and he thanked me gratefully for my help. His thanks were welcome but unnecessary – had the situation been reversed he would have done the same for me in an instant such is the camaraderie you find when embarking on such a challenging adventure with potentially life-threatening obstacles to overcome.

I managed to complete the final leg up to Base Camp in around four hours and twenty-five minutes, a time which surprised some of the more proficient members of the team as much as it surprised myself. I'd never climbed before –

never mind climbing at these altitudes – and it felt good to have accomplished something which only a few weeks before hadn't even crossed my mind as being something I was capable of.

But I was foolish to rest upon my laurels so soon: after passing the 5,364-metre point and arriving at Base Camp, the effects of altitude started to kick in.

When we first arrived at the camp it was almost impossible to walk without it becoming difficult to breathe and the two days, we spent there were as much about acclimatising as anything else.

And yet, the experience of Base Camp and the vast landscape which surrounds you, is something that is almost impossible to put into words. It is a place where no photograph can reproduce the immense scale of those ever-expanding vistas of countless mountain tops stretching across the horizon's full breadth (and at this altitude it's hard to guess exactly how far the horizon lies).

At night the glacier on which we slept shifted imperceptibly, the very planet beneath us subtly reconfiguring itself in an endless process of tectonic alterations, putting our brief and insignificant place in the scheme of existence into a new kind of perspective which would be unheard of in civilisation. It might not have completely diminished the sense of achievement I felt for having accomplished my goal of climbing to Base Camp, but it certainly offered a new point of view, both literally – upon the world as I had never seen it before – and metaphorically, towards a kind of serenity impossible to attain living in bustling, heavily populated cities.

I had conquered Everest, if not the very peak then certainly the goal I had set out to reach, and I had never felt better. The stillness of the air surrounding Base Camp was serene and seemed to encourage self-reflection, and I couldn't help but think of the mystical monks of ancient times who would ascend these treacherous slopes in order to meditate in seclusion.

My own reflections might not have reached the same spiritual heights, but I had good cause to be content. I'd made it up the climb in spite of my lack of training and brain injury, and not only that, I had done so whilst assisting Sally as she suffered from altitude sickness and helped Simon when he'd gone through the same condition. I might have been a few thousand feet shy of the literal top of the world, but my spirit was soaring higher than it had ever been before.

Unbeknown to me I had been put on a new path and begun another journey, one of deeper discovery towards my true purpose in life which I had arrived at following an arduous trek to the top of the world. It had been a long and winding road to this point with many life lessons which had become more difficult each time I ignored the signs and had blundered on regardless.

They say that fools rush in where angels fear to tread and I realised that while I wasn't a fool, I had been acting like one, nonetheless. I had focused intently on trying to help people in my private life under the impression that this was my true path, but in reality I was only detracting from the real me, and I vowed to myself that as I travelled this new path I would be true to myself.

Looking back on this trek the fullness of the experience came to me:

We all travelled a long distance to trek a mountain to prove to ourselves that our insecurities were not real; but the true journey and adventure was the one of self-discovery.

We all have our own mountain to climb, but if we put one step in front of the other then the journey is a foot.

The moment Jade walked into the bar will be one I'll remember for the rest of my life.

I might have been enjoying the success of running Red Zebra and loving the life of the entrepreneur, but she knocked me for six with her Audrey Hepburn glasses, behind which her large, warm eyes reminiscent of the cat from the animated movie Shrek gazed back at me.

I remember the moment vividly. It was the start of a whirlwind romance-to-be which would shake me to the core and nearly kill me. Part of me knew at that very moment that Jade and I would be together – it was a feeling from deep in my gut, something preternatural and intuitive. Even though I was with Allison at the time it felt like predestination.

Yet Allison was the first to notice something which I completely missed. It was a twist in the tail which was to catch up with me further down my path: Jade was painfully thin, and it took me a while before I understood why this was.

She was an exceptionally diligent worker with a streak of Obsessive-Compulsive Disorder (OCD) which manifested in an immaculate attention to detail. She also took a shine to myself and we often talked at some length about my photography and the conversation skills I'd developed through running a business and engaging with so many customers. After a while, many hours had passed when we weren't caught up in work and would talk to one another about a wide range of subjects.

If Jade was caught up in her OCD and other issues, for me it was the saviour complex which was emerging in my life. It led me to see how amazing she could be and as much as I tried to resist the pull towards her it was hopeless – she

145

continued to draw me in; like a spellbound child my wits and logic went straight out of the window.

This was to be to my detriment and would come back to haunt me in more ways than one.

As Jade and I continued to get to know one another, and Allison and I separated, we decided to move in with one another. Jade conveniently had a house to rent so I moved in there, marking the beginning of a new and crazy journey. I was drawn to Jade considerably more once we were living together; I was eager to help her, slowly supporting her during the tough road which lay ahead. It started to dawn on me even more just how ill she was and how severe the anorexia had affected her health, both mentally and physically.

Jade had been battling anorexia for ten years. It had nearly beat her a couple of times and is a story she may well tell herself one day, which will certainly inspire others to face such a challenge with their heads held high. I dedicated my time to her recovery and with my love, support and energy she returned to a healthy body weight.

She was happy in herself for the first time in many years and I believe now that in retrospect that the role in life I'm now playing could well have helped her more then. Still, I felt truly blessed to have had the chance to see her blossom into what I had envisaged when I first found out about her condition. I'd imagined her fully recovered, healthy and glowing with vibrancy. I imagined a future of the two of us stood side by side, her fierce intellect helping to build an empire for our children. It felt as if we could have conquered the world. But this shadow of the future was only a glimpse of one of many potential paths.

Looking back, so much happened in such a condensed space of time that to be emotionally detached from it or remain silent about it is difficult. Even from a distance, detaching my perspective and striving for objectivity is impossible. However, I will try my utmost to relate with accuracy what transpired in that period of my life.

It was a part of my journey when I felt unsettled, constantly creating new projects to focus on; always looking for the next distraction. I was doing everything possible to avoid facing the issues I'd had for a long time. It was also to become an indicator to me, allowing me to realise that I could remedy it and move on to a calmer and more serene place.

But everything is about timing and this cycle in my life still had lessons to teach me.
It was also a missing year in my life – a lost year which drew out into three of the longest years I've experienced.

After thinking that all my trauma was over and that the consequences of the head injury were finally behind me, I thought I now had the perfect woman in my life. Combined with everything else which had transpired – the successful business, the money and all the great things I'd been able to buy – it seemed as if my life was complete. Jade was someone whom I knew in my heart of hearts would be someone I could settle down with and have children together. But a cruel twist was on the horizon; a turn of events which would teach me the toughest lesson of my life.

One day, while I was staying at her house, I noticed a photograph on one of the notice boards in the living room which looked familiar from a distance. I approached it to see it more clearly, then pulled back in disbelief as I recognised the face in the image.

It was Lindsay, the woman I'd met when just a youthful soldier setting out to serve in the forces. I couldn't believe the chance coincidence when I saw her face. But then it occurred to me that it might be a higher power eluding to the inner conflict which exists in everyone's search for that perfect love. Love is perhaps the most evasive concept humans have ever dreamt up, but it felt to me as if the universe was giving me a hint of my true desires, and my real-life journey for the quest for the first pure love.

Being my first true love, Lindsay had remained something of an ideal in my imagination. The relationship we'd had when it was at its best was what I'd aspired to my entire life since. It was characterised by the kind of enthusiasm and simplicity that young lovers often exhibit, and I was naïve for thinking

147

that this was a flame which could be rekindled. Naivety and youthful hope are familiar bedfellows.

This perception of love is much like any other mirage one builds in their mind. When you finally get there to drink from the cool, refreshing water, you realise it's nothing more than sand.

The grass is never greener – it's only a fleeting aspect of your perception. We never really live in the present moment, since often we'd much rather talk about the past and the future. But in reality, the most precious thing any of us has is the present moment.

Jade and I became much closer over the time I started looking after her myself. When she was with me, she confided about her illness. We stayed together while I was making arrangements for the new apartment at the mill and over the next few months I would move back and forth from one home to another. Sometimes I would stay at the mill then move away, but I always seemed to return to the mill sooner or later. It felt like my safe haven – a place which drew me back to it like a powerful magnet.

During this time, we talked to one another for hours on end and I took her out as often as I could so that we didn't get cabin fever. I would drive up to Chatsworth, one of the most picturesque regions of Derbyshire, renowned for its extravagant hall and gardens, surrounded by tree-lined rolling green hills. Jade often slept in the car on the way there and back, but once we arrived, we'd walk amongst the grounds and talk.

We were present in the moment; two human beings trying to figure out life and improve it for one another.

She opened up to me about her condition and when we weren't talking, she slept a great deal. Lacking the energy and mental fortitude to do anything took it out of her and drained her more than I could imagine. The amount of time we were spending together increased over time. When Jade was spending time in the clinic, I would drive for hours a day so that I could be with her and support her during her recovery. I was preparing for my trip to Everest around this time, but it didn't stop me from seeing her daily.

I watched her grow as a person in every way possible.

I watched her facing her demons with true bravery.

Yet I never expressed to her just how proud I was of her for the immense courage she'd demonstrated during that fight. In hindsight I doubt there are the words to do this justice. She'd gone through the experience of staying in residential care – and the long, drawn out process of treatment – with a zest for life and energy which was formidable. It proved to me that only when we face true adversity and emerge triumphant do, we become a stronger and more grounded person. Adversity overcome gives us a wealth of experiences to draw new strength from.

During those weeks we'd grown together, strengthening a bond the likes of which I'd never felt before.

I knew then that I loved her.

While I busy was making preparations for the Everest trek, Jade and I had a devastating argument. I'd discovered that Jade might have leaked certain information to an old business contact. She knew how much I valued my privacy and kept my cards close to my chest, so such an act on her part had seemed to me to be an incredible betrayal. The concept of privacy is perhaps one of the strongest markers of my personality – a value I hold deep in my core – and I couldn't believe Jade would violate this principle.

By the time I boarded the plane for Nepal I found myself questioning everything that had happened. A great deal had been said between us in the heat of the moment; far more than simply the usual cutting remarks to be expected in a run-of-the-mill argument. These were words which had cut to the core, leaving me with the feeling that she had betrayed my trust in the worst way imaginable.

As it later turned out, there were certain things she hadn't said at all. They were rumours which had been spread by third parties, the kind of people who wield daggers behind your back and seek to plunge them in deep when you're vulnerable.

But I knew none of this on the flight to Everest. The argument was still fresh in my mind, and I hoped the trek to Base Camp and the challenge ahead would clear it and offer some fresh perspective.

By the time I returned from the trek it was obvious that Jade and I had missed one another immensely. One thing which was clearer than anything else was that we were falling in love.

I can still vividly recall when I came back from Base Camp and arrived in the United Kingdom; the moment when I met her at the clinic, and she walked down the stairs. The clinic was established in an old house with a grand, ostentatious curved staircase, and as Jade descended wearing a flowing summer dress and a radiant smile, I knew that the love I felt for her was sincere.

Jade had made the decision to really beat the illness while I was away, and the difference was immediately striking. Not only was she clearly physically healthy, but her mood seemed infinitely lighter and happier. There was a glow to her which I'd never seen in another human being.

We started seeing each other more often and soon she recovered to the point where she was able to move out of the clinic for good. The battle appeared to be over and we moved in together. After I'd moved to the city centre so I could be in the local area I'd rented a spacious apartment, and had arranged for a delivery of her favourite flowers for her home coming.

I wanted it to be perfect and for some time we lived a dreamlike life. We were drunk on love and wished it would last for an eternity.

We had a favourite restaurant just a stone's throw away from our apartment where we would often go for meals or a few drinks. In fact, we frequented the establishment so often that we ended up with our own table and were good friends with the owner Marco, a wonderful, pleasant and relaxed guy. We dressed the part as always whenever we dined out, with Jade adopting a 1930s style of attire which was stylish and elegant, reminding me of the knockout gangster's moll from old movies.

Many happy hours were spent in that restaurant. But I'd sold the camper van and was living off the profit, so inevitably sustaining such a lifestyle couldn't last forever. In effect we were living on borrowed time. I hadn't worked for a year and was effectively frozen out of my business, but fortunately I had savings to help tide me over.

But finances aside, the memories we had together over the course of a year were priceless. Those were the days of amazing highs, where we felt as if we were floating on top of the world. Perhaps inevitably, these were followed by low periods, and I realise now that everything requires balance; without this there's no chance for stability to assert itself.

You can shoot for the stars and achieve your dreams, but in order to do so a solid, grounded foundation is required. Being grounded allows you to launch yourself towards your ambitions, as well as allowing the flow of abundance.

I bought a cute little Mini for Jade, having owned one in the past and remember just how cool and quirky they were. It was difficult to track down the correct model and I ended up looking all over the country, eventually having to travel up to Scotland to collect it. It had to be perfect and I obsessed over the details (wherein lies the devil!), but I was starting to notice that I was repeating my old patterns of materialism.

It certainly wasn't all about possessions, though – more often than not we'd go on long walks together, driving out into the countryside or to scenic historic towns where we would stroll idly around the landmarks, talking about anything and everything. Life was about freedom for us, since it seemed as if we had all the time in the world. We'd wake up in the morning and decide on the day what we were going to do together, hardly caring about anything else in the world other than being in each other's company.

It was a time of growth for us both and as Jade started to recover, I smiled as I noticed her mind coming alive with passion. Before, due to the starvation of fuel to her body, she would show brief moments of clarity where her true intelligence shone through. Now, this intelligence was a near-constant, animated presence.

We were in our own little bubble, hoping it would never pop.

When we weren't taking long walks in the countryside we often sat at our window in the apartment, talking with one another at length as the world passed us by outside. No subject was out of bounds and I often look back on these memories with a lot of fondness. We might have been through a great deal together, but there was a lot of love there and plenty of moments to cherish had transpired.

Sometimes we would discuss books which we'd found interesting, sharing our views. She loved listening to me discussing subjects I felt passionate about and seemed to absorb the depth of knowledge I had on certain issues. She became increasingly proficient at photography as I continued to show her the ropes and improve her technical understanding. Jade already had a creative eye – something which cannot be taught – and it was thrilling to see her improving and enjoying this art form.

We often visited our favourite park, lying in the sun with her head on my chest as I read to her, watching the clouds gently drifting across the sky above. I still think of those days and have sometimes imagined returning to them. It would have been wonderful to be able to read to her my collection of poetry, inspired by the feelings she instilled in me.

I often looked back on these memories and thought of them as the happiest moments of my life. But now I understand that memories have flags on them; the emotions we attach to them is what highlights the memories we use from the millions of memories we have.

The unconscious mind is a vast storage space cluttered with all of our memories. It is effectively infinite in size and yet we have so many memories which stay in the unconscious that we don't ever recollect. There are traumatic memories and others with unprocessed emotions, and these emotions operate like a red flag on those memories. Until we deal with it we will continue to repeat the sub-routines and the destructive patterns that it has created.

However, once we deal with these emotions through regression, we can effectively allow the memory to be flattened, removing the red flag and thus allowing the interaction of the event to change, rendering it unimportant. Then, the memory of this event blends back into the millions of other memories in the unconscious mind. The red flag is removed and in a sense the file path to this piece of data goes with it.

Clients I have used this process on in my hypnotherapy courses have noticed a massive improvement in their functioning capacity in just a short period of time. They have reported that the memory is retained but has changed to black and white; present in their minds but no longer having an effect on them.

Over time, Jade's urge to control her eating in order to stay on top of her anorexia shifted towards controlling her environment and her OCD started going into overdrive. She started focusing excessively on cleanliness and I would be sent out on my bike while she spent hours cleaning an already clean and tidy apartment. To a degree it was a part of her therapy – and by extension a part of her life – and I was accepting of this and other issues relating to her recovery, taking a back step on a lot of issues.

But then things took another turn and we separated for a few weeks. Since she'd come out of the clinic her obsessive-compulsive tendencies had caused her to become increasingly controlling. While the illness had been beaten, her underlying control issues had transferred into our home environment. It was an incursion on my lifestyle I found difficult to adjust to as things worsened. For one thing, it was a stark reminder of the regimentation of the military, and by now I'd become more of a free spirit, inherently resistant to any forms of control or coercion.

Jade's desire for order and structure was inevitably going to conflict with my desire for freedom without being held down by the constraints of society. But Jade's illness made this sense of structure equally inevitable and I fully understand why this was the case. Yet the feeling of restraint and the echoes of life in the army – a memory of a confined past – swayed my decision and caused a temporary rift between us. When we separated somehow, we knew this was to give us both the space we required to grow before we could grow together.

I did what I always did in such circumstances and sought to change something in my life. Since I didn't have to work and had the freedom to do as I wanted, I got a new apartment and car (that familiar routine, as if changing the objects in my life helped to reorient a new direction) and continued with my life.

We were separated for a month but still bumped into each other, since we still lived close by. It felt like a strange magnetism and each time we encountered one another if was as if we rekindled a small light inside one another; small rays of love shining into the room. We both felt this love radiating and when we were apart, I felt incomplete, as if half of myself wasn't there.

I thought to myself that if Jade was the love of my life and yet for some reason it wasn't meant to be, I was still blessed to have experienced with her all that I had. It was a painful thought to consider in many ways, but pain is often the greatest teacher we have. Pain is one of the few things which reminds us that we are truly alive.

Because I'd moved away from all of my family and friends, I didn't know anyone, I had started reading a lot of books to pass them time and teach me about new avenues to explore. It was as much a way of distracting myself from thoughts of Jade as it was about expanding my mind, but few distractions are more worthwhile than reading.

But then Jade and I got back together again.

After a chance meeting at our favourite Starbucks one day, we started to talk and realised that we belonged together and suddenly my life spiralled forwards. Within a few weeks we had started planning our wedding. I bought her a wedding dress and began to make arrangements for a small and intimate affair. As with the Red Zebra business venture, I took it upon myself to make all of the arrangements myself, partly paying for it by selling my prized possession: my chopper.

After selling the chopper and handing over the keys I almost felt like crying, especially as I was selling it for less than it was worth. It was even more painful to see the buyer selling it on for a profit of thousands just a short while later. But this was another lesson in materialism, and the old maxim which tells us that if we don't have the money for something, we should probably wait for it.

In one sense, the bike was far more than just a possession – it stood for the freedoms I'd been enjoying; a metallic ode to the spirit of a life on the road. Another pattern in my life became clear to me, where I would buy a new motorbike when I ended a relationship to signify another rebellious phase. It was a pattern I promised to myself I would leave behind me once my daughter was born.

I wanted Jade to enjoy a dream Christmas wedding, and despite the fact that she was now working and could have contributed to the costs, I was happy to foot the bill. I even discovered later that Jade had a selection of credit cards without balance and could have assisted financially, but my eagerness to cover this spoke volumes about my commitment to our relationship (although I think it's clear I'd preferred to have kept the motorbike!)

Jade had chosen her dream dress with no expense spared and the plans were set in motion. All that remained was the outcome. Leading up to the wedding there were a few signs which I chose to ignore, even though they seemed to predict the sequence of events which would later unfold.

The main sign – cryptic and yet to me full of meaning – was when the wedding dress turned up with a mark on it. An instinct which seemed to come from deep within my soul forewarned me of the path I was about to take, but I dismissed it as little more than a coincidence. But inside my intuition was performing backflips, screaming at me as I stubbornly ignored the signs. The stain personified imperfection, but instead of confronting the symbolic significance I simply spoke to the hotel concierge and got him to track down an emergency dry cleaner.

The wedding was a small affair with only around fifteen people there, with most of these family and friends from Jade's side. But Jade was happy, and we had a beautiful wedding and honeymoon in the Lake District.

After the hectic process of getting everything organised this turned out to be one of the most perfect weeks I had ever had. The location was simply stunning, and we stayed in a beautiful cottage which felt like a home away from home. The food and drink were also on a par with anything I'd had before. In short, I can't recall a better Christmas I've had in my entire life.

We'd driven to the Lake District after the wedding in the Range Rover, with Michael Bublé singing Christmas carols on the car stereo. It felt as if I had reached the height of what I perceived to be success and luxury, but in many ways it was still a superficial show of materialism which wouldn't even scratch the surface of my true feelings and reflections once I started to work with people as a hypnotherapist.

But there was no denying that the cottage we were staying in was idyllic. When we weren't relaxing there, we'd take Rufus the Range Rover out for a spin, or go for long walks in the countryside, savouring the quintessential English rolling hills and feeling blessed to be alive. I'd bought Jade a top of the range camera and had begun teaching her photography, and I can still see the expression on her face when she had opened it. It's an image which burned into my mind's eye with all the clarity of a camera's sensors.

In retrospect it was the time itself which was the most precious. Material objects inevitably come and go, leaving our memories as the most valuable things we possess. This was the happiest I had ever been until the birth of Hope. I'd cook for Jade each day, something which I was pretty good at but only seemed to excel at when cooking for others. It was heaven on earth, but in the back of my mind a gremlin sat telling me it wasn't going to last.

Now I had to ask myself, if I had silenced this voice of doubt would the outcome have been any different? Would events still have transpired the way they did?

New Year came around and we were newlyweds together. Shortly after we discovered that Jade was pregnant, we were going to have a daughter and it filled me with a kind of joy I didn't know I was capable of experiencing. Everything I'd yearned for in life was beginning to manifest itself into reality. We'd already thought of a name for her: Sophia. We wanted to name her after the Greek goddess of wisdom and hoped she would grow into a loving person with wisdom beyond her years. But Jade was still recovering from ten years of major trauma to her body and it came as a terrible shock to learn that her body

wasn't capable of carrying and sustaining another life yet. She became increasingly ill as the pregnancy continued. Her blood levels went haywire and she became highly anaemic.

Then we lost the baby.

Feeling completely devastated by the news, we tried our best to deal with the situation as Jade recovered in the hospital. But rather than pulling together and providing one another with a beacon of strength, we drifted apart. Much to my shame, I didn't know how to deal with it.

After twelve weeks of pregnancy, the dream I'd had all of my life – of being a happily married man with an intelligent, sassy wife and a gorgeous daughter – was shattered. The unborn Sophia collected her wings and after feeling her soul being conceived into this world, I then wept as I felt it pass out of this world and on to the next.

The experience left Jade and I with deep scars which will never truly heal.

The day after we'd lost our child, we were both asleep in bed when I suddenly woke up. There were two small faces which I recognised floating above Jade. For some reason I wasn't at all scared by this vision – something inside told me that they had come to assure me that Sophia was safe and that they would take care of her spirit.

On one level these apparitions instilled deep inside me a calm feeling of assuredness, on another, I couldn't help but question what I was seeing before me. I think anyone in the same situation would find themselves completely conflicted internally, especially given the heart-wrenching circumstances.

But I knew that these were my guides, showing me that regardless of how bad things might seem, everything would be okay. Was I ready at this point in my life to take this step towards fatherhood? Perhaps not – perhaps this is why events played out in the manner they did.

I believe everything comes down to divine timing. Any attempts to rush or fast- track your destiny can lead to disastrous consequences.
Nevertheless, I fell apart in the days and weeks after Sophia's passing. Jade's anaemia continued to worsen, her health deteriorating to the point where I was incapable of coping with it all.

I distracted myself in any way I could think of - fixing my broken car from dawn to dusk, locking myself up in a cold and damp garage, while Jade lay in bed trying to recover. We should have been pulling together, but the grief and sickness served to act as a wedge, driving itself between us and refusing to budge.

There exists a belief with soul mates that the twin flames are the highest calling. Once incarnated together, they bring light to the darkness; illuminating what was once concealed. I'd believed that Jade was my twin flame and as anyone who has had this feeling about someone they love can attest to, such a realisation can be a scary thing. Confronted with the possibility of being hurt on a scale you've never before imagined can cause one of the souls to run. I was such a soul.

158

To this day the love I felt for Jade at this time hasn't truly dissipated. But I also know that we weren't meant to be together. I was left in a confused state of mind; a residual hang-over from being drunk on love for so long. Perhaps inevitably, I tried to transpose these feelings onto my next relationships, but it is impossible to move forwards in life when one is anchored firmly to the past.

Our past holds on just as the roots of a tree cling to the earth and only when we understand that we carry the keys to our own prison are we able to set ourselves free.

The man I became after the death of Sophia was a mere shadow of my former self.
I lost all of the pride I'd had in my appearance, putting on two stone in weight and no longer buying clothes or paying any attention to how I dressed. Having focused so much time and energy on helping Jade, I hadn't found any time to look after myself.

I'd missed out on the crucial element of balance in life. One of the principle rules of first aid is to not become a casualty yourself. I'd ignored this completely and put Jade first and my apparent selflessness had only caused me personal suffering as well, which ultimately benefitted neither of us.

But I know now that what I felt were selfless acts on my part were in fact for my own benefit as much as hers. I'd expected something in return, but true and heartfelt selflessness comes from a place where nothing is expected in return, neither from the person the actions are directed towards, nor the situation the people are caught up in. As the saying goes, "Fools rush in where angels fear to tread", and these words were ringing in my mind, an incessant reminder of the folly of our actions borne from good intentions.

I didn't consider myself to be a fool, but why had I acted in the way I had? Maybe I was just another fool looking for love. It's a familiar story we've all heard, but this love would never manifest itself in my life as long as I wasn't happy with who I was.

Only when I was comfortable in my own skin would I be ready to find the love I'd been searching for.

I went through several weeks which can only be described as Hell on Earth.

Jade had moved out of our apartment and was recovering in a bedsit, and I was trying to find work. I ended up teaching at a rough college full of unruly, hyperactive teenagers which would have been stressful under the best of circumstances but given my grieving mind-set became unbearable very soon. Before Jade had moved out, I'd done everything I could think of to console her, but every time we were together it quickly descended into an argument. I didn't know what to do to make things better for us both and felt as if I was trapped in purgatory with no way of escape.

I ended up blaming myself for lacking the strength needed to help us both through these terrible times. I never told Jade this, but I thought that if I hadn't been selfish and we had waited for a year or so after the wedding before trying for a child, she would have been fully recovered, and the pregnancy wouldn't have cost Sophia her life.

But everything happens for a reason.

Events emerge in our lives which at the time seem too horrific to overcome, but these are often catalysts which turn us into the people we are now. These life lessons continue to arise as and when they're needed. The message becomes refined, until eventually the life cycles and patterns are broken for good and we can move on.

I made the decision to leave Jade and spare both of us from the spiralling descent which we'd found ourselves in. It was a relationship in freefall, characterised by lengthy arguments in which neither of us would back down, often over things which truly didn't matter.

I'd helped her through the hardest part of her recovery from anorexia and seen her recover completely. But now, in her deepest and darkest hour of need, I left her. There are few things in my life I'm less proud of, but during this period my own health – both mental and physical – was also beginning to deteriorate.

The teaching I was doing involved a lot of commuting, which added extra stress to the highly stressful teaching itself. My mental acuity was through the floor. I was constantly tired, regardless of how much sleep I managed to get, and my weight continued to balloon. Despite the fact I was supposed to be only working for fifteen hours a week, I was putting in closer to sixty. I was responsible for sorting all the paperwork out to ensure that everything was up to date and correct for the end of the year, checking to make sure the students were going to pass.

Eventually this became untenable – if I continued at the rate I was, and the stress continued to mount I could well have suffered from a nervous breakdown. Much of the stress was on account of departmental politics which has the ability to grind a person down as much as anything. I'd landed into a highly disorganised role and my predecessor's desk was piled two feet high with paperwork.

Even in my diminished capacity I was able to get this paperwork in order, learning all of the students' names – something which most people who taught only seemed to get around to in their second year. In a sense I ended up becoming a victim of my own efficiency and rather than perceive me as a useful ally some of my colleagues instead saw me as a potential threat.

When I eventually explained to one of my co-workers at the college that I was going to leave to write a book, he thought I was making it up. Yet here I am, putting pen to paper to tell my story and contribute something to our understanding of trauma and recovery. After the experiences in Kosovo and the traumatic recovery following on from the head injury – and everything else which had taken place; the accumulation of events leading to this point in my life – the biggest contributing factor towards changing my life had been my relationship with Jade and the loss of my daughter, Sophia.

If I hadn't left Jade, I'm certain that we would have come close to destroying one another. Sometimes relationships reach a point where they become so chaotic that to perpetuate them serves only to perpetuate and increase the heartache felt on both sides. The cost of this decision has weighed heavily on my mind ever since, and while part of me knew that I had to leave her to save her recovery, I was not proud of this. I know that this decision is one that I will live with until the day I die. But we'd come too far to allow Jade to slip back into old habits, and I'd left the relationship a shattered and broken man.

As I lived alone following our separation, I wanted the pain to stop. Part of me thought that only death would be the solution, but I knew that this wasn't the way. I'd been there before following the death of my mother, stood next to the deep pond with a sack full of rocks contemplating drowning after my head injury, and had vowed never to be in that position again. Even in despair there remains a glimmer of hope and light in your life. This shining light – however dim it may appear – is the only way you can adjust your perception and see things from a different angle.

I spent nearly a year living alone, not seeing anyone and drinking every day in an attempt to block out the pain I was feeling. Even during this time, I somehow had the self-awareness to question my reason for existing, begging myself to release me from the pain I was feeling. I pleaded for death to come, and when it failed to happen, I learned to live again.

I somehow knew that everything I was going through was a test of my character; a test of faith in myself and what the world had to offer.
Each day I tried with all my willpower to process everything that had happened to me. But with my head clouded by grief and addled by alcohol I know now that it wasn't the right place or time for me to truly appreciate the lessons. With wounds still fresh, more time was needed for me to heal; more distance from these events was needed for me to reflect from a point of objectivity and understand the true underlying meanings.

It felt as if I had fallen into purgatory. Having established a large barrier between myself and other people – keeping them at bay emotionally as well as physically – I fell into a new, desolate routine. Each day I would go to the same

162

place for two hours just so I could be around people. But I didn't talk to them; instead I just sat and listened to their conversations. It became one of my comfort patterns, and even at the time I started to question my sanity, wondering if I was on the autistic spectrum.

But words like autism are in a sense just labels. What really matters are the underlying causes. I'd been through hell and back and had lost all of my support network. The only way I knew how to cope with the situation was the familiar response of isolating myself.

But the voice in my head returned and told me to not give up. Move forwards, it urged, reminding me that while I may be feeling emotionally dead I was in fact alive. The way we perceive any trauma in life affects how we function in the world, but if we don't change this perception over time, the trauma becomes deep seated and far more psychologically damaging. It wasn't until much later that I was to finally discover the tools to change my perception and finally grasp the reasons why I had gone through all of this. These life lessons would turn out to be perfect training for the path I was going to walk.

These times of darkness saw the return of nightmares in which I was visited by demons. They sensed that my energy was low and sought to prey upon it. No doubt the alcohol I was drinking at the time wasn't doing my overall health much good, but it prevented these dreams and allowed me to sleep through until the next day in a deep slumber.

So, I would get up each day and begin the routine over again. I'd head out on the motorbike and drink coffee for a couple of hours while I observed the people around me. Then I'd drop the bike back at the apartment and go to the local pub, drinking from around 4pm until it closed. At the pub I'd drink myself into a stupor, each gulp slowly numbing my mind and dulling the pain I was feeling.

It didn't take long for my image to completely shift away from the smart businessman I had once inhabited. The way I was now dressing appeared to keep people away, many of whom took me for an unruly biker. They didn't know just how much my external image had changed in such a short space of time. My business suits were gone and without the smart attire all they saw was the shell of the man I once was.

I found it fascinating how readily people judge others by their appearance. Some people wouldn't come near to me, and yet, when I returned to the business world and had my hair cut short restoring my former smart appearance, these interactions changed instantly. It was as if the suit was a book cover, dictating to those around me the contents of my character. Again, I thought of the old adage about judging books by their covers. The time I spent with long hair and biker gear became almost a social experiment, my observations teaching me more about the power of expectation.

People tend to see what you want them to see. They form their opinions largely from non-verbal communications, allowing them to form their judgments on the way others dress, not how they really are as an individual.

But I had certainly changed in many ways and it took a long period of study and introspection, in which I gazed deep into the abyss of my life and came to perceive the gulf between the person I was before my accident and the person I had become. I realised that I had become a person I didn't like and wanted to distance myself from this manifestation. I saw that my actions had a huge effect on the people around me, in ways which I'd never noticed before, and started to carefully assess every action of my life. I studied all the relationships I'd been through and felt a great remorse for everything I'd done and each interaction I could have changed.

Understandably, my recollections of this period are hazy and indistinct. My zest for life had vanished and it had taken with it everything which I had believed in. I truly wished to return to Jade and tell her how sorry I was for everything that had happened. A large part of me still loved her dearly, but I knew that if I'd stayed, we'd have ended up devouring one another completely, and our destruction would have been inevitable.

The period of my life spent in the mill was akin to the dark ages. But from darkness emerges light. Over this time, I began to understand what it was I wanted in a relationship and slowly but surely, I crept out of my shell until I finally met someone.

Over the months of recuperation, I started to build up a new group of friends, changing my image again and trying to put the past behind me. I met a local woman called Claire and it seemed as if my life was starting to come into focus again. I felt myself coming back to life, finally rejuvenated after a long absence in the social wilderness. I cut my shoulder length hair to a fashionable short style and even the hairdresser noticed a transformative change in me. When I'd walked into the barbers no one had paid me any attention, but after the hair was gone it seemed to open up my face to the world.

I was ready to engage with the world again and sure enough, things started to move quicker than expected. For a while I thought to myself that this was finally it: I had finally arrived home and it was time to be happy. After everything I'd been through, it seemed the light at the end of the tunnel was shining bright.

But then things faltered again. As much as I thought I was ready to move on with my life, I rushed things and wasn't ready at all. The pace of my relationship with Claire was going at lightning speed and before long we announced our engagement. Despite the fact that deep down I knew I still had so many loose ends to tie up, here I was creating another. Within two months Claire and I were engaged – already we were making plans for the wedding just three months down the line. It was too much too soon and the cracks in me began to accelerate and I started to fall apart. I was still far too hurt and damaged from my relationship with Jade – quite simply, I wasn't ready for this at all.

Claire rightly understood my situation and, knowing I was damaged goods, ended up walking away from the relationship. In one fell swoop I lost nearly all of the friends I'd spent the last fourteen months working to build up, as I flapped around like an emotionally drowning man, desperate for help but unable to find it.

To make matters more emotionally confusing, I'd had a funny feeling about Claire and the manner she interacted with a close friend of ours. He was married, yet Claire would often play fight with him in a manner which felt completely inappropriate. Not long after we separated, they got together and are now married with their first child on the way.

It was as if Claire had come into my life to prevent me from reconciling with Jade and coming to terms with what I'd been through. The friends I'd recently made did not want to get involved in any relationship issues, leaving me totally alone again. As fragile as my emotional state was at this time, I took this very hard and closed up again.

It felt as if life refused to give me any leeway and for a while, I thought I'd never break free of this feeling of despondency.

Then fate intervened and I was offered a temporary contract assessing at Leicester College. The staff were amazing, and it didn't take long before my faith in human nature was restored.

Slowly but surely, I started to return to the person I should be, interacting with people properly for the first time in months. Whereas before I had held the people in my life at arm's length, now I started trusting people again. I began to see once again that we can only be truly known or loved by another if we allow them to see who we truly are.

After Jade and I had separated I had ended up with all the contents of our storage locker. While there were many things in here which were sentimental, the most symbolic of all was Jade's wedding dress.

It was still covered in grime and other marks from our wedding day. Most brides would have guarded their dress and kept it spotless - this might be because they would have spent a long time saving to buy it, but clearly this dress hadn't meant the same to Jade. I had the dress hanging up in the closet as a stark reminder of what had come to pass. I left it there until I thought I was ready to move on with my life and considered getting it clean before returning it to Jade.

But for some reason I decided to hand clean it myself. The process was a mixture of torture and therapy in equal measure (or perhaps more likely the torturous feeling was the therapy itself). Every mark and stain on the dress felt like a memory engrained in my mind. As I began to wash each stain away, it felt as if my past was also cleansing in the process.

In hypnosis there are many techniques which can be employed to change the feelings attached to a given memory, which then go on to change our interaction of the memory itself. Using Neuro Linguistic Programming (NLP) techniques, it's possible to effectively strip out the emotion and flatten the memory, thus allowing the person to reintegrate it without its traumatic aspects.

Jade's wedding dress stood as a clear metaphor for this process, each stain an isolated memory which faded from my mind just as the stain faded from the surface of the dress. Soon, the collective events the marks on the dress represented took on a different, brighter meaning to me. It was a cathartic process and a turning point in my life.

Eventually I returned the clean dress to Jade's father, along with all her other possessions which had been kept in storage. I tried to enquire after Jade's health and well-being, but he wasn't interested in talking to me. He never wanted to know my version of events – let alone try to understand my point of view – and to the outside world it seemed as if Jade had lost the baby and I'd just walked away. I appeared to them to be the villain of the piece, but even though this didn't sit well at all with me I decided to let it lie.

It is only now that I feel able to reflect back on this and confront what happened and what it implies.

One day I received a call from Jade. We talked for what felt like hours, just as we'd done when we first met, and it felt like I had been transported to the past. I knew I still loved her deeply and I believed she felt the same way, so we agreed to meet up.

It was eight months since we'd split up when we finally met again. Jade looked radiant and healthy and I realised any concerns I'd had that she might have relapsed were completely unfounded. We talked about everything that had happened between us and discussed the possibility of getting back together. I apologised to her from the bottom of my heart for leaving the way I did and as our conversation continued, I finally saw the sequence of events through her eyes.

I'd been so consumed by my own grief that I never realised how badly losing the child had affected Jade. It had changed her in many ways and even though I wasn't responsible for the loss of Sophia, I nevertheless felt guilt for imposing that on her. But the conversation we had gave me a new hope that we might be able to reconcile our differences and I left that meeting with a song in my heart.

We met again the following week, arranging lunch in our old hometown. As we walked around arm in arm it felt just like old times. It all felt so natural and I truly believed that we'd now grown stronger because of our experiences and had a chance to make it work out this time.

But it wasn't to be. Fate intervened for a good reason, even though it wasn't apparent to me at the time. The last time we met up for a lunch in Nottingham was a sombre affair in comparison to our previous meetings. The food was good and the conversation pleasant, but as I walked her to the train, I could tell that something was amiss.

As Jade stepped onto the train, I knew that this would be the last time I saw her. The train pulled out of the station as tears began to stream down my face. It surprised me to feel myself weeping, as I rarely showed any emotions.

I composed myself and got on a bus, since I'd been drinking at lunch, and another wave of loss hit me. I started to cry again and sobbed longer and harder than I'd ever done before. I hadn't cried this much since the death of my mother and it felt as if all the emotions I'd been holding back and denying an outlet had rushed to the surface in an instant. It felt like a huge release of pent up feelings had burst a dam; all the emotional events I'd been through were coming out at once.

It needed to happen. Having always bottled things up and avoided sharing my true feelings with others, now I had no choice in the matter, and everything was coming out.

I headed back to my local pub so I could do the only thing I knew – drown these unwanted emotions in a glass of beer. But instead of drinking myself into another stupor, I broke down and cried on the bar in front of everyone. For a man who always considered himself to be fully in control, this was a very strange experience, and when I woke up the next day, I immediately decided it was time to pick myself up and move on with my life. It would take time to rebuild, but I couldn't remain stagnated and consumed with grief and self-pity any longer.

The last time I contacted Jade I wrote her a poem and sent it to her via email. It encapsulated how I felt about her and everything we'd been through.

Jade never responded to the email, so here is the poem for posterity:

My mind, my spirt, my love, my soul.
To be with you, the ultimate goal.
The passion the love of life,
To dream of you to be my wife.
What once has been and gone before
That always seemed a solemn chore,
I thought that once I was before
The man who lost which still endures.
To start to breath, to feel again,
To see you in my life again.
The pain that burns in my soul
The feeling that once was whole
But no only in deep despair
To look to find and not see you there.
To lie with you upon my chest,
To hear your breath when at rest,
To see you only in dreams
It tears my heart at the seams.
One day again we both shall be
For then it will last an eternity.

All my life had been lived up until this point with a barrier erected around me to prevent people from getting in. It was the armour I used to protect myself from the outside world; it was the mask I wore to conceal the real me.
It wasn't until my relationship with Jade that all the barriers and armour I'd constructed were stripped away entirely, returning me to my bare essence. Only now did I begin to live an authentic life, realising the true purpose of human interaction and connections which make us stronger and allow us to thrive.

Our internal worlds are mirrored by the people around us. Up until now, my state of mind had led me to blame any misfortunes I suffered on other people or bad luck. But now I faced a stark and uncomfortable truth: it was the darkness which lay inside me which attracted all these traumas into being. As uncomfortable as this truth was, it was the catalyst for much-needed change and transformation in my life.

Once I looked deep into my own soul, I realised that I had to learn to love myself, faults and all. I had to learn to accept myself truly and only then would I find the peace of mind and happiness for which I'd yearned for so long.

In spiritualism, people search everywhere in an effort to seek out enlightenment. But the clue lies in the title – the light we seek out can't be found in the external world since it lies within us. Like a lost set of keys, enlightenment is often in the last place we look – once we realise that no one has the answers we're looking for, to questions about the nature of the soul, we finally learn to reflect inwards.

Some people experience a glowing epiphany – a kind of light bulb moment of instant awareness. For me it happened in slow stages, with each trauma I experienced, stripping my ego bare until in the end my true essence was able to shine through. As I was going through these traumatic events, I'd considered myself to be unlucky – or perhaps even cursed – but now I understand that in a way I was blessed to have gone through these life changes.

I had learned to grow as a human being. I was finally able to see the truth of my situation and why I had gone through these hard times.

To appreciate the light, you have to experience the darkness.

Sophia, the name of my unborn daughter, is Greek for wisdom. Through reflection I had managed to gain a small wisdom of my own. Despite the despair and pain, I'd felt at the time, I could now look back on what had happened as a time of learning some truly invaluable life lessons.

I never expressed to Jade just how truly I had loved her, and I mourned the loss of our daughter and the relationship we'd had for a long time. Maybe I could have changed. Perhaps I could have been stronger. Perhaps our lives could have been different. But we are an accumulation of our life experiences. They shape us, forming our identities through each step we take.

But they don't define our actions. Only we choose how to act out our lives in the world. Sometimes our decisions are right, sometimes not. But since we're only human all we can do is try to make the best choices with the information we have at the time.

I believe Sophia is always with me and I continue to keep her alive in my thoughts and in my heart. In this sense, she never dies. We carry the people we love with us in our hearts and it is this eternal place for love which makes us more than mortal beings. The vessel may perish but the contents continue on.

The soul abides in the minds of others, witnessing the world through their eyes.

Chapter 8 Isolation

After a year of total elation and bliss with Jade, crashing
down to earth with such a bang was the most painful
experience of my life. Where once my life had felt like a
blissful dream, the reality of an empty bank account, home
and life in general drove me back through a mixture of fate
and comfort to the only place I knew: the mill.

It was an old lace mill – at one point in history the largest in
Europe – featuring vast industrial windows which seemed to
represent the mill's eyes reflecting its soul. A Grade 2 listed
building, the mill's traditional brick structure spanned three
floors. It was this old, industrial architecture which drew me
towards it, and I felt a sense of solace within its walls the first
time I stepped inside.

From the south end view the mill took on the appearance of
a ship, navigating its way through the English landscape.
This imagery inevitably linked to thoughts of the ocean and I
can see now how this may have subconsciously affected my
tendency to be near water whenever I was dealing with
trauma. It was an imposing building, towering over the
houses which surrounded it; a beacon of strength which
called me towards it.

In a cruel twist of fate, I ended up living in the apartment next
door to the one I'd lived in when Jade had first walked into
my life. With my soul broken and heart destroyed, I struggled
to exist for months. My attempts to impose a normal routine
on my life, for instance working three days a week at
Leicester College, were too much to sustain. With my energy
levels through the floor I was completely drained and the
only thing I could do was quit work and focus intently on
rebuilding the shattered remains of my life.

As traumatic as some life experiences can be, the only way we can truly overcome them is to reflect on them honestly and sincerely. It was only through looking back on this year and attempting to unpack the causes and effects at play that I was finally able to reconcile the trauma and integrate it into my life.

It certainly wasn't easy.

At the time I was going to the pub and drinking on a daily basis, remaining uncommunicative and effectively keeping myself to myself in order to obliterate the pain and heartache. On some days I would find myself on the floor of the apartment begging for the pain to end. I'd sunk to the deepest depths of despair and felt like I was living in Hell. I wondered what it was I had done to deserve such pain and only now can see the simple truth.

I had tried to change someone else's path in life at the cost of my own well- being.

The excessive alcohol consumption was an exercise in futility which only pulled me deeper into the pit of loneliness and despair. Most people self- medicate with alcohol as a means of forgetting and I was no exception. But the reality is that alcohol is a chemical depressant and ultimately the road to further ruin. Whilst drunk the time passes, but you inevitably emerge the other side of this drunken stupor in a foggy haze. Meanwhile, the unprocessed emotions you're trying to escape remain to be dealt with.

Begging for everything to end whilst slumped on the floor in a pool of tears had become the norm for some time. When I wasn't drinking, I slept a great deal, both as an escape from conscious reflection on my lot in life and to slowly regain my energy. I had invested so much of my energy into helping Jade with her recovery, which, combined with the loss of Sophia, had left me completely drained of life's vitality.

While now I'm capable of placing Sophia's passing into a wider context – even though the memory is still a painful one – at the time it weighed heavily on my soul. I thought that with prudent thought and action I might have been able to avoid this awful sequence of events. The moment Sophia moved on from this world I'd felt her soul pass over. This feeling was validated by the message I'd received in a dream state, telling me that she was safe, and sound being taken care of in the next life. But I was still beating myself up for failing to see the writing on the wall.

I'd briefly contemplated seeing a counsellor for grief in the weeks following on from Sophia's passing. But then I remembered the aftereffects of this process when I'd lost my mother. It had ended up creating more problems than solutions, so I'd opted instead to lock away the traumatic events rather than deal with them properly. I was fortunate to have discovered a way to return to them later and deal with them for good.

There were at least ten different events during the period leading up to my wedding with Jade which had served as red flags warning me of the impending trouble. Some might have seemed insignificant on the surface, for instance the stains on the wedding dress, but they amounted to a series of conscious and subconscious markers which could have altered my path in life. Only fools rush in where angels fear to tread and my bull-headed stubbornness led me to brush these warnings aside and carry on regardless.

In one sense it was as if Jade had cast a spell on me from the moment she walked into Red Zebra. I was powerless to resist, and was swept up in a

euphoric whirlwind in which I lived, laughed and loved. But as with any period of euphoria, sooner or later the whirlwind will send you crashing back down to earth, just when you least expect it.

The picture in my mind of the last time I saw Jade departing on the train will remain with me forever, just as I will always feel a residual trace on my cheeks of the tears, I'd shred on the bus travelling home. But the reality was we weren't meant to be together, and while our paths had intimately crossed, our destiny lay in different directions. I sincerely believe that one of my purposes in life has been to help her to recover from her illness, but in the process of doing this I fell deeply in love with her. It felt as if I'd finally found the

175

woman I'd been searching for my entire life, but when you've been out in the metaphorical desert for so long the mind starts to play tricks on the soul.

One particularly telling incident, which, in a strange twist of circumstances, echoed the past whilst hinting at a new path to the future happened when I first went to Jade's house and spotted the photograph of Lindsay on the wall. At the time I'd been most taken aback by the coincidence that Jade and Lindsay knew one another. But thinking back on her expression in the photograph – her enigmatic smile illuminating the room, as if to say, "have faith and all will be as it is meant to be" – seemed to hint towards something approaching divine timing.

Lindsay had always been present in my mind, both consciously and unconsciously and it occurred to me that this could be the reason why no relationship had worked out for me.

Was I being held back emotionally by my first love?

During the long periods of time I spent in my own company, I would often dream of my relationship with Lindsay, imagining we'd settled down and got married, living in a wonderful home with a white picket fence. I pictured the two of us with two beautiful children of our own: an idyllic life filled with love and laughter. While I knew deep down that this wouldn't happen with Lindsay, the thought that it could manifest in life with someone else seemed to ease the pain whenever I was going through a period of emotional torment.

Since everything which has come to pass, I have occasionally bumped into Lindsay when out and about in Derby. It had sometimes felt as if that magnetic pull between us remained, exerting a strong attraction between the two of us. But there was also something else stronger holding us away from each other – it was the wrong time and place now, and either she was with her current partner or I was with someone else, and the moment quickly faded as we went on with our lives.

If we try to force our way down a path we shouldn't be on, fighting against divine timing and changing our free will, we end up creating an illusion. This illusion feels real at first, but eventually it breaks down and we see it wasn't meant to truly exist.

Each of us has the power to create our own happiness. But each of us are equally capable of setting into motion events which cause us misery and I had subconsciously chosen misery. Reality is largely something we create ourselves, both through our intentions and our actions. We craft these by holding our intention on the images we create in our mind's eye, willing it into existence in our daily lives.

In spiritual parlance, this is called the Law of Attraction. Roughly speaking one can think of it as a radio mast mounted in our minds, bouncing out into the collective unconscious whatever we happen to be thinking of. Just as the energy wave from our thoughts is sent out into the world, so too are signals being sent towards us. Like the stone thrown across a still pond, each skip – each thought – sends out ripples far and wide, radiating out far beyond their point of conception.

Perhaps at a sub-atomic level I understood my true path, but at the time I'd coped by establishing a routine which denied me the path to progress. But this routine of coffee and lunch at the same place, drowning my sorrows in booze and going for daily rides on my Harley-Davidson was what allowed me to cope.

At least, that's how I had seen it at the time.

I became dishevelled and grew my hair past my shoulders. This, combined with the biker's clothes, was enough to keep people away from me and the interactions of people due to the way I presented myself during that period of time was very amusing. Before, when I'd worn smart suits and had a tidy haircut, people would look me confidently in the eye as we spoke. Now they seemed to look right through me, as if I had become a ghost of a man, which in many ways I had. Even more interesting was that women wouldn't look twice at me, which was perhaps something I subconsciously desired. I'd made a drastic change to my appearance, which inevitably changed the impression others had of me in a radical way.

I became a recluse in many aspects of my life, but when I was out and about the appearance of a biker seemed to function perfectly as a camouflage designed to keep people away. I was afraid of being hurt, and consequently didn't want anyone to approach me. The thought of engaging with other people felt was something I found difficult to bear.

I hardly spoke to anyone and for a while I couldn't recall any moments in which I'd smiled. I no longer cared about myself and this was reflected in my appearance – if you understand the right way to present yourself in appearances and actions, it's easy to blend into the background. I became something of an expert at this ability to disappear from view, reducing my energy while putting up an invisible barrier which few people were able to cross.
Only on rare occasions would I lower it for anyone and even when I was in the pub drinking I'd often keep to myself. This put me in a position where I could sit and watch the interactions, which was often amusing in and of itself and helped to keep me sane. Despite my state of mind, some good came from it, and I learned a great deal from observing the social interactions around me.

But eventually I realised it was time to begin looking after myself again. I still had a successful business which I took to winning Derby's best bar for second year, but the passion for business was no longer there. So much had changed for me since I'd set up the business and the materialistic items and the success, I'd experienced no longer satisfied the ever-widening hole in my heart and soul. I'd won the award for best bar, but now if felt like a hollow victory; another empty gesture which on the surface satisfied my ego but deep down was superficial and meaningless.

I was longing for something much deeper and more profound in my life now. I finally understood that materialistic possessions are no replacement for the love of friends and family and that true wealth can't be measured by the digits on your bank account. But while I'd changed for the better, many people around me still appeared to be stuck in the old materialistic world, clinging to their possessions in the misguided belief that these were representative of their value to society.

I'd seen how my own materialistic urges when I'd been running the bar had affected how some people perceived me. For example, an old military friend of mine had become more distant towards me as my success had grown, and I discovered he'd assumed that the business was entirely down to the settlement I'd received from the head injury accident. But while the settlement had helped me financially, the bar's success came from the hard work I had put into the project. But because they hadn't seen this for themselves, they failed to appreciate it.

Realising the importance of family and friends was just the first step in bringing about a true transformation in my life. Having put up barriers throughout my life, I'd become estranged from my family and hadn't invited them to my wedding with Jade. I had, at best, fleeting and sporadic interactions with my family, the connections weakening over the years, and a sad consequence of going through the darkest phase of my life meant that, through my own design, I was truly alone.

I've since began to slowly rebuild the relationships I once had, constructing a bridge between myself and my family as best I can despite the shaky foundations I had to build upon.

My family have never been able to fully understand the depths of despair I sank to, but this is in part because I never felt able to tell them exactly what was happening. This self-defeating lack of communication on my part is most likely a consequence of my time in the military; a place where a stubborn attitude is often one which can cause more problems than it solves.

But unless you ask people for help in times of suffering and let them know when you're in pain, there's nothing they can do to try and make things better. Without the help of others there is only one other place you can turn to for a solution: yourself. I'd been looking for answers everywhere, yet they continued to elude me. Looking into my own character and focusing on myself was the last place I looked, but once I did this the answers started to become clear.

All it takes is a quietening of the mind – a separation from the noise and distractions of the world around us – and the present moment becomes paramount. From this place of acceptance for the now, stripped of past and future meanings, we're able to seek out true meaning. It's an incredibly powerful place to find yourself in, and once you've realised that the past has gone and the future doesn't yet exist, this new focus can change the tempo of your life forever.

The traumas of my life up until this point were at least becoming transformed into lessons which I could learn from. They were putting me on a path to a new, exciting destiny. I still wasn't sure where this was going to lead me, but I knew that it was going to be far away from the familiar destructive cycle I'd been following for some time. I was starting to function as a human being, interacting with other people again and regaining the confidence I'd formerly had.

The passion I had for always exploring new projects and learning new concepts was often misinterpreted by the people in my life as a sign of indecisiveness. But really it was an underlying urge I'd had for many years to learn new things while occupying my mind. The mill turned out to be the perfect place for this process of introspection and discovery. I would spend many long nights here when sleep eluded me with my head buried in a book until the early hours of the morning. Each night, when most people were tucked up in bed soundly asleep, I would read vociferously, researching a wide range of topics which caught my attention.

Reading helped to pass the time during the many long and sleepless nights I went through, distracting my mind until I was able to fall asleep. This taught me about how we can deal with insomnia more effectively, but now through my hypnotherapy training I am able to treat insomnia far more effectively and have aided my clients in getting a good night's sleep. Without experiencing it for myself, I might not have fully grasped the effects of cognitive functioning on a person's sleep pattern. As draining as it was to go through a period of insomnia like this, I learned a lot about the psychological mechanisms at play.

When I finally did fall asleep the nightmares would return with a vengeance, and flashbacks to the horrific day in Kosovo, stuck in traffic and helpless to do anything other than watch an angry mob tear people to shreds with machetes would fill me with night terrors. During times of particularly high stress the nightmares would be more violent and distressing. My mind was doing everything it could to process the trauma and deal with the emotions attached to these memories, but it took a while for me to release these demons for good, and they tortured my dreams for some time.

It was only recently that I realised that I was going through all the symptoms of post-traumatic stress disorder, initiated by my experiences of war, compounded by my head injury and exacerbated by the loss of my unborn daughter, Sophia. I have no doubt that I had been experiencing PTSD symptoms even more so since the head injury, but as I was drinking heavily when this worsened – as well as isolating myself from the people who might have been able to help – I'd been blind to this fact.

When I was finally able to honestly revisit these events, I found that the issues triggering these bouts of PTSD could be processed and would quickly subside. Having been self-medicating with alcohol, moments of extreme stress brought about dreams of being destroyed by forces of pure evil, the night terror of that tragic afternoon in Kosovo still haunting me. Alcohol's role in this was clear and is very common amongst other people who are also suffering from PTSD.

There are numerous studies which have investigated the link between PTSD and alcohol and its use to attempt to control the symptoms. PTSD sufferers are far more likely to self-medicate with alcohol and other drugs, which not only fails to accomplish the task but also gives rise to a secondary problem – the addiction to the drug itself. The person is then left with a dual diagnosis, with a serious psychiatric disorder co-existing with an addictive disorder, each one amplifying the other.

The combination of the trauma along with the coping mechanism common for people who serve in the military ended up turning me into a mess. I'd sealed all these traumas into boxes, shoving them to the back of the attic of my mind. But traumatic events cannot be repressed forever and occasionally they would escape from their boxes and play havoc on my subconscious.

The space in the attic was reaching bursting point and I didn't know how long I could continue to contain the monsters. It haunted me during my waking hours, finding its way through the fog until I had no alternative left other than to consciously open the boxes myself and face the horrors within. For too long I'd considered it a sign of weakness to admit what these boxes contained, but only when you lay the contents bare can you deal with them head on.

It takes true strength to attempt to acknowledge, overcome and integrate traumatic life events. Many of us would much rather live life with our heads in the sand, comfortably numb to the cold realities we've faced and suppressed. But the cost of such ignorance is to live a life with a shadow cast over it and once you confront your inner demons you can then be truly free of the past.

I'd spent most of my adult life pursuing a path based on what I thought others had wanted me to do. Now I knew that the best course of action was to trust my instincts and follow my own path.

Reading also played a significant role in overcoming the pain and suffering I was feeling. I read books on everything from psychology to conspiracy theories, studying and learning as much as I could about the various theories out there; occupying my mind during the long hours of sleeplessness. I also learned about the significance of the time we awake at night from my investigation of Chinese medicine. The hour you awake correlates to a certain energy system in the body: for example, if you wake up between 1am and 2am it relates to the liver and indicates that you are suffering from stress or anger.

I learned a great deal from these books about the world outside me, but equally, if not more, about the world which lay inside me. This information would also inform the path my life would take in the future. While at the time these long hours spent awake at night felt like torture, dealing with this insomnia by reading every night provided an intellectual challenge which kept me going.

I have had many periods since in which my ability to learn along with my intelligence has grown, each occurrence reinforcing the idea that we hold all the answers within ourselves. Once we know how to quieten our minds, we're able to listen to the information that lies within. Having gone through a long and tortuous process of self-denial, questioning whether I even deserved any happiness, I knew that I would have to atone for my losses.

I also asked the question most of us ask ourselves when we face traumatic events: why me? At one point I considered the possibility that I had been evil in a previous life and this was my punishment for transgressions from the distant past. But now I see it as the most instructive and illuminating experience I've ever had. It has equipped me to help other people – and to understand other people better and approach my interactions with them from a position of compassion. Understanding how it felt to be at a point which I perceived to be utterly hopeless has given me new eyes to see through; eyes which show me hope for the future.

I hope that I can help to inspire others who have reached rock bottom in their lives, by teaching them something about what I've learned in life and all the woes and painful experiences I've overcome. I never felt like I was sinking into depression. If anything, the unhealthy spiral of constantly drinking myself into a chemically induced haze had the effect of numbing me to feelings of any kind.

Analysing the nightmares, I had also proved to be incredibly insightful. As the visits in the night from these strange visitors increased and deepened, they told me that they were trying their best to destroy me. The characteristics of these nightmares were consistent: a burning scene would morph into that day in Kosovo, opening up a path which led to a door in my mind. This door would burst open, revealing a view of my inner anguish, represented as a hellish place of intense fire and suffering. Once the dreams had stopped and I was able to reflect on them I realised that there was a strong analogy to be unearthed. The door in my mind represented the opening up of the possibility of change – if I didn't change my behaviour, I would end up destroying myself.

But I realise that something only ever has the power you give it, and this applied to these nocturnal visitors as much as anything else. In fact, these demonic visions which were apparently sent to destroy me, were little more than symbolic emblems from my subconscious, and the underlying message was that I hadn't been dealing with my past and this was where my problems lay.

During the Rapid Eye Movement (REM) phase of sleep the mind begins to attempt to process the events of the day, and by the same token, this is also when the day's emotions are processed too. Failure to process these events and their attendant emotions is what leads to unwanted problems and inevitable changes in our behaviour. From here, behaviour loops are generated, leading to self- destructive patterns. Only through dealing with the underlying message can we escape from these new behavioural patterns.

In times of crisis I would revert into a series of set patterns; these routines provided me with temporary comfort zones which inevitably couldn't be sustained for too long. Looking back I realise how unhealthy these were – and yet, at the time they helped me to weather the storms I found myself adrift upon.

The mill itself was an emblem for this comfort zone, but also the place where I confronted my demons and overcame them.

It felt surreal when I moved back into the mill after breaking up with Jade, settling into the apartment next door to where we had lived together. I'd come a long way and accomplished a great deal and coming full circle back to the mill felt comforting. Whether or not this was by chance or design is perhaps irrelevant – either way, it proved to be a much-needed sanctuary. The old building was like a lighthouse for my weary soul; a beacon from a well- travelled road where I could sort out my life and clear up the issues from my past.

The job I'd taken at Leicester College teaching Electrical Installations allowed me to exist in the real world as well as reintroducing me to being around and interacting with people on a daily basis. My energy was still low, and I was functioning well below my full capabilities, but one thing I took from it was my passion for teaching students.

I've taught throughout my life in one capacity or another. The moments when you can tell that a student has grasped the concept you're explaining – the light bulb going off above their heads lit up by a light in their eyes as they make the connection – are mutually inspiring. I always seemed to be drawn back to teaching, as if the natural structure of the subjects was a perfect match for my habit of filling my mind with information.

I've taught many subjects but at the college in Leicester I started feeling that teaching electrical engineering was coming to a close. It didn't fill me with passion, and I wasn't speaking from my heart. By contrast, when I now talk about hypnosis, I know I'm doing the right thing, since my soul resonates strongly with the subject. If you don't feel truly engaged with the material you're discussing, the words coming out of your mouth are just that. But when you're impassioned by the subject matter those words take wing and spread ideas far and wide.

Once we find the spark which ignites our passions, our strength grows and, through a slow process of re-engaging our thought processes, we regain the energy to effect positive changes in our lives and those around us.

These changes came to me in a series of waves over a period of several months.

It was only when I was able to spend a long time alone and withdraw from the general noise of daily life that I was able to refocus in on new thought processes. It felt as if my mind had evolved, the synapses inside my brain literally re-wiring themselves in order to reorient my view of the world. As this process continued, the amount of alcohol I was drinking began to decrease in parallel with the increase in focus and intention.

I was slowly but surely returning to a frame of mind similar to that which I'd had when setting up the Red Zebra bar. The ideas were starting to flow, and I got involved the Red Zebra again, taking a more active role than I had for some time. Reviewing all the accounts, I streamlined the business, as well as putting energy into getting the venue redecorated in time for the upcoming business awards. It took time, but as my involvement in the business grew so too did my confidence, and soon the bar was running very well.

Becoming more involved in the bar also ironically helped me to deal with the issues I'd had with alcohol. It might be literally available on tap, but it is impossible to run a business effectively unless you are sharp and focused. Obviously, this means drinking at work is a no-no; and besides, watching the people around me getting drunk had the effect of changing my interaction with the drug and seeing it in a new light.

I realised I'd done my time with alcohol and since emerging from this period of recovery at the mill I now only drink alcohol on very rare and special occasions. No longer requiring the two or three days to recover from a drinking, my mind had become clear again.

There were a few more key things to take away from my experiences of coming back to a business I had neglected. Allison had led people to believe that all the design work for Red Zebra was her own, negating the hard work and time I'd invested in the Moroccan theme. I also noticed an overpayment of the staff which I quickly rectified, bringing the business back in line with the correct model and making it shine again.

But a combination of how it felt to have been kept out of the loop and not been given the credit I'd deserved for my role in creating the bar, coupled with a newfound desire to move on to pastures new following my long absence, led me to seek a way out from the business venture. I needed a fresh start, so I asked Allison to sell me her share of the business. The situation became entrenched and she demanded twice the market value, we only managed to break this deadlock by agreeing to put it on the market and go our separate ways.

Still, I learned a great deal from my time at Red Zebra, including many new life skills about running a business. More importantly I learned a great deal about myself, discovering a wider range of skill sets than I knew I had, as well as the ability to put together a concept and execute it effectively. Perhaps most importantly of all, I understood how working for yourself and doing things your own way is the best way to guarantee the outcome you desire. It's a principle which has currency in life in general, not just in the business world.

Cutting my losses, I decided the best thing to do with respect of the business was to sell it and move on with my life. Having been put on the market for a quick sale, the bar ended up being purchased by investors with plans to turn it into a restaurant, changing the whole ethos and rebranding it to a new design. Once again, I'd built something amazing only to walk away, allowing it to disappear into nothing. I felt conflicted: even though I was moving on I decided not to think too much about Red Zebra and have seldom discussed it since.

Yet I'm still told by people how great the concept was and have been asked if I'd consider doing it again. But having moved forwards to my true vocation I realised that I'd learned all the lessons I could from running the bar and that it was time to put what I had learned towards helping others. The business had been ahead of its time, but ultimately it was about creating a space where people could relax.

When I'd been running Red Zebra, I'd often watched people coming in after a stressful day from work, noticing how much alcohol can work to alleviate the stress from a day's grind in the office. But now, I realised that this was due to more than just the alcohol – it was as much about relaxed atmosphere and music, and the ambience which was conducive to relaxation.

I certainly didn't know it at the time, but the hours I'd spent listening to their conversations and observing their behaviour was also perfect training for my future role.

building up a new group of friends and making an offer on an apartment I'd found. Combined with the new job I felt hopeful for the first time in months.

After I'd been seeing Claire for a while we had discussed moving in together. It was nice being around someone whose company I enjoyed. I missed the small details in life more than anything, for instance the simple yet meaningful gestures we experience from the partners in our relationships – the cup of tea in the morning or the hug when we return home from work.

But the relationship with Claire was moving too fast for me and I now see that I wasn't really ready for something so serious so soon. I was still living in the aftermath of my two previous relationships with Jade and Allison, both of which had issues I'd yet to resolve. I knew I had to face the fact that I needed closure on these before I would be ready to move forwards and find love again.

I'd made so many rash decisions during this period, wearing my heart on my sleeve time and time again, until my heart had been completely hardened by the pain and torment of failed relationships and the collateral damage which had followed on.

How would I ever put this all behind me and move on?

It was a question which needed answering, and with Claire I was just repeating a pattern I knew I had to break free of.

Once the relationship with Claire was over, I moved away from the village which I had started to call my home. It was the only thing I could do, since places are so tightly bound to our memories and habits. Part of me wanted to remain, but common sense told me that moving on was the best thing to do.

Fortune shined for me when a friend approached me, telling me he had a boat I could rent from him. I'd often thought living on a boat would be very appealing. Being close to water had always seemed to boost my creativity and even though I was still drinking following on from the split from

Claire, before getting the boat I'd frequented the marina on many occasions while looking for new renovation projects.

A life on the water spelled a life of escapism and the boat became my new safe haven where I could find a new focus and explore my creative urges.

When Emma and I were together I'd wanted to get an Airedale, but Emma had vetoed the idea and we'd got Dylan the Welsh terrier instead. Now that I was alone on my boat, I could finally get the breed of dog I'd always wanted. Angus came from Jude Averis, a breeder renowned throughout the UK who had won Crufts several times. I went to choose him on my motorbike and on the way back a car drove into the back of me – fortunately I was not hurt but the shock was enough for me to be very cautious on the bike again.

I tried to find the mental energy to begin writing this book and collecting my thoughts into something coherent. But my mind was still too crowded to focus on the writing and instead settled into a more sedated routine in which I would take my dog Angus on long walks in an effort to thin the crowd of ideas swimming in my mind. I'd take Angus out twice a day, strolling around the marina where my boat was moored and down the banks of the canal. These walks had an effect similar to meditation and I started to fully process the events which had happened to me.

I felt ready for change, but I was still short of reaching a place where I could exorcise my demons for good.

I knew what I wanted but I couldn't find the way to get there.

In November of 2013, one of the most devastating natural disasters in the history of mankind took place in South East Asia. It was called Typhoon Haiyan, although for many who witnessed the intense devastation it caused it will be remembered by its other more accurate name: Super Typhoon Haiyan.

We all saw the images on television, looking on in horror as wave after wave smashed up against beach fronts, hotels, fishing harbours and countless homes. Destroying virtually everything in its path, the typhoon was a stark reminder of the power of nature and the insignificance of humanity's technological and structural prowess.

The bulk of the damage done by Typhoon Haiyan occurred in the Philippines, where it hit the coast with sustained winds far stronger than anything else the country had experienced before. The damage was so absolute that authorities were still discovering more corpses well into the following year.

I'd watched the news footage of this disaster unfolding in horror and like many other people a feeling of helplessness washed over me as the television showed footage of the destruction the typhoon had left in its wake. It made me put my own personal tragedies into a different perspective – while all suffering is upsetting, when it is carried out on such a vast scale as this and affects hundreds of thousands of people, it becomes something almost archetypal in its meaning.

Before I'd heard this news, I'd been looking around for a new project to invest my time in and alleviate boredom. Then out of the blue a friend made a post on Facebook, looking for someone who was willing to assist with the deployment of ex-military engineers to the Philippines, in an effort to provide additional humanitarian aid relief.

I contacted Clint who was running the operation to let him know of my intentions to help out with the campaign. As we continued exchanging emails discussing the plans, my brain started to go into overdrive. It had been some time since I'd found myself with a project which I felt like I could invest my full energy and I wasn't going to miss the opportunity to do what I could to help the many people suffering across the South Pacific.

I set up the registered charity and had the website designed and online within a week. Then, I secured a shipment of top of the range equipment to be sent down from Roy Ripon, whose details I had got from a mutual contact. Roy was an ex- engineer himself and owned a company which supplied military equipment called Top of the Range. This equipment ranged from all-weather clothing for the teams, sleeping equipment and Bergan's in which to carry everything.

In essence, it was a quick deployment bag containing two sets of clothes – the bare essentials for a mission, but essentials, nevertheless. More importantly, it was top of the range when it came to quality, crucial for both comfort and the effective use in a disaster zone.

As part of the branding for the website and charity I had t-shirts designed and embroidered, featuring the image of Hurricane Haiyan on the emblem and the website for the charity on the back. This would assist with media operations, particularly when the team were on the ground, and help to get the charity mission into the limelight.

I also handled the publicity side of the charity, securing a feature on the work we had planned and our appeal for funding on East Midlands Today and Radio Derby. My contact at the BBC, James Robison, did a fantastic job of interviewing me in my apartment, my photographs framed in the backdrop, the interview was conducted with perfect timing

I'd had a feeling that the equipment which I'd ordered for the expedition was going to arrive while James was at the apartment and sure enough it turned up right on cue. Thanks to this fortuitous timing he was able to gather footage of me loading the large air portable boxes into a high-top van, ready and waiting for deployment. It felt a little like being back in the military again and I didn't realise how a part of me had missed the rush of adrenaline when getting fired up for a big mission.

This time it was different – I was in charge, even if the only person I was issuing orders to was myself.

Unfortunately, when I heard from James after the interview had been wrapped up, I discovered that the audio feed had failed, and the interview was therefore unusable. This may well have been the first warning sign that not everything was right with the project, but at the time I ploughed on irrespective of this hiccup, determined to get the charity off the ground without being distracted by superstitions.

At this point in time I was personally funding the establishment of the charity, which as anyone knows who has set up a charity is a catch-22 situation, since on the one hand you start without any donations but on the other you still need to be in a position to raise awareness to the cause, leading to the donations required to keep the charity afloat.

Everything was moving at a million miles per hour. Clint and I were communicating even more as the charity started to build momentum. Both of us were ex-military and appeared to share similar ideologies. I thought he was a trustworthy man, like myself, just trying to do something for a good cause.

In the run-up to Christmas that year I was leading a hectic life, running around doing what I could to drum up more funding for Unseen Heroes. I was still trying to pull myself back together following on from the breakup and living in isolation at the mill but focusing on Unseen Heroes gave me the drive and dedication to continue onwards.

Because I assumed, I'd be going away on deployment for six months, I packed up all of my equipment in preparation. I also sold a lot of furniture in order to help pay for a personal satellite phone and an additional three thousand pounds on additional equipment I required, placing a personal marker on the equipment coming from Roy. Since I had connections in the old boys' network from my days in the military, my word was good enough to secure the equipment on the condition this was either returned or paid for.

I started putting my affairs in order, the time for action was approaching. I waited patiently for the moment to set out for the Philippines.

Some elaboration on the intricacies of the Unseen Heroes charity will help to clarify exactly what we had in mind.

The basic concept was to deploy ex-military engineers and other former servicemen, each possessing a specific skill set relevant to operating in the field, to post-natural disaster zones around the globe. More often than not, as relief aid swamps a country in the aftermath of a natural disaster, it doesn't get distributed correctly. This is due to a variety of factors, including the inevitable congestion – or complete destruction – of basic infrastructures used to move around the terrain, theft (where it finds its way quickly to the black market), or being locked away by corrupt officials who use the resources for their own financial gain.

Clint and I were joined by another ex-military who had served as a Warrant Officer, he was a resources specialist, Les. He suggested our first priority should be to deploy a small team as a forward base while continuing the funding drive back in the UK. A presence there would give us the opportunity to provide concrete evidence of our intentions on the ground. I'd already spoken to The Times newspaper about media coverage, but they wanted to see some proof of concept before committing to a feature, so having a team in the Philippines would be a major boost.

I also went to visit the director of the company Aquabox in Matlock, Derbyshire. Aquabox manufactured superb boxed water filters which can be used as community water points, capable of providing 18,000 litres of clean water. They weighed just fifteen kilos and required practically no skill to set up; they would prove to be invaluable for thousands of people stranded without drinking water in the wake of the typhoon.

Aquabox's director, a fantastic guy named Mike Tomlinson, was happy to provide us with six boxes for free, ready to deploy with the team. Each one of these boxes would provide potable water for up to five hundred people, a small fraction of the total number of displaced people but still a significant contribution to providing relief.

Aquabox was very keen to collaborate with us further, since they had been deploying their products to natural disaster zones themselves via alternative agencies which had proven to be less than effective. If all went to plan, our streamlined and highly trained operation could plug the gap and provide an efficient service.

With our supplies sorted, it was time to deploy the team to the Philippines.

Clint, who had been a Mechanic during his time in the army, oversaw coordinating the operation, but wasn't giving me much in the way of solid information on how the operation was going to be conducted. The basic plan was to meet up at Stansted Airport and take a flight along with equipment to Manila International Airport, where they could travel from there to the key areas of devastation affected by the typhoon.

Having loaded up a large van with all the equipment the team required, I picked up Les, who was to form part of the forward reconnaissance team. We hit the road and soon arrived at Stansted, meeting up with Clint and the other members of the team. Les was a wiry man in his late fifties, with that sharp sense of humour found in long-serving members of the military. He was passionate about the mission at hand and his knowledge of supply lines and acquisition proved to be invaluable to the mission.

The first thing we did was go through the equipment and issue it to the members of the team. Clint was dismayed to see that his Bergan was the wrong size for the trousers and waterproof Berghaus jacket. But there was something more going on which I couldn't quite put my finger on at first. His initial reaction when we met suggested that something was amiss and that the situation wasn't what I'd thought it was. He seemed very surprised to see me arrive with so much equipment and equally surprised when he found out I'd set up the website as well.

Then we hit another snag.

After speaking to one of the officials representing the major airline, we were using we were dismayed to hear that they couldn't help facilitating our flight prices because we simply had far too much equipment. Weighing in at around 300kgs we were clearly over the limit and in hindsight we should have been better prepared to cover the additional expenses.

After discussing our options, we made the decision to send Clint and Les ahead to forward base, leaving myself to make my way back home to Long Eaton. Here I could continue working on rear operations, including acquiring the rest of the equipment the team would need and establishing more media contacts to kick start the donations.

Once they'd landed in the Philippines and contacted the assets we had on the ground, communication between Clint, Les and me became scant, as might be expected when placing oneself in such a chaotic environment. I'd given Clint my satellite phone – along with some of my personal kit – but when I handed it to him it was clear that he wasn't sure how to use it. This set off another alarm bell ringing in my mind, leading me to question his suitability for the task at hand.

With communication breaking down across the oceans, I started to get conflicting reports back from the Philippines. Clint was telling me one thing, but when I spoke to Les I'd hear something completely different. It led me to lose confidence in the ability of the team to carry out what was being asked of them, but since I was thousands of miles away there was nothing I could do to intervene and set things back on course.

When Clint decided to send Les back to the UK, it felt clear by this point that Clint had ulterior motives for going to the Philippines. It was also apparent that his own agenda came from a difference in ideology as to exactly what the charity was supposed to be about.

After discussing this with Clint at great length over a series of sporadic yet increasingly frustrating conversations, it became obvious that we did indeed have very different conceptions about Unseen Heroes and the direction it should go in. Since I had already put my name to it and made personal guarantees along with the financial commitments, we mutually agreed that I would take control of the charity.

In effect I was left carrying the can, while Clint had earned a free flight out to the Philippines, where he had taken photographs which he'd ended up using for his personal business. In addition to investing in all the equipment for the team, I'd also funded a generator for one of the hospitals out of my own pocket and I was grateful to hear that at least this aspect of my investment had gone according to plan.

195

Clint had deployed from Manila with the generator and had secured from the military a helicopter flight to a local hospital in the Philippines. He then had the generator set up to provide power to the hospital's emergency room to allow the facility to operate 24 hours a day. Considering everything that had happened it felt good to know that we had achieved our aim and save people's lives.

Nevertheless, this left me drained of my own finances in the run-up to Christmas, to the point where I ended up eating through the rations which I'd originally bought for the teams to deploy with. Needless to say, it was one of the worst Christmases of my life. I was sat in an unfurnished apartment eating rations which could have been put to much better use, saddled with a large debt around my neck which hadn't contributed to the good cause in the way it was supposed to have done.

Having put others first in my rush to become involved with implementing a great idea for a noble cause, I'd unwittingly left myself in a position where I was struggling to look after myself. I'd done it again and had neglected my own self-worth without thinking about risk management and exposing myself to unforeseen circumstances.

The time, effort and money I'd invested in the project – and the far from satisfactory outcome – left me feeling stressed and deflated. To make matters worse, salt was rubbed into the wounds when Clint decided to take all the credit for the charity, since he was the man on the ground and there was nothing, I could do to speak up and explain my role in setting up the entire infrastructure of Unseen Heroes.

In spite of everything I'd done, it was Clint who received a letter of commendation from the Mayor of Manila. There might be something to be said for performing a selfless act for the sake of it, not for praise, but the expression "credit where credit is due" seemed fitting.

The final straw came when Clint informed me that he had dumped the bulk of the equipment which had been taken to the Philippines in Manila. He gave me the contact details of the person with whom he'd left it, but they simply told me that it was too expensive to return any of it to the UK. The thousands of pounds I'd coughed up to get the charity off the ground was gone and I'd learned a costly lesson in the nature of trust.

In spite of everything that went wrong with Unseen Heroes, the concept itself remains a solid and worthwhile idea with a great deal of value to the untold thousands of people who are affected by natural disasters. It provided a perfect infrastructural model for disaster zones, circumventing the bureaucratic red tape and deployment barriers faced by many of the larger relief agencies.

It is also a charity I'll be revisiting in the future, in the hopes of fitting into the niche market and doing the concept justice. While many national charities based in the UK deploy aid all around the world, few have the infrastructure in place to affect a speedy transition of aid. Often it can take between two and three weeks to arrive, during which time countless innocent people may die due to lack of essentials. Most often this is due to the lack of potable water, giving rise to an increase in communicable diseases.

The time I had spent living alone at the mill had taught me many lessons, some of which were still being processed by my unconscious mind. But while the data was still formulating into an opinion or lifestyle choices, the depth of knowledge I'd accumulated as a consequence of these experiences was now there, ready for me to access at any point.

I learned a valuable lesson from both Red Zebra and Unseen Heroes, one which taught me to keep my business ideas to myself in the future. I realised that this was the only way that I could avoid other people taking the credit for my work, and that other people were only too happy to take recognition for the hard work of others. I resolved to keep the details of my next business venture very close to my chest and I would be the only person involved in every day running of the project. This way I would be certain that the benefits of my hard work and ideas would go to myself and my daughter, whom I was yet to meet but was about to come into my life.

The lessons I learned from the trauma I'd experienced and the process of recovery I'd gone through are ones I now use in my daily life. When helping others and seeing their lives improve, I often reflect upon those life lessons and appreciate how blessed I am to have them to draw upon, giving me both strength and wisdom.

Chapter 9 Clarity

I had sold my business and had the funds sat in my bank
prior to booking New York. I had done my usual materialistic
thing and changed my car. I gone from a reliable cheap Ford
to a flash and luxurious Range Rover, it was a strange time.
I was attracting the thing I thought would make me happy,
but they changed, I wanted the thing I longed for all my life. I
did enjoy driving the Range Rover, but it was a silly
extravagance that I should not have bought. I should have
focused on the next move for a house, but this would
happen when the time was right. I booked a holiday in New
York as a treat to an end of a manic phase of my life. I met
Hope's mum just a month before New York, things of the
next phase where about to unfold fast.

I was sat in the airport, waiting for my flight to New York.

My flight was scheduled on the anniversary of 9/11. People
asked me why I had chosen that day to fly and if the
prospect scared me at all, but I thought that if anything it
would be one of the safest days of the year to fly. No doubt
the day would feature heightened security, reducing the
chances further of anything happening. Truth be told;
however, the relevance of the date hadn't occurred to me. I'd
been so busy dealing with such a manic point in my life and
trying to clear the decks that I'd only seen the connection
once it had been pointed out to me.

It was a smooth flight and as I came into land I watched as
the terrain started to come into focus in the distance. As we
approached, I tried to get my bearings and see if I could spot
any recognisable landmarks. Maybe this was an old military
habit creeping back in – a practical desire for orientation.
Foolishly I thought I could see New York as we began to fly
over a sea of buildings, but then I remembered that as you
fly in from across the Atlantic Ocean the flight path takes you
over Long Beach before touchdown at JFK Airport.

Looking down on the grid patterns of the city, I found it interesting to try and put the maps of New York I'd studied into context for when I was on the ground. Like my life itself, this was another way for me to view things from a different angle and gain a new perspective. It was the same city but felt very different from the ground. From the plane it had felt so small, like studying a miniature town constructed in a hobbyist's basement. But seeing it all from the ground had put that illusion into perspective and I realised I had to look at my past in the same light.

I disembarked from the plane and made my way through to the airport, keen to take in the full effects of New York. As a single male with a military stance and sense of awareness, it wasn't long before I was instructed to move to a different queue, where I felt eyes watching me from behind mirrored glass. Even though I hadn't done anything wrong, I still felt my nerves rattling slightly as they scanned my fingers for prints and added me to their database. The security guard looked like he was expecting a positive identification, but of course nothing came back as I had never been caught up in any trouble.

As I watched people coming and going in the bustling airport, I realised that for the first time in as long as I could remember, I'd finally gained clarity and focus. I knew with certainty that I was capable of far more than I had ever given myself credit for. It felt as if I'd finally awoken from the slow drudge of madness which had consumed me for the past two years.

After what had happened to Sophia, this period of time was the necessary evil needed for my transformation; it was also a time when I would punish myself by being unkind towards myself, wasting large amounts of energy in an effort to atone for my sins. Sophia's name meaning had given me the literal life lesson - I thought she would bring wisdom to the world and in a way she did. She brought, through her loss, the wisdom out in me, pain can be one of the best teachers. It can focus the mind and allow you to push yourself hard during the time of suffering, but the real gift is when you process the pain and allow the lessons into your daily life. So

Sophia had bought me many gifts and lessons but not in the way I thought she would. In life it's not always about controlling the outcome, it is the process which we go through that can cause the most profound shifts.

It was a period of self-flagellation and psychic turmoil which has finally now come to pass. The pain has lessened while the loss still bears heavily upon my soul.

I had questioned for so long why I had to suffer such anguish and pain, but the reason was to be revealed. Like everything, we can't see the reason at the time, but with time and perspective we can gain a clearer insight. When we are in the fog of trauma our rational mind is suppressed by the fog of emotion and trauma we are in engulfed by. It's not until we emerge the other side that we can see where we have been and where we intend to go. Life trauma can be one of the greatest gifts to us as it makes us change our interactions with ourselves and if we're lucky we come out a better person.

I believe that I found the keys to unlock and process lock in trauma and these were in the form of hypnosis techniques, I had done my usual process. I learned a new subject and then the engineer in me said now you've got the knowledge, let's deconstruct this. I studied the subject until I had all the knowledge that was currently out there, then I let my engineering brain take it all apart and reconstruct my current treatment modality. I realised in the process the true potential that this treatment can have on people, I was fortunate to learn a lot about me. I had finally, by helping others in a professional capacity, learnt to come to peace with who and what I am. I learnt to celebrate my differences and I even got to grips with the darkest parts of my mind that I did not like. I came to accept myself as the whole person that I am now, with the parts working independently, but the whole working in unison.

The fortunate – or perhaps it was fated – arrival of peace was in part due to the research I was doing for this book. Through setting out to learn for this book and answer questions, I inadvertently stumbled upon my own reason for being. I thought that studying to become a hypnotherapist was just another learning curve for me to master, but the more knowledge I added to my growing database of information, the clearer it became that through helping other people I could also help myself.

I had not touched my camera in a long while and the scenery in New York allowed me to reconnect with the creative side of my brain. I found the skills were still there and my eye, I could still see the photos in my mind before I took them. I took a daily photo inventory and then looking at these daily, I used it to review the day. My inner monologue was whirring at million miles an hour, because if you spend a lot a time alone, you internalise a lot. But this process allowed me to reconnect with my inner self and allowed the creative side to expand.

The photographs always reminded me of my life, I always seemed to be watching life through lenses with filters. I was always detached from the picture and remained this way till Hope came along. I had felt that during these times I was here only to observe, but in observing you learn how to really live, however, to really live you have to engage in life and feel it to your core. Children have this amazing ability to grab your heart strings and take charge of your life.

Finally, I could process the demons from my past and set myself free. It was a process still in motion and some of my old patterns were still there, but now I had the ability to see them for what they were, giving me the fortitude to move forwards.

Finally, I was able to make sense of the torment and suffering I'd been consumed by. Now I could cast a light upon the darkened path I'd been taking so far in life and see a clear way forward. It was the best training I had ever received, giving me a depth of knowledge and understanding to draw from. But it also provided me with a model I could show to my hypnotherapy clients; proof that you can beat the odds no matter how high they appear to be stacked against you.

Everything that transpired now feels almost like a distant memory; a blurring of events and energies into something amorphous. Following on from grief and loss of this magnitude, I now realise that I functioned during this time at the bare minimum of what was required just to survive. Yet even the slow decline into isolation, reaching the point where I started to question my own sanity, was a necessary part of this survival instinct. Without this withdrawal from society I would never have been able to retrospectively analyse the things which mattered the most.

I spent many hours of reflection raking over the ashes of what once was, and shall be again, a gifted mind. The slow, traumatic onset from the aftermath of the ghost which had tormented my soul had combined with the ever-present questioning of what I had done to deserve such a turbulent existence. It had taken some time to quieten the voices which had kept me awake at night, ever since the moment – or rather, the string of sequential moments – which had altered the very course and fabric of my world.

I learned what the lessons had to teach, sometimes making the same mistakes time and time again. Each time the punishment for these mistakes increased, until I came to the last, final break from society. In order for us to be able to evolve as individuals we need to fully take on board the lessons of the life cycle we go through – only then can we enter into the next phase of our lives and pursue the happiness we seek. Once we have learned to love ourselves, we are finally able to calm our minds, allowing self-love and peace to roam free.

It took me eighteen years and three failed marriages (not to mention numerous other relationships) until I learned these lessons for myself. As I'd embarked on the flight to New York, I'd wondered what destinies lay in store for the thousands of other people flying from the airport on that day, I realised that the personal journey I'd set out on had nearly come full circle, back to where it started.

At last, the end was almost in sight.

New York was a magical place to experience, both in terms of the incredible architecture and the melting pot of inhabitants who lived there, and it was a shame that I was there on my own. During my time there I walked endlessly down its grand avenues and took in many of the main sights, partly wishing I had company but nevertheless in awe of this iconic city.

One stroll led me onto Brooklyn Bridge, its vast steel construction – part cable- stayed, part suspension bridge – spanning the depths of the East River and providing a link between Manhattan and Brooklyn. I recognised the bridge from countless films, and it reminded me just how indelibly New York has been etched into our minds through decades of popular culture.

Part way across the bridge I came across a field of love locks attached to the bridge's sidewalk. In a relatively recent tradition (in comparison to how old the bridge was), lovers have been attaching "love" padlocks to the bridge intended to stand as a lasting testament to their betrothed. I looked at them and contemplated buying one myself, placing it on the bridge along with the thousands of other locks as a mark of my feelings for Lindsay.

But then I realised that in doing so I might be tying myself to a promise I wouldn't be able to keep, feeding an idea that might never happen. As it turned out, the city of New York soon became fed up of lovers leaving their trinkets to show their affections and clamped down on the practice; simple gestures of sentiment wiped out by an unfeeling bureaucracy.

I spotted a policeman and approached him, asking him if I'd be in trouble if I took a few steps out onto one of the girders which straddled the traffic below.

He replied with a gruff, "What do you think?"

Ironically, it turned out that Lindsay had also been in New York the same week as I. Was this another coincidence? Or something more congruent? Perhaps only time will tell.

After walking over Brooklyn Bridge and then into Harlem, I could see the stark change in buildings.

The stark contrast in the change of wealth as walked around Harlem, I felt slightly unnerved.

It was not a large geographical distance, but I could feel the shift. Most people don't go that far off the bridge, but the walk took me round to the other bridge where I noticed a beautiful carousel at the bottom of the bridge peers. It was a classic Victorian one, that had been painstakingly restored and loved. It made me think of the small things in life that make us happy, like the infectious laugh of a child. It can be so simple when growing up as everything is magical and a new experience. It's only when you go off the beaten path in life do you come across these hidden treasures.

I walked back through Little Italy and was very surprised it was only two streets, ironic really. But there was a carnival and the streets were full of people and couples enjoying the food and culture. The smell of excitement and energy hung in the air mixed with all the different smells from the food.

I made my way back, taking a parallel rail bridge to allow for much better panoramic shots of Brooklyn Bridge, since taking a clear shot whilst stood on it clearly wasn't possible, and I wanted to capture its true scale.

It was a shame, since it would have been an amazing shot.

Coming full circle back onto Brooklyn Bridge reminded me how in many ways my evaluation of my life had also come full circle; reaching that goal and beginning a fresh, new cycle of life meant a return to Lindsay. She was my first love and I realise now that my heart has always belonged to her.

In and of itself this wasn't a re-evaluation of my heart, but my brain had taken me along a very protracted route to where I should be. Lindsay is happy now in a relationship of long standing and as a decent human being I am ethically bound to not interfere with her life. If it is our destiny to be together – as I believe it is – then I can simply allow free will to decide the outcome. If by some miracle she decides to be with me then I can assume the gods have been smiling on me after all.

As in hypnosis, Lindsay had almost become a metaphor for my happiness. I was still reflecting on my first pure love, supporting myself through dark times with the memories we shared. But in reality, Lindsay and I's time had probably passed. Still, as with my clients, I used these happy memories as a resource to assist with my own therapy, but in reality, these memories were distant ones of a time long since passed. The time of living in the past was over – it was now time to set the ideal free and transform it into a new reality.

I'd been searching my entire life for the one thing that was once right in front of me and had loved me dearly in return. In a cruel twist of fate, it has taken me an amazing journey and a lot of trauma to fully understand my true path in life and what I have been aspiring to achieve for all these years: to be a loving husband, father and friend. I'd come so close many times on all but one of these and the father issue had also been a very close call, but since I'd affected free will this wasn't sustainable. I'd rode the rollercoaster of life at full speed, fought and overcome difficult battles and traumas, grasping onto the steering wheel at breakneck speed.

It may be that, had I taken more time to stop and pay attention to the signs, I would have arrived at the same destination earlier. But I'm inclined to believe everything has a divine plan and that the timing is outside of our control: my path was set from the very beginning and I was merely a passenger in the ride called life. But I can say with certainty that, even during the lowest of the low moments – of which there have been many – I wouldn't change a second of it. Without all of these moments I wouldn't have arrived at my current state of mind. This state of mind has been honed by each experience and moment, giving me a depth and wealth of life experiences with which I can equip myself for my role in life.

The long path and all the life lessons which came along with it has brought me to my role as a hypnotherapist and now the reason behind each of these lessons has become crystal clear. I now realise why those moments of despair, during which I questioned "Why?" and thought I was cursed in life, happened. Without those moments I would never have had the depth of knowledge to draw upon for my clients and I see how I have been blessed to experience these events as preparation for my life's work. Through this work I can help others and by helping others we're able to learn, understand and evolve to the point where we can let our inner demons go.

While I was in New York I was still searching for this role.

By that point in my life I knew it was coming, since we are all the master or mistress of our own destiny. We are the architect who designs the structure and the builder who constructs it; we control the flow and manifestation of our own personal reality.

I know now that my fairy tale ending is on the horizon, and the more I think about it the faster it will manifest itself. Until that moment arrives, I will continue to make amends for my past – and all the interactions of which I am not proud of – and try my best to live a humble and honest life with meaning at its core.

The elusive woman whom I hoped to meet at some point in my future could be the physical embodiment of Lindsay, or perhaps it was simply the first premise of her. But I realised that life is fluid and very rarely stands still, and once you have just got abreast of the current the tide can turn very easily, as if acting on unseen whims.

During my period of recovery and introspection I was able to spend many hours observing life quietly from the side-lines, pondering the meaning of life before finally realising one crucial thing: before we can find love, we must first look inwards and discover the fundamental drive of our being. Only once we understand what it is that drives us are, we then best placed to lead a harmonious life.

True serenity comes from within and even the most enlightened souls' mankind has known have had to suffer along the darkest paths in life before they can arm themselves for the arduous battle of life and fulfil their destiny. We see this clearly in the lives of spiritual guides such as Jesus Christ and the Buddha, both of whom suffered and sacrificed in order to illuminate this universal truth. And we also see it in real life heroes who have suffered for greatness, for instance

Stephen Hawking, whose physical trials far outweigh his life-altering scientific accomplishments.

With each battle fought and overcome, a new piece of wisdom is imparted. Through this wisdom we can avoid being caught in a continuous loop, teaching the same lesson but never fully learning the underlying principle, as well as help others to defeat their own demons. When we finally understand these principles and apply them to everyday life, the true miracle of life becomes clear.

This feeling of true wonderment often reminds me of my dog Angus the Airedale. I often watch the way he jumps into the air to feel the wind on his face and see that he is living in the moment. For Angus, there is no past that's disappeared, nor a future which hasn't been set. Just like Angus, all any of us really have is the current moment – the present second, we are experiencing right now – and once you let go of the past you become free of the ghosts which torment you.

I repeated many mistakes over the years, which created a whole lot of demons for me to confront. But the more I live in the moment, the quicker those demons are fading. The scars will remain on my soul but over time the pain lessens, and I've been both unfortunate and fortunate to have experienced most of the major life traumas.

Having taken the time to explain these over the course of the previous chapters, I hope the life I have led so far can be understood. Charmed and cursed in equal measure, these events have made me the person I am today.

If I could change one thing only in my life, what would I change?

The answer to this is easy to arrive at: I would change nothing. The reason behind this is very simple, as each of these moments has become part of the foundations to this book. I've been writing this book for three years and it has taken on many forms as it's developed. As any creative person will tell you, often what you set out with in the beginning is nothing close to what makes it into the final manuscript. Like my life, this book has also been a journey of discovery, and being the consummate perfectionist, I wouldn't let it see the light of day until I was certain it was ready.

But now I am at the point in my life where I'm able to focus on the book and unlike before, the fits and starts of writer's block have melted away. Perhaps it was divine timing, or maybe I simply required the time to rest and gather my mental fortitude. I suppose the answer to this is one I'll never know, but I understood how I needed my life to be clear of distractions before I could write clearly. My life isn't entirely free of distractions, but I have no partner or job beyond the teaching which helps to financially support me until this book comes to fruition.

Should I have taken the gamble I did and made that leap of faith that this book would be published?

I can answer this with a resounding "yes", because the only person who will stop you in life is yourself. Only you will put up the mental barriers which turn into physical barriers, because ultimately only you will create the thoughts which lead to intentions.
I had thought about it many times and even self-doubt crept into my mind and I thought "will anyone read it or buy it?", but without self-belief from the start you won't achieve your dreams and make the impossible happen.

Everything is about timing, and the creative process of writing won't happen if you're not in the right mental place where the words can flow. Having once been caught up in writer's block, I'm now in a place where I struggle to keep up with my thoughts and put them to paper. Far from wondering what to say, being in a place of clarity and inner calm has given me boundless enthusiasm to express my thoughts in words.

The last five days of my stay in New York were spent in deep contemplation of the current state of affairs in my life. I didn't realise it until I took this trip, but I'd neglected my basic needs and requirements for a long time. The mess of the previous two years had driven me down an unknown path – now, for the first time in a while I realised, I'd finally awoken from a terrible dream, leaving me open to a period of the most exciting times in my life.

The original plan was to go to New York City with a friend, but as it turned out going alone was the best thing I could have ever done. I got to wander the streets on my own, clearing my head and gathering my thoughts in readiness to collect the fortitude required to write this book. Having met some interesting people and been through some life changing experiences, I realised that it was finally time to let go of the old and embrace the new.

Like the seasons, my winter had been a cold and bitter one – a self-imposed bleak landscape which I was desperate to escape from. Now the snow which covered my mind in thick layers was starting to melt, allowing me to look forward to the future with fresh eyes full of hope.

I had now emerged into the spring of my life and the summer was yet to come, full of excitement, I could feel that I had changed - I had become more grounded and went with the flow more. During my time here I was just getting up and going with my instincts for that day, I went where I felt I had to. This was the closest I had to freedom for a long while and it was so refreshing.

I was at peace – it was a strange feeling of tranquillity which washed over me and cleared away the despair of the past. I felt invigorated; born again as if into a religion. Indeed, despite my own personal lack of religious convictions I could suddenly relate to the term "born again". I too felt reborn, seeing the world with fresh eyes and feeling my faith in mankind renewed.

I finally loved the person I had become. Acknowledging this love for myself had up until now been a tough battle which I'd struggled with to the point of self-destruction. Now this feeling – this overbearing burden – was gone, and it was time for me to build an amazing future.

I had not realised but this massive shift was on the announcement of the birth of Hope (my daughter) and it really change me in so many ways. I now had a reason to love myself and build something for us both to enjoy. I had, up to this point, always had this feeling I had to do things for others first, but now it was time to put me first.

I always seemed to build amazing things for other people as I did not truly believe I deserved love. Hope changed that from the first moment I saw her, my heart that was encased in stone suddenly melted. From that moment forward it belonged to her, she had only just been born and she was teaching me to be a better man. I had up to now been successful, had money and houses but nothing compared to this. I was now the richest and wealthiest man, because I had true love and that is the purest of commodities. I also knew that now the days of building things and letting others take them was now gone, I had someone very special to provide for now. She had filled a whole in my soul that Sophia had opened and now I was complete again, I could really start to be amazing.

For much of my life, particularly when I was running Red Zebra and speaking to the clientele on a daily basis, I'd given advice and words of wisdom to others. But I'd never extended myself the same courtesy, ignoring the primary rule of first aid to not become a casualty yourself and sporting the physical and mental scars to my detriment. But these scars brought me to the point I arrived at in New York, that light bulb shining bright in my mind allowing me to formulate my experiences into a congruent structure.
I had always found that people gravitated towards me for help and I seemed to heal with my kind words or advice, if I could have only advised myself. Then maybe it would have been a path of less resistance and it would have been an easier journey.
But, I would have missed out on these amazing lessons that I learnt and the ability to now see how truly blessed I am.

This structure is one which I intend to apply to every situation I encounter for the rest of my life and I feel blessed at this moment to have finally arrived at the clarity where I can see the path and work set out before me. It was to become the basis of the sessions I ran when I set up my hypnotherapy practice, after realising that I was naturally trained in talking to people and understanding their points of view.

Like a battle-hardened soldier ready to set out to war, I know I have the strength and fortitude with my life lessons to set out for the battle. The lull that was my time in the metaphorical desert has come to pass – whatever doesn't kill you only makes you stronger.

Having been forged in the fires of Hell itself, the time for a new purpose in life was now. As if by divine timing, the virtue of patience paid its dividends and the wait was finally over.

Almost ten years had passed since I'd suffered the head injury, and three years since I had started down a spiritual path. Who would have thought that a short break in New York City would have provided the catalyst to unlock my creative flow?

I'd spent many months in anguish as I'd tried to put down my thoughts and experiences into this book. But they say that when a book is ready it will write itself, and thanks to New York, this book was able to flow onto the page with a fluidity like never before.

I believe that on the fateful day of the head injury, that a part of me died and it has taken up until now to become the person I was always meant to be. It was a literal reboot and it has taken all this time and experience to rewrite my programming to evolve into my current mind-set. People believe that you can't change, but you can effectively re-wire your brain, this is simply done by changing your thought process.

On a sunny and calm Sunday, I walked around Central Park. The experience was almost a metaphor for my life up until this point. For such a long time I had longed for a mind like this: on the one hand there was the city, busy and full of noises which merge into an incoherent drone; yet inside this

212

lies the park, with its soft ambience and sense of tranquillity a reminder that this was the day of rest.

I can see a mother playing with a child in the sun and the little girl is laughing, I almost see the future and I can't wait to see Hope and hear her laugh. For the

moment frozen in time, nothing else exists or matters, life is simply boiled down to its pure essence and that is family. The connection we make as humans is what defines our lives and our life paths, when we look back from the finish point, we will only remember that happy moments of our lives, maybe the regrets as well.

Finally, my mind resembled the peacefulness of the park, secluded from the chaos of the external world. For such a long time I had got the balance the wrong way around, filling my head with clutter it didn't need. I'd been so busy and chaotic as for so long that, like New York City itself, I could no longer hear anything above all of the noise. Now my mind had shifted dramatically away and resembled Central Park. It was quiet and still, possessing a restfulness which allowed me to finally hear the true voice of my mind.

I was absolutely surprised when this clarity hit home, seeing how this calm state encouraged a fluidity of writing I'd never experienced before. I discovered the inner abundance I'd been searching for so long, seeing that it was within me all along. Like the park itself, I needed to enjoy this quiet time and soaked up the scenery so I could make sense of the bigger picture. My life had been a huge unsolved jigsaw, but the pieces were slotting into place and the picture was coming into focus.

A simple Sunday morning strolling in the park was all it took to make me realise that I had to take time out from the daily noise of everyday life to be able to truly listen and focus. I found in New York something I had never realised before – in all the time I'd spent searching for love in others, I'd failed to love the most important person in my life: myself. When we find self-love and accept who we are, warts and all, we can truly be happy in the moment.

Walking the streets of New York alone was a cathartic moment, as if clearing the pathways which crisscrossed my mind. Through removing the past, a new flow of positive energy began to surge through my brain, recharging my soul. I found that I had a deeply creative connection with the city, one which is world famous for its diversity of culture and expression.

Something else which stood out as I wandered the streets of New York was just how passionate about talking to people and helping them I'd become. I hadn't felt this degree of enthusiasm for a long time and as I talked it felt as if I'd become an expert in my field, with knowledgeable words flowing effortlessly from my lips. It was as if my purpose in life was to speak to and help others and all it had taken for this to finally register was a chance encounter with a stranger in a bar.

I had, during the isolation in the mill, almost forgotten what human connection was like. I had built that barrier that people could not penetrate, it had protected me during my hour of need but now I longed to know real love.

I'd discovered a wonderful Irish bar which I would visit on most evenings. It reminded me of my service across the water in Northern Ireland, with an electric atmosphere in which I was surrounded by friendly punters. One evening I started chatting to a group of people and before long the conversation turned to religion. One woman in particular was very devout and I had a lengthy discussion with her about the books and scriptures I'd been studying the two couples of which both the guys were police detectives in Louisiana, it was one of their birthdays and they invited me over. As I was alone, we had started to talk and, as the night evolved, so did the conversation. They had asked why I was here alone, this led to the abridged version of what happened with Jade. They could see the pain in my eyes and one of the wives had said about me falling out with the divine. This led to me realising that I had lost my connection and I started to discuss the subject in depth.

Judging by the way I was speaking, some of the people in the group thought I was a preacher, since I spoke with such passion and eloquence. This surprised me at first, but the more I thought of it, the more the idea started to resonate with me. I'd always tried my best to help people in one way or another, but the thought that I might be able to help people directly by drawing on my life experiences was like a dream come true. At this point it struck home completely just how at home I was talking and that I had a gift when it came to speaking to people. The religious woman I'd been talking to thought that I'd fallen out with the divine and lost my way. In a way she was correct. I'd failed to accept my own connection after Sophia had passed away, but now I understood this conversation as a clear message telling me that the time for mourning had passed. I now understand completely when people say that they've seen the light – thanks to my time in New York, my life up until this point suddenly made perfect sense.

I had other work to do now if I wished to reconnect with the divine. I'd been set upon a new path, forged by the life lessons I'd been through in order to help me to help others, in the process overcoming my own issues as well. Helping my clients and seeing the changes which came about has since become a privilege to watch, and it was this moment in the bar, talking openly and honestly with open-minded strangers, which told me to let go and move forwards.

It was time to start helping people in my daily life.

It was the perception of finding the key to unlock my mind which opened up the floodgates, allowing me to reflect and forgive myself. Only once I'd forgiven myself was the weight finally lifted and the creative gates opened up. I had been punishing myself spiritually, emotionally and physically for Sophia for so long that I'd convinced myself that I'd deserved this purgatory.

I'd also made a mistake with Jade which would change me as a man forever. I was supposed to help her recover from her illness, showing her the way to a healthy and happy life, but in the process, I'd fallen in love with her. For this transgression I had paid the highest price of all – my daughter Sophia.

But this version of me no longer existed; a distant nightmare of a person who has now died, leaving a new version of myself occupying the same body. My mind is different now and ever since the alteration of these memories through hypnotherapy I've finally been able to put these events to rest.

It was a surprisingly swift process. I found that content free regression hypnosis was the key to this success and I now use this myself to help others put events of their own past to rest. In a sense, these events are like concrete blocks which a person is chained to. The chain represents the unprocessed emotion of the past and once we release the chains, we are able to move forward into the future. We alter the way we interact with the memory, no longer bound to it once the emotion has been processed.

Often you have to experience such a volume of trauma and heartache to the point where you simply wish to die, but then realise that you can't because suicide is a mortal sin and a selfish waste of life. The anguish, pain and torment pushes you to the point where it feels like there is no end in sight – and then you realise that you are the only person with the power to end it.

Transformation of this kind can be daunting, and the simplest way is to take small steps each day. Then the days turn into weeks, and the weeks into years. The pain lessens as you forget how to feel the emotions attached to the trauma. You remember how to interact with people and enjoy the company of others. You start to laugh and smile and begin to feel love and hope.

It's a slow process and if you're not careful all of a sudden you can be blindsided by the realisation of what you had become – a shell of a former man. You see the same face in the mirror every day, but other people sense the pain and torture in your eyes and avoid you. You start to avoid them, leading back to an ugly cycle which deepens until you become a hermit living on a boat with a dog for company.

I had unwittingly built my own Hell, isolating myself from the reality of the situation as well as becoming the judge, jury and executioner of my fate. But for the grace of God I was saved. I finally saw that all the time I had spent going through a period of grief, compounded with other life choices and combined with the nature of my mind – my stubbornness and my propensity to never ask anyone for help – had very nearly led me to becoming a permanent hermit, lost in self-pity and despair.

I have been lucky, and my guardian angels have saved me for the purpose of paying it forward. Karma is partly about giving people help whether they ask or require it, and, if each and every one of us performed one random act of kindness, the world would certainly be a better place. I remember on my birthday being alone and sitting in my comfort zone of my café. I sat in that café for five years. I half expected Jade to walk in and we'd forgive each other, but that was never going to happen - I tormented myself with that too much. It was time to finally let her go and move forward. While sitting there people watching and drinking coffee, the waitress Chelsea was very kind. On my birthday she asked how I was, I said it was my birthday and she bought me a piece of cake. It's random acts of kindness like this that allowed my faith in humanity to stay alight.

Such a shift in our mind-set, perpetuating a cycle of peace, could – and most likely would – usher in a time of greatness not known since the legendary Atlantean period. If each of us, as a member of the human race, took the time to think about our actions on other before we acted, the end result could be a Utopian society on Earth.

It may seem like an unachievable task but, like a great lake or sea, it starts with one drop of water, so one act combines with another and changes the tide of Humanity forever. It could ripple out into the surrounding environment and each person helping another for no reward but because it's the right thing to do. The combined energy or thought of the collective is greater than the single individual, but change can be bought about by one single intention with the right mind and will.

You have to let the deep water stand still for a long time in contemplation.
Only once they have become very still does all the sediment settle, this allows you to see the bottom of your well. This can be likened to when you have trauma and it churns up the sediment and clouds our judgment or paths in life. The

emotional turmoil that we go through can be the underlying current that stirs the sediment or our behaviours. These patterns or behavioural programs lie in the unconscious mind, affecting everything we do and are. It's not until we access these programs that we can truly effect change, we are re-wiring our brains in the process. Our brain changes every day with every interaction and memory, the memory changes each time we interact with it. It's almost like we encode and decode the memory in the brain using the process of neurological brain chemistry and protein strains.

But each process changes the interaction with the memories, they're not carved in stone but are actually fluid. Tibetan monks have been shown using MRI scans to have larger frontal lobes - this is due to mediation. Effectively the brain is like a muscle, the more we use and understand it, the better it becomes at operating and making new neural pathways.

The Museum of Modern Art or MOMA is a place I always wanted to visit to view the art and bask in the creativeness. The building alone is visually stunning, a piece of art in itself, holding a wonder of creative works. These inspired my creative side and I stored ideas ready for when I next do a project and require visual stimulation. I always used my photographs as my creative art, as I could not paint, but I often toyed with the idea of metal water sculptures and I have the design ready in my mind. I may make some for myself just to engage in the creative process that I find very cathartic for my soul. I find many depressed people that have given up the creative side become more depressed, but when they go back to their passion their creativeness lifts the veil of dark and they become lighter again.

To be able to see the clarity of what is in plain sight, but sometimes we are too busy to notice that what is beneath our very noses. We take the long path in life when we could easily look and listen to the truth in the situation and free ourselves from the unnecessary heartache and pain.

My time in New York had given me the focus to see and the space to think about what I wanted; I went back to start the next chapter of my life. This was the thing I had been working towards for so long, becoming a father, and I thought maybe now life will settle down and become quieter. But in reality, becoming a father was the easy part, to be a good dad was going to be my life's work. She shifted and changed my life, because when you become a parent it's no longer your life any more. Your life becomes their life and you make sure that everything you do is with them in mind, she is my first waking and last thought of the day. People don't realise how your responsibility changes when you become a parent, they are forever directly connected to your heart and mind. The way they laugh, the way the look or smile, it is all burned into your life and memories.

Do you know who makes the best hypnotherapist?

It is your parents of course, because before seven years old they install all your life programs. You learn how to act, behave and think by observing your parents. Some of this programming can be unsupportive, for example if you say don't do this or you can't do that. If you remove the negative reinforcement with the interaction with your child, then they can truly achieve anything. In hypnosis there is a barrier between the conscious and the unconscious mind, this is called the critical factor. Its job is to filter the information between the two and allow the control of information, but the strange thing is, the critical factor is not formed until children are seven years old. So, there is an argument as to whether we require this filter to change our perception of the world? Current research would say yes, as without its conditions like autism exist, but how do we manage to the age of seven before it comes into action?

Children up to this age see the world as a magical place and they are very intuitive, it seems we condition them out of this. I made the decision a long time ago that I would never tell Hope what she is or what she can achieve. I would always support and help her to achieve her dreams, because if we dream it, it can happen, all it takes is believing. If we all believed in our dreams and never gave up on them, it would be a magical world in which we live. It is only once you've had trauma that you realise what you can truly achieve with your life, you realise that if you put your mind to it, you can achieve anything. We are conditioned via self-doubt that we have to settle for a mundane life, but if we follow our dreams, we can live with no regrets.

This is when you notice, and you become very surprised at the congruent events that start to occur when you pursue what makes you really happy. We hold the keys to our own kingdoms and can build our dreams and make them a reality, all we have to do is believe it. Then we can allow the unconscious mind to work out the details and allow the solutions to permeate to the conscious mind. We just have to have self-belief and faith in our dreams. If I had listened to all the negative people when creating my new projects, I would have never let them get past a thought. But it's the constant thought and energy towards each one that allowed these projects to leap from my mind and into the real world. I visualised the end goal before I started - with this book I saw myself holding it in my hand. The more you do this and the more details you add, you'll be surprised how the answers and solutions come to you.

This process in hypnosis is called future pacing and it is used a lot by Olympic athletes; before the event they see themselves visualising the race and winning. They see themselves receiving the gold medal and practice all the finer details in their mind. It's a very powerful tool, not only for athletes but for life coaching as well. My time in New York had almost become the catalyst for the clarity of all my ideas forming together in a single lucid idea. This, and the impeding birth of my daughter, had changed me at soul level, I never thought after Sophia that the pain would go. Hope was not to replace Sophia, but she was to teach me the true meaning of love and she'd not even been born yet. I'd often dreamed before with Sophia about the simple things, like taking her to the park and playing on the swings and slides. Now it was like the universe was giving me a second chance with Hope, as if it eluded that I learnt the lesson from Sophia.

Now I can learn all the lessons that Hope will bring. I am sure there will be many lessons and lots to learn but the privilege of being with the thing I yearned for so long, will drive me on to the be best father I can be. I am sure she will be a lot like me and hopefully have my intelligence and my piercing blue eyes, but whatever she brings, I will love her unconditionally and be there no matter what transpires. I am finally going to be the one thing I chased all my life. Now the question is, am I up to the challenge? I believe the answer is yes, as otherwise it would not be the right time. I believe the protracted path I have taken has equipped me with patience, strength, wisdom and fortitude.

Chapter 10 Hope

Things developed very quickly between me and Sarah, she announced she was pregnant and that changed my world. The thing I yearned for, for so long, was within reach again, but I was detached as I was still haunted by the past and Sophia.

I went into the relationship, that was planned on her part, before I realised she was pregnant with my daughter and soon after moved to the sofa to sleep.

The relationship was over before it started, yet I blundered on doing what I thought was the right thing for nearly a year. I was working so hard in a job I could not stand, that I buried my head in the sand and ignored all my instincts. I felt like I was a mere pawn in her game to achieve what she wanted, once my daughter was born Sarah had the control over me, she believed she required.

Due to the Electrical Consultant job I was doing, I was away from home all week and only coming back at the weekend. This was to be the nomadic life again, but I yearned for the house full of laughter and love. The building of a home and roots had started; it was happening as a child is the best thing to ground one to the reality of situations.

Still, the emotional turmoil of Sophia was in my inner world and affected my out world, the content free regression with Chris was soon to put this to an end. So, I missed out on the pregnancy, Sarah become very distant and blamed the pregnancy. The relationship was over before it had begun, but I had a daughter with her and tried to heal the rift.

I had always had this dream that when I met the love of my life, we would work together to provide a beautiful home, this would provide the very place for our children to grow up in, but until my inner world had been resolved I was only seeming to attract the chaos which still lay inside me. I wanted so deeply for calmness to exist.

222

It would eventually come but it meant going back to basic foundations and rebuilding my life from scratch. For now, I was just going from one messy relationship to another and it was taking its toll on who I was.

I had gone from outgoing and grounded to being isolated and lonely, almost lost adrift as unsettled inside. It was a difficult time for me, but my only focus was providing for my daughter and being there for her. I had always envisioned being present and supportive during the pregnancy, but this was not meant to be this time. In realty I was away during most of the pregnancy, I was in a job I no longer suited, and I was resenting it. It was well paid but as I was working away, I was paying for everything back at home and lived in hotel rooms again. I felt that I was working very hard for something I could not yet see; I was living a basic lifestyle. Putting others first and leaving nothing or very little for myself. I was just existing again and going through the motions, I found this an unsettling period again.

I continued with this routine for seven months until the politics at work had become unbearable. I had been promised promotion and my own team, but the people I recruited had formed an alliance with the directors and as I spoke my mind, my days were numbered. I later found out that one of the people I interviewed and employed got the manages job and the team I had built. But I could not have stayed there as the travel and work environment was highly stressful and draining me, so in the end I felt I had no choice but to resign and move forward - I felt the release straight away and free again.

I had to find another job as soon as possible and I took the easy option of going back to lecturing Electrical Engineering; I once loved the subject but now I was just going through the motions. I was being pulled in many directions and yet again found myself organising the electrical section and the apprentice structure.

I was in one of the lonely places of my life, to be with someone and be alone is the worst place to be. I considered my options but had a daughter to think of, we then moved into a complete house renovation project. Talk about a glutton for punishment, I had given up the job travelling the country and taken a job at the local college so I could be near home.

I would have, and did, work myself into the ground renovating the dilapidated house for 16 hours a day, seven days a week. I was also holding down a full-time job an Electrical Lecturer at a nearby college - I was in a very dark tunnel again and could not see the light

But I appeared to be efficient at my job and spoke my mind freely again to managers and the directors, I was seen more as threat than an asset. This was a long period which in reality only lasted eight months before I resigned again, it was making me very ill.

This is the period when the month of madness started, very long workdays of building and restoring the house so it was habitable for Hope to live in. In thirty days, I had to rip out the kitchen, bathroom, a wall and the bathroom floor and joist, then re-instate it all before Hope was born. I was still working full time as well, so fitted this in during holidays and out of work hours. I spent the long hard hours alone in solitude, I felt like my purgatory for what had transpired with Sophia.

I felt the symptoms of burn out and asked Sarah for help, but none came. So, I left just before Hope was born, again mentally and physically shattered. I started to build myself again but when Hope was born my life changed forever. I believe that was the lowest point of my life, I was mentally tired and if I had not left, I think I would have had a breakdown. I truly believe I was on the edge of a meltdown that would have made me seriously ill.

I bought a new boat and furnished it, but even though it was beautiful, it was like me at that time. I had achieved what most people desired, a luxury brand new boat that I lived on, but it was just a boat and not a home; the thing I longed for the most was still at my house. I remember putting a Wi-Fi antenna on the roof and an older couple asking if I was a tradesman, I replied no its my boat with pride. I realised that the materialistic items were a lesson linked directly to ego. The only person you are in competition within life is yourself, once you realise that there is no competition.

224

I would see people walking around the marina as couples looking at boats and commenting how amazing my boat was while I was inside thinking I would trade this boat for the family and happiness that they seemed to have. Each morning I'd sit with my coffee on the deck, trying to write this book and people watching. It was during this time that I sought guidance, and after reading a book on past life regression, I booked an appointment in Glastonbury. The place had resonated with me when I visited it with a familiar feeling of coming home. I thought I will end up living here one day. The appointment for the past life regression was with a woman called Atasha, it was my first introduction to hypnosis. From the very first moment, I realised the power of hypnosis. I

realised I had to follow the steps in the sequence and started to look for a hypnosis school.

I had left because me and Sarah did not work, but I missed Hope so much. I even missed her first Christmas, something I will never get back; I will just have to compensate with time. The boat was something I wanted for a very long time and the stars aligned and I got an amazing deal. But it was after a while I realised it was just another materialistic goal, it left me hollow inside and a deeper longing was calling. I had this amazing thing to enjoy but I had no one to enjoy it with and my time with Hope was more precious than anything on this planet.

I was empty and felt nothing, it was time to start addressing all the issues that I had, the baggage stored away in the attic of my mind. Christmas came and went. I went to my family's on Christmas Day, but I was missing out on my daughter's first Christmas. It made me realise that I never wanted to miss another Christmas, birthday or special moment of her life.

I eventual reconciled with Sarah, sold my boat and moved back into the house. Things changed briefly, but then it was back to grind of me working and working on the house.

I thought at last that we would be able to work together and achieve a lifestyle that allowed us to be there for the children. But this was not meant to be, it had allowed me though to finally put roots down.

The final revelation and blessing of a yearning all of my adult life, not sure if the drive to be a father was the lack of the presence of my own growing up and promising once if blessed would never make the same mistakes. In his own way my father was the best teacher I had ever had, his lack of interest in my life after conception made me vow, I would never be like him.

This stubbornness, with the drive to be a father, cost me dearly in relationships, thinking that I only deserved what I endured. This made most of my adult relationships very harsh - with two I stayed too long for the wrong reasons. When I finally met Sarah, I was worn down by the life lessons I had endured and my defences were very low.

I allowed the pursuit and drive of what I thought was the most important thing in my life to be a parent, you'd think after the trauma of Sophia I would have learned.

I realised in retrospect that the yearning to be loved from a young age, compounded with an empathic nature, had driven me to abandon my sharp instincts and trust people who I should not have.
The run up to Hope's birth was very disturbing for me, the past haunting me still - the moment Sophia passed made a mark that stayed on my soul for eternity. It kept me awake at night praying Hope would be born with no complications. The signs were there again, as with Jade, but I buried my head deep in my work.

Sarah slept on the sofa shortly after conception. I realised that we had become acquaintances and not in love. I was working away for the first five months and staying in hotels up and down the country. This was a very sad lonely existence, I spent most of my adult life alone, even I was with someone I felt alone.

There was a song "you built your walls so high nobody can climb them" or was I being a typical Cancerian and hiding behind my shell. I think the reality after Jade was that I had

nothing left to give until Hope came along and restored me to the living world giving my focus and drive back, but the true clarity would happen with the year of solitude.
There was something not right but I ignored the warning signs, when we went to the Antenatal appointment it seemed like a challenge, my instincts were telling me that it was not right.

I knew this was not all, but medical confidence would not allow me to uncover the truth, that combined with the nagging question of paternity was driving me crazy.

I had worked very hard at a job I could not understand, and all Sarah seemed bothered about was the money I was bringing home. Even though she was working, and I was giving her a generous amount a month for housekeeping, she always seemed to have no money or not have any expensive vices. The web of lies began to untangle as I refurbished my first home, after a month of 16-hour days, close to mental burn out and a physical wreck, I left and moved in with my brother. It was three weeks before Hope's birth and I was not allowed at the birth, I had to wait in reception whilst her aunt was with her. The staff giving me the same look of contempt as before, I had been isolated out of one of the most magical events of my life.

I been here before and, not trusting my instincts, I went to discuss things with a friend who advised me about Jade, which I ignored, and she was right. So, this time I heeded the warnings and called off the wedding. Maybe after Sophia, when I felt the conception of her soul to this world and also her departure from this world, had changed the way I felt about being a father, but it was more much more the sums and all the details did not add up. Sarah did not seem concerned I was working myself into the ground, not sleeping and spending everything on the

house. We did not go out; we didn't talk, and we did not share any romance or affection. For a whole year I just functioned in the darkness and built a home single-handedly, with no support or love.

I had become a servant to the ideology of being a good father, a slave to my own idealism. But like the old adage the straw that broke the camel's back, I waited and planned.

I went back to live with her after 3 months apart, but things weren't right, she slept downstairs with Hope who was dependent on Sarah for breast milk. I was that tired I could not think straight, sleep or function like I should. I buried myself again in work and working on the house again doing every trade and project managing. I did what I excelled at and got two amazing fireplaces from eBay. I installed the first one and after three weeks of hard work and heartache, we had an open fireplace.Then the second fireplace was bought for a princely sum and collected from an Edwardian manor house, a thing of absolute beauty, well-cared for in the years in had been installed. I had the mantle delivered to the house and removed the old fireplace. Within 12 hours of being in the house it was scratched (I sighed again as I was trying to build a beautiful home and was alone).

It was not so much the fireplaces getting damaged but the counter of my trying to build us a beautiful home, while I was alone in this idea.
That was the final straw of many, I kissed my daughter that Wednesday morning, told her I loved her, packed the car and left. I asked for a sign to say I'd done the right thing, as I felt awful for my actions, Sarah's words ringing in my ears "You're just like your dad".

Sarah knew where to strike to the inner core of my heart. When I said I love you to Hope she head-butted me as if to say I know what you're doing. This was one of the lowest ebbs again, I'd got the daughter I longed for but missed out on all the nice things so far. It was a week before Christmas and I was here a 39-year-old alone and staying in hotels again, a pattern that happened with Allison and Jade. I promised myself in that moment I would get my own home and never miss another Christmas of my daughter's again. I started to enact a plan from five years ago before meeting Jade - I intended to buy a boat. I started looking and found a Dutch Barge. My offer was swiftly refused, so with a deep heart I asked for guidance and a conversation I had with Louise, my hairdresser, popped into my mind "How about Mercia Marina?" The words resonated in my head, so I looked online at the boats for sale.

228

The events that happened next, I can only explain as miraculous - I found my dream boat. When I looked at building a boat, this had the exact specification and style I would have built, so I rang the boat yard and arranged a viewing. The boat was almost new with only six hours on the engine, it was pure luxury. I walked in and Ian (boat brokerage dealer) could tell by my face that I wanted the boat, the only question was the price. I had the funds to pay the full price, but the businessman in me negotiated and I got the boat of my dreams for an amazing deal.

The deal was done, and funds transferred the next day. Whilst in the bank going through the security procedures with the new cashier (as the amount I was transferring was large), she said "hang on, I need to go and get another member of staff to verify you identify". She disappeared out the back only to reappear with Charlotte who I knew.

Charlotte said, "So James what are you buying now?" and I replied
"Well, you know me Charlotte, always a business deal in mind".

It was sort of ironic as I had known Charlotte from when I owned Red Zebra; a customer and then a business acquaintance, the boy from Spondon had come a long way in the business world.

I was once told by an acquaintance about the child's nursery rhyme. "Row row row your boat, gently down the stream. Merrily merrily merrily, merrily, life is but a dream"

It took me many life lessons and heartache to realise the true meaning of this simple rhythm - if you're going against the current life is very hard, if you're on the right path, life should just flow.

By leaving Sarah and going back to where I should be, life became magical very quickly, I filled my mind with beautiful things, and they happened. The book I had been writing for four years and always let relationships take priority over was now to be finished.

The periods of coming back to it, then getting deeply involved with females was over, the main focus of my life now was to build a future for Hope.

Ironically her name is what it meant to me in my life, she gives me hope and purpose to be the man I should always have been. I will lead by example and make sure, through my work, that she has opportunities growing up that I could have only dreamed of.

Ironically after a month of relaxing and taking care of myself, I found myself looking for my deeper calling. Say all of sudden you had all the free time in the world without the financial constraints of the rest of the world, what would you do?

When I first took the new boat out with no formal training, I felt out of control almost lost without direction, my ego said you'll be fine, it was only a 57ft by 12ft and 30-ton boat what could go wrong? The next 15 minutes were very surprising, it can only be likened to steering an articulated lorry from the rear with no brakes.

I managed to get it to the fuel point with only a few minor bumps. When I first took it off the sales mooring, I was heading for all the new boats, all lined up worth millions in total. Luckily, I only bumped the fenders of one. It must have been so comical for anyone watching as here was me in a large new boat, that I could not even operate. I was like a metaphor for my life, that whilst appearing to have what everyone else wanted on the surface, below the water I was drifting out of control.

I thought I would be able to handle the boat easily, I had the knowledge to operate it, but not the skill. In those scary 15 minutes, I vowed I would never be out of control like that again. I would always ensure that knowledge was backed up by skill or by acquired skill and if required, I would ask for help.

I started to read book after book on spiritual awareness and mindfulness, I had more answers than questions. I knew I could do this for a living but the leap of faith and the divine spark to find the passion that was extinguished when me and Jade separated. From now I will refer to these as the

230

Dark Ages, I wanted to reignite my passion, my soul calling but how and doing what? I had seen most of the best people in the country on stage and I just felt a knowingness that this was my calling but how to make that big leap of faith.

I knew the really gifted people and the people who were in it just for the money, they lost the true meaning a long time ago. I searched for the answer to take my gift to the next level to help people, but it seemed to elude me, then it struck me I was required to heal myself first.

So, I set myself on a path with the faith and belief in my instincts that I had been sent down this path for a reason to teach. I could see myself on a stage speaking to a packed auditorium, them hanging on my profound words of wisdom, earned through all the life lessons I endured, the training if you will, to speak from experiences and with conviction.

For the first time in my life I felt something that had eluded me all my adult life, it was a deep contentment with just being in the present moment. I sat there on the back of boat, the world walking past with the sun rays on my face and I felt true peace; it was like heaven on earth.

I had raged, fought and struggled against the current of life for so long, it was second nature but now I let it ebb through my soul and take me on its journey. This journey on which you join me at the start of. Where it will lead me, I have seen in my vivid dreams, almost like echoes of a long lost knowledge of the place I won't be.

It's only now, with clarity, that I see what has always been there, I just required to disengage from the busy hectic life. I have seen the signs many times, simply live your life and do the things that make you happy. Only in doing this you realise how many distractions in life are there to take you off your true path. Sure, I'd like to lose the weight I acquired whilst with Sarah, maybe two or three stone, but like before when I followed a vegetarian diet and did what I loved. The weight just melted off me within two months last time, this is because when we are stressed it lowers our energy levels and makes us crave junk food we don't really require.

I found being a vegetarian before made me come alive, physically and mentally, it enriched my creative side and during this time I was able to manifest everything that I put energy into very quickly. This is because like the nursery rhyme, life can be the dream you wish it be it just by focusing on the positive and shifting your state of mind to achieve this.

The idealism of stripping back the layers of your life, like an onion, to get to the true core of your being. Most people accumulate traumas and never deal with them. They think 'why me?', 'why am I always having bad luck?', but really they're storing negative energy in their aura. It takes time to realise everything in life is a lesson and that once you learn the lesson you move onto the next stage of your life. Most get stuck in a cycle as they never learn the values of the lesson and they repeat it again and again, they make the same mistakes and plough on regardless. Its only through times of crisis with profound introspection and soul searching that we realise the meaning of the lesson.

I have had many life lessons and I got stuck in a cycle with my saviour complex towards women and it cost me dearly on every level. It is the sum of the parts and your experience that make you who you are, that person is truly unique and very special. It is only with time out and introspection that you can put all the pieces of the jigsaw together to create and see the whole picture.

This is called Gestalt Therapy in hypnosis and is also known as Parts Therapy, where you get the parts to communicate as a whole again.

This was my time to walk out of the shadows and into the light to help others in the shadows and show them the way through my experiences. The purpose of my pain and my anguish was to share through my lessons and help people, what better a teacher that's been there, done it and healed the scars. Like the phoenix I have raised my life from the ashes, many times due to tenacity and self-belief.

The nightmares have faded to leave a surprising state of mind that is balanced, to laugh at yourself before others, to never take yourself too seriously and to deflate your ego as it will be your downfall. I find pleasure in helping others and without being asked, it is a selfless act that if we all did would change the human race over night. Maybe one day one act at a time to shift the paradigm from negative to positive, for each human to help each other and the end of all starvation and hunger.

It's all achievable, but first we have to address the issues of greed and money, if we all lived with what we require rather than what we think need we would solve these problems very quickly. The shift of the planet would be towards the positive; imagine seven billion humans focusing on one united goal, how quickly could that be achieved with all that energy focused on it.

War, famine and disease would be consigned to the past where they belong, as we make our own universe, we all have the ability to change every aspect of our life. But to first do this we must be in the present moment and strip away any distractions in life.

I managed to do this as I sat on the boat for a month - I only talked to people I wanted to and had very few visitors. This self-imposed isolation was the key to calming my mind and only then could I hear my inner voice guiding me.
I just started to see every interaction with fresh eyes, like a new baby, I saw the magic of every aspect of the miracle of life. The true interactions between people which boils down to basic energy exchanges at every level. I became that quiet observer of life watching it pass me by as I interpreted what the meaning was, the conclusion I came to is do what makes you happy and do this with love.

During this time, due to the tiredness of my mind and my low energy levels, I was only barely operating on an intellectual level. It would not be until much later that once I dealt with all these past issues, that I started to recognise my true capacity and my cognitive function increased dramatically.

I really started to feel for the first time in my life I belonged somewhere and with purpose it helped me get stronger. Whilst lecturing I found my dream dog and the key to sanity, Angus the Airedale, like before with Dylan, he helped me reintegrate into society.

233

I had vowed that Hope would always have me in her life and I would always provide her with a home that she could flourish in. I believe that when you have children, you strive to give them the things you didn't have growing up. I had the home with love provided by mum, but never that father figure. That is possibly why it been had so important to me to be a father. Hope had finally brought me back to life and you don't know true love till you have a child, she had taught me so much and the meaning of love. She reminded me of how simple life can be and when you have a child your life priorities shift and move to theirs.

The simple thing in life that gives me the greatest pleasure is to see my daughter laugh or smile - that is absolutely priceless. To walk in the park with her on a sunny day replaces all the years of loneliness and the search for my life purpose, I now not only live in the moment, but I enjoy being present. I believe I encased my heart in concrete when Sophia passed, but Hope has smashed that away and it has started to feel and love again.

I have searched all my life for this great love and being the hopeless romantic I am, thought it would be like a classic novel. But in reality the love of my life is my daughter, the bond between father and daughter is unique. I will always be there to support and love her, advise her and guide her. She had, through her very being, given me the hope to go out into the world again. I have called my hypnotherapy business after her as I believe if we can inspire hope in others then anything is possible.

Even in the darkest hour, if you still hold hope in your heart, then you can go through the fires and turn adversity into the catalyst for profound changes in your life. We all have the power to change our lives and effectively our programming, this can be by changing our habits and routines. Allowing yourself to get out of a rut, firstly you have to believe that you can achieve your dreams. Once you can cut the ties to the anchors in the past, you can move very quickly to calmer waters and sail into your very bright future. Whilst finishing this book and speaking to others, I keep hearing the word "Inspirational", if we can each inspire others through our actions and life stories then what an amazing world we would live in.

If I manage to inspire people, through my work and my life story, then I feel that my journey has been a privilege and success. This book started as a just a title and a few random pages, then sat there for nearly five years, until I made the conscious effort to make it come to fruition. From that point it seemed to fall into place naturally as if it was the correct time for me write this book. Anyone can write a book, all it requires is discipline, routine and a life filled with events. Then all you have to do is break it down to bite size chunks, for example two pages a day. Within six months you will soon have the book in draft form.

If you apply this same technique to any goal you wish to achieve, then it will soon become a reality. I have realised that the sum of all my experiences, which I can draw upon them for wisdom, don't define me or control who I am. The journey we take through life is our path, but we ultimately choose the scenery that we look at along the way. When we reach our final destination, we t look back and only the important memories will stand out, so why not make every day special and magical. I found that the birth of Hope allowed me to see the world through fresh eyes, the eyes of a child with wonderment and magic, but with the knowledge I have acquired.

This fresh perspective gives me the best of both worlds, I can imagine what is possible and combine it with the ideas I have already learnt. When we are born, we start as a blank book, with possibly genetic memories or programs in place. But we become who we are by our experiences that create memories and with any traumatic events, we attach unprocessed emotions to these memories. It is understanding this that I finally found how to process and release the person from the underlying effects that this has on us. I had gone to learn hypnosis as I thought the research would be good for the book, little did I know it was the missing piece, not only to this book, but to me and the inner peace I searched for so long.

I had done the usual research and due diligence and found what I believed to be the best qualification being taught. This was the Hypnosis Practitioner Diploma (HPD) and it was currently the gold standard in hypnosis. I arranged the initial formal interview with Meirion, who was running the course. He had to assess suitability for the course as I would be working with vulnerable people. The interview went very well, and we hit it off straightaway, I joked that I was doing it for research for my book and he retorted he would make a hypnotherapist out of me. I think he knew when he met me that I would be ideal for this line of work. After the interview I was accepted onto the course and awaited the course to start with excitement, I could not explain this as I had done many courses but this one seemed to resonate deeply with my soul.

I went back to my day job and I really started to realise how much I was wasting my mind. I loved setting up the structure and lessons but after I'd done all the hard work it was not challenging enough. I had seemed to drift after the military, I had rebuilt Red Zebra but after Sophia I lost my focus and just seem to drift from job to job. I could not stay in positions because I had taken jobs I could do while on auto pilot; this became a problem when my intellect came back. I started to realise I was capable of so much more; I had a plan to qualify in hypnotherapy and work from home. This was so I could get the work life balance correct and be there to watch Hope grow up. The drive for the success and money had been replaced by the riches that money can't ever buy - the memories and my daughter's laughter.
Had I finally learnt the lessons I should have a long time ago? I believe that everything that transpired was to make me prepared to be a patient father.

I was faced with a choice of self-belief while writing this book, to take the easy path and go back to teaching engineering or to wait. By waiting and focusing on what I really wanted I could bring about self-belief and really change in my life, not just go back to my default safety pattern. It was time to move forward into an area of fresh territory for me, to have peace and happiness. Because if you believe in your dreams, it can actually surprise you when you achieve them. I could finally now, because of Hope, live the life I was meant to with freedom and choices of my life path. It had all come about from a very long journey and now Hope had put the clarity and fire back into my soul. I could see me achieving the goals I set out a long time ago and many more, I could achieve the dream and help people along the way.

236

I started to realise that I could now, with Hope's love, build an empire and this time it was sustainable. This was down to the old adage "love gives you wings",

Well, now Hope had given me the wings to soar. I realised in the first year of her life, while chasing the business idea to give her a good start in life, I had missed out on the precious moments. I will never, regardless of all the money and success, ever get that time back. It's only when we have time to stop and think, we realise what truly matters in life, I was shedding the old faucets of my old ways. I had been blessed with the biggest gift ever, my driving force for most of my adult life Now was the time to be present and love, laugh but more than that, to live. Not to observe life and analyse what it could mean.

Children have this innate way of getting into your soul and changing your interactions. Long gone was the ego driven businessman, I'm now the man in the park that makes silly noises and faces and no longer cares what others think about me. My focus, my life, my reason to be, is the very thing that delivered me from the dark times and put light and love back in my life. I would now make memories of positive impacts on her life and my own life, she had lit me up with love and pride. I remember when she was born and I held her for the first time, I felt from that point on, as any dad will testify, that I had become her protector and guardian. I cried after her birth - it was tears of joy which was a new thing for me.

After experiencing so much sadness, now was the time to experience happiness and true love. I had started to assemble all the pieces of my life and build some solid foundations, using hypnosis I had freed myself of my past Then Hope had come along and showed me my future prospects and the love of her gave me the drive for the future. I was finally free to do what I was meant to. The chance or fated path that lead me to the hypnosis course in Wales allowed me to meet who was to become a very good friend, Chris.

He was very intelligent and a former director in corporate banking world and was on the course with me, he got into hypnosis by using his annual training budget to do NLP course. This lead on too many other courses on hypnosis and now he'd left the banking world and was on this course to formalise his knowledge. His father was a GP who had used hypnosis and Chris had many books on the subject, it was like we were meant to meet. Often on the course we discussed many subjects from hypnosis to philosophy.

We had the same black sense of humour and we often made each other laugh in class. I would find during the lessons I was asking many questions that the teacher could not answer. It was almost like I was deconstructing the pieces as I learnt each new subject. I also came up with many ideas on how to implement these and use these during my practice when I was qualified. I felt during this time there was resentment over my intellect, but this was the alpha male issue again. I kept bumping into people's egos all the time - the issues were not mine but theirs. I found the weeks on the course were very engrossing, I was staying locally in a hotel and talking to Sarah on FaceTime most nights, but the rift was getting wider.

This pained me deeply as I thought I had now finally got the child I so longed for but I was probably not going to be living with her mum. This would resolve itself during the next year, so for now I was focusing on completing my course. While doing the course I came up with the idea to set up a new business - to restore classic cars in my garage. I been on a three weeks specialist bodywork and panel beating course and I learnt the other skills required.

The idea being that I would restore the car in my spare time and then maybe sell the car, with the funds pay off sections of the mortgage. I had a five-year plan for the business and to be mortgage free and working from home with a happy life balance. But I was starting to do it again and pushing myself in too many directions at once. I was up and down the country and when the car arrived it was put in storage as the garage, I was having built was not ready -I seemed to be juggling many balls and on my own again.

Sarah seemed more detached than before and it started to make me ill, so we separated again. I was at the point where I had nowhere to go, no funds for hotels and I had sunk to the depths again. I decided this happened to make me realise many lessons again, the first was that I required solid foundations to build from. Then I could do one project at a time. I would go back to some of these ideas but when I was clearer in my mind and free to pursue them. So after a big argument me and Sarah separated, I went to stay at my friend's house. It was my 40th birthday, I was alone and sleeping on my friend's barn floor. I vowed that night this was the end of the turbulence in my life and now only a happy, stable life would be for me.

But I had to get to that point before coming to the point of making the final changes required for inner peace and the foundations to build from. Shortly after this I went to see my old military friends - they were more like family and I had hardly seen them since leaving - my best friend Danny, who I served with in Northern Ireland, his wife Shelly, and their amazing kids. I stayed for a week and it made me realise what I wanted was the simple easy and happy family life. Shelly spoke to me during that week and she pointed out that I was pushing myself too hard again.

I had imported a classic car to work on, which was my dream car but there was no point having a dream car in an empty house, so when I got back I decided to make many changes, the car was sold and I used the money to finish the house. This allowed me then to set up my clinic and work from home, but it gave me many other things I did not see until now.
I finally built a home for me and Hope, somewhere she would always have and I put roots down and started to really change. I let go of all the materialistic items that I once held so dear, my riches now were to spend time with my daughter and hear her laugh.

After the separation from Hope's mum, I seemed to spend a year in isolation again. In reality this was a period of self-discovery and setting foundations for my daughter. I spent two years rebuilding a house to make a home and now it was finished I lived in it alone with my memories. But it gave me the required space and time to formulate and work out who I am and where I was going next. In time spent alone we get to look at who we really are and if we keep making the same patterns and mistakes in life, we can change them. I spent this time as before, to learn who I am and why I have come down this path, I realised that I can use all my life experiences as a wealth of knowledge for therapy.

I started to work on my hypnosis methodology and realised that the points I said on the course would establish the basis of my working methods. During this time, I questioned the silence, but it's only in silence that you can hear the truth of your mind. I was eating well and looking after myself and for the first time in a long time, I become teetotal, as alcohol fogged my mind. I started to get to the next phase of my life. I could see the stormy dark waters were now a thing of the past and I could see the light, clear water now in front of me.

I believe that this time of trauma was to put me through a stage of evolution and self-growth, as each one made me rebuild stronger. I became more grounded and calmer after each event and had a deeper well of clear resources to draw from, but the drought was now in the past and a bright future lay ahead. I read many books and studied all the information I could on hypnosis, which allowed me to build a very robust working model that works with most clients. I finally found not only my calling in life, but the love of my daughter and the foundations I put down.

This allowed me to enter a new peaceful phase of my life that was to give me the inner peace I had been searching for. Once I finally stopped fighting the change and let go of my old patterns, I found my inner world, as my outer world, changed significantly.

I found these changes brought me in line with the true person I wanted to be, with compassion and love. I had become lighter and brighter and now helping other people in a professional capacity. I was very privileged to watch the change in my clients, as I helped them release the darkness from the past. I was clear and now free just to be present in the current moment, the love of Hope and my life gave me peace. This was such a revelation after so many years of turbulence and troubled waters, these now calm and clear waters refreshed my mind. I had finally found the key to true love, this in part was my daughter, but it made me realise that I had to love myself first. With this new self-love, I can be at peace and happy with the person I now see in the mirror. The time of being my own worst critic is gone and

now I am my own supporter. This is because now I know
Anything is possible.

Printed in Great Britain
by Amazon

42572205R00138